Music from the Tang Court 6

This volume continues the transcription and historical description of items of Tang Court Entertainment Music from twelfth-century zither, lute and mouth-organ scores. These are from two mode-key groups: twenty three pieces in *Ichikotsu-chō* and eight in *Sada-chō*.

Of particular interest are: a tune for a birthplace-ode by the Taizong Emperor composed in 632 AD, music for a collective spear-throwing exercise and a piece imitating calls between sexual partners in a flock of geese.

Important appendices discuss stylistic differences between music of the Tang and imitative Japanese compositions, relationships between a group of Tang compositions with imperial military associations, and evidence of interrelatedness between movements in suites from the Tang.

Music from the Tang Court · 6

edited by

Laurence E. R. Picken and Noël J. Nickson

with Rembrandt F. Wolpert, Allan J. Marett, Elizabeth J. Markham,
Stephen Jones and Yōko Mitani

A primary study of the original, unpublished, Sino-
Japanese manuscripts, together with a survey of relevant
historical sources, both Chinese and Japanese, with full
critical commentary and detailed structural analysis of
all items transcribed

CAMBRIDGE
UNIVERSITY PRESS

CAMBRIDGE UNIVERSITY PRESS
Cambridge, New York, Melbourne, Madrid, Cape Town, Singapore, São Paulo

Cambridge University Press
The Edinburgh Building, Cambridge CB2 8RU, UK

Published in the United States of America by Cambridge University Press, New York

www.cambridge.org
Information on this title: www.cambridge.org/9780521621007

First published 1997
This digitally printed version 2007

A catalogue record for this publication is available from the British Library

ISBN 978-0-521-62100-7 hardback
ISBN 978-0-521-04452-3 paperback

To the memory of

Alice Matilda Bevan

Who taught with love

Contents

Preface

The reader seeking a general introduction to the series, and to the scheme adopted for the organization of the contents, is referred to the introduction to the first fascicle (1981). There, information will be found relating to the manuscript sources, to problems of transcription, to the development of our 'Tang Music Group', and to our ideas with regard to the history of the manuscript tradition in Japan.

Those responsible for transcriptions published in this volume from manuscript Sino-Japanese instrumental scores in tablature are: E.J.M. (zither); R.F.W. (lute); L.E.R.P. (mouth-organ).

Change to computerised origination of musical notations has meant it is no longer possible, by inserting Chinese characters or other symbols into the musical text, to furnish as much information as hitherto about the structure of scores in manuscript. Fascicles 1 to 5 have already furnished detailed evidence of that structure.

The abbreviated forms of many Chinese characters in use in Japanese are often not abbreviations in Chinese use. We make apology for substituting Chinese forms where Japanese equivalents are not available to us. Most particularly we apologise where a friend may be displeased to see a family name transformed. In extenuation, we plead that the extended Chinese original confers a certain antique distinction wherever it is used.

In quotations from Japanese texts, our use of the *katakana* or *hiragana* syllabaries follows the usage of the original.

In the original mouth-organ scores, bass-drumbeats are shown as large, vermilion-red dots; here they are marked as **O**. 'Small beats' (*kobyōshi* 小 拍 子) are now omitted, and intracolumnary, binary markers are no longer shown. Mordents are indicated by a standard Western sign.

In scores for plucked strings, bass-drumbeats are still marked as *hyaku/bai* 百. Where notes are repeated at the same pitch in lute transcriptions (see Markham, 1983,1; p.49), open-string notes are shown with tails down – regardless of the position of the notehead on the stave. In octave leaps, open-string notes are again shown with tails down. Pitch glides in zither ornaments are no longer marked.

This volume completes publication of transcriptions of items for *gaku biwa* from the fifth and sixth scrolls of Fujiwara no Moronaga's *SGYR*, from the

Karyaku copy of 1328, and of items for *gaku sō* from an eighteenth-century copy of his *JCYR*, both manuscripts from the Library of the Imperial Palace (Tōkyō) *Kunaichō Shoryōbu* 宮內廳書陵部. The contents of these two manuscripts represent those items from the Tang Music (*Tōgaku/Tangyue* 唐樂) repertory, assigned to the mode-keys *Ichikotsu-chō/Yiyuediao* 壹越調 and *Sada-chō/Shatuodiao* 沙陀調.

In 1981 we omitted explanation of our use of a neologism: 'mode-key'. Its use, in relation both to Chinese music and to the *Tōgaku/Tangyue* repertory of Japan, is occasioned by Chinese practice, dating at least from the Tang, of giving different names to modal octave note-sets that are the same – in respect of the sequence of intervals between successive pitches – but differ in key. As an example, the basic *Shang* pentatonic, modal note-set on the second degree of the scale [obtained by inversion of a 123.56 *Gong* pentatonic note-set on *C*] may be represented as *D E G A C'*. In its heptatonic form, on the same final *D*, this is *D E F♯ G A B C'* – that is to say, a Mixo-Lydian set with tones and semitones distributed as T T S T T T S. In the Tang, seven different versions of the heptatonic Shang mode were distinguished, of which the three most common were *Yuediao* on *D*, *Dashidiao* 大石調 (the Tajik mode) on *E*, and *Shuangdiao* 雙調 on *G*. (See Picken, 1969, p.98.)

To translate *diao* 調 as 'mode' is convenient, but always in some degree misleading. As used in the context of music, the term means a *class* of tunes, as defined only by intervallic relationships between notes in the sequence of the octave note-set, and by the pitch of the final in relation to the final of the entire system of absolute pitches – for the Tang: *D*, the 'Yellow Bell' *Huangzhong* 黃鍾. The same lexigraph also means 'a tune' or 'to tune', so that (conceivably) the notion of a 'tune-type' lies behind this conception of 'mode', as elsewhere in the world of music. The right-hand side of the lexigraph, with 'mouth' added as classifier: 啁 (Karlgren, 1957: **1083 j**) means 'to twitter', or 'noise'; but this same right-hand side by itself is the lexigraph for the dynasty: 'Zhou', and perhaps originally represented a city, with streets laid out, running East-West, North-South. Maybe the character was 'borrowed' for the sake of its sound – itself meaning, originally, just that: a kind of sound. Unease in using it as the equivalent of 'mode' springs from the wide range of meanings that the sound had in the Tang (and indeed earlier), meanings among which it is difficult to recognise a common semantic element. Even today the monosyllabic word *diao* (調) may carry a host of meanings, specified in speech by aspiration or non-aspiration of the initial, by segmental tone, and of course by context.

This and the succeeding volume are not intended to be read from cover to cover, as continuous texts. The Appendices should be read as outgrowths from materials made accessible both in previous fascicles in this series, and in other of our publications bearing on particular topics. Occasional redundancies between

Appendices have arisen in the attempt to ensure that each Appendix is comprehensible within its own limits, without reference to other parts of the text.

In *Music from the Tang Court, 5*, p.1, explanation was offered of how the Chinese title 'Prince of the Grave Mound' (蘭 陵 王) became 'Prince of Luoling' (羅 陵 王) in Japan. In this volume, the Sino-Japanese forms of the title and its variant, in their Chinese *pinyin* romanisations, are used for the most part: 'Prince of Luoling' (*Luoling Wang* 羅 陵 王) and 'A New "Prince of Luoling" ' (*Xin Luoling Wang* 新 羅 陵 王). For brevity's sake, the shortened Japanese reading of the former is also used: *Ryō-ō* (= *Ling Wang* = Prince of the Grave Mound).

Acknowledgements

For help of many different kinds we are indebted to Dr C.J. Adkins, Dr Karel Brušák, Dr Ian Cross, Professor Christopher Darwin, Michael Good, Dr P.A. Herbert, David Hindley, Dr Graeme Lawson, John Moffett, Dr Nobuko Ishii, Michiko Matthews, Richard Ranft, Dr Richard Skaer, Professor Denis Twitchett and Robert Walker.

Sadly, a friend, Dr Rajeczky Benjamin (formerly of the Népzene Kutató Csoport of the Hungarian Academy of Sciences, already named in Fascicle 1, 1981, p.6) is dead. He had been a greatly valued supporter of the Tang Music Project, even before the project itself came to enjoy sponsorship by the American Council of Learnèd Societies and financial support from the Andrew W. Mellon Foundation. It was a crucial piece of information from Father Rajeczky that led to an investigation of the history of the names of notes in modal note-sets (*Music from the Tang Court 7*, Chapter 4, in preparation).

The final stages in the preparation of this volume for publication could not have been completed without the generous and sustained help and support, given by Stuart Barr and Mark Etherington.

Abbreviations

Sino-Japanese primary manuscript sources

CORYF	*Chū Ōga ryūteki yōroku-fu* (*c.*1320) Yamanoi no Kagemitsu
HFF	*Hakuga no fue-fu* (966) Minamoto no Hiromasa
JCYR	*Jinchi-yōroku* (*c.*1171) Fujiwara no Moronaga
KCF	*Kaichū-fu* (*c.*1095) Ōga no Koresue
KF/HSF/RK	*Kofu/Hōshō-fu ryokan* (1201) Toyohara no Toshiaki
RJSF	*Ruijū sō-fu* (11th century) Fujiwara no Morozane
RSCY	*Ruisō-chiyō* (*c.*1261)
RTHKF	*Ryūteki hikyoku-fu* (1287) Fujiwara no Nagamasa
SGYR	*Sango-yōroku* (*c.*1171) Fujiwara no Moronaga
SSSTF	*Shinsen shō-teki-fu* (1303)

Chinese and Japanese historical sources

BS	*Beishi* (7th century) Li Tingshou
DNHS	*Dainihonshi* (1810-50) Tokugawa Mitsukuni and others
[D]TLD	*[Da] Tang huidian*
GKMR	*Gakukō mokuroku* (see *GKR*)
GKR	*Gakkaroku* (1690) Abe no Suenao
HPGS	*Honpōgakusetsu* (see *GKR*)
JFJ	*Jiaofangji* (*c.*758) Cui Lingqin
JGL	*Jiegulu* (*c.*848-50) Nan Zhuo
JTS	*Jiu Tangshu* (945) Liu Xu
KKCMJ	*Kokonchomonjū* (1254) Tachibana Narisue
KKS	*Kyōkunshō* (*c.*1233) Koma no Chikazane
RMS	*Ryūmeishō* (1133) Ōga no Motomasa
STJH	*Sui Tang jia hua* (early 8th century) Liu Su
TD	*Tongdian* (801, 803) Du You
TGS	*Taigenshō* (1510-12) Toyohara no Sumiaki
THY	*Tang huiyao* (961) Wang Pu
TPGJ	*Taiping guangji* (978) Li Fang
TSJC	*Tushu jicheng* (1726) Chen Menglei and others
WMRJS	*Wamyō-ruijū-shō* (in part, late 10th century) Minamoto Jun
WXTK	*Wenxian tongkao* (*c.*1308) Ma Duanlin
YFSJ	*Yuefu shiji* (Song dynasty, before 1101) Guo Maoqian
YFZL	*Yuefu zalu* (890-900) Duan Anjie
ZKKS	*Zoku-Kyōkunshō* (late 13th century) Koma no Asakuzu
ZZTJ	*Zizhi Tongjian* (1087) Sima Guang

Glossary of signs

The change to computer-assisted music origination and the reduction in page size
of this volume have necessitated omission of a majority of Chinese and Japanese
lexigraphs and Japanese syllabary signs from items transcribed in quasi fullscore
form. As a reminder of the extent of detailed information present in the
manuscripts in tablature, the substance of the glossary of signs supplied in
Fascicles 1-5 is reprinted here. In this way, the reader may be reminded both of
what the manuscripts provide and of our interpretation thereof.

( )   Round brackets in transcribed scores or translations enclose notes, etc., to
be omitted.

[ ]   Square brackets enclose notes and/or explanatory material editorially
supplied.

由   Chinese lexigraph, romanised as *yu* in Sino-Japanese, as *you* in Chinese
pinyin, borrowed as sign for a shake. Where the lute, at the same locus,
shows a plucked descending mordent, and the zither a slurred mordent, the
mouth-organ shake is to be executed as a matching mordent. Though the
lexigraph is Chinese, its use in a musical significance is Japanese, as set out
in detail in Picken and Mitani, 1979, pp.98-108. The change from the
earlier form of the conjunctive base *yushi*, to the form *yuri* as used today,
probably occurred in the tenth century.

引   This lexigraph, read *hiku* in Sino-Japanese (*yin* in Chinese) written both as
here and abbreviated in various ways, originally meant 'to stretch' (as a
bow-string), hence 'to lengthen'. When the sign functions as a
prolongation sign, the duration of the note that corresponds to the
preceding tablature sign is doubled. This lexigraph may also be used as a
binary marker.

延   The two source manuscripts for mouth-organ tablatures, transcribed in this
series, both make use of this lexigraph (read *nobe/yan*), also meaning 'to
lengthen', seemingly as a replacement for *hiku*. Like *hiku*, too, *nobe* seems
also to be used, on occasion, as a binary marker. Its most frequent use,
however, is as an indicator of tempo – 'slow', in contrast to 'quick'.

二   In mouth-organ tablatures, the numeral 'two' written after a pitch sign indicates that the note is to be repeated. The duration of the repeated note, and the durations of both notes, depend on relationships between all tablature signs within the binary unit.

早   This and the preceding lexigraph are more commonly used in descriptive preliminary notes that precede items in score, or in descriptive passages in the handbooks, than in the scores in tablature. Read *haya/zao* it means 'quick', 'fast', 'speedy'.

火   This lexigraph, read *ka/huo*, 'fire' is a metaphor for speed. In the *MS* known as *Hakuga no fue-fu* (*HFF*) (Fascicle 1, p.9; Marett 1976, 1977) 火 is equated with the lexigraph 急. This last has a range of meanings, all related to 'swiftly', both in Chinese and Japanese. When written immediately after a pitch sign, *ka* halves the duration of that note. If written between two pitch signs, the duration of both is halved. In all contexts, the precise significance of *ka* is determined by relationships between pitch signs within a binary unit. Thus, if there are only two such signs within the unit, and if the second is followed by *ka*, this latter note is halved, and the binary unit is completed by a rest. Marett (1977, p.20) sets out a number of variant uses of 火. In the context of predominantly crotchet/quarter-note movement, for example, sequences of quavers/eighth-notes can be specified by the insertion of *ka* between pitch symbols.

丁   This sign (*tei/ding*) – probably deriving from *ting* 停 'to stop' – is defined as a short pause in the *Hakuga no fue-fu* (Fascicle 1, pp.13,16). It may be no more than a break in sound-continuity on the part of a wind instrument, marking the end of an extended phrase or section. It is used also in tablatures for stringed instruments with the meaning of a pause of one or two beats duration.

| Read *ichi* in Sino-Japanese, this sign functions as a binary marker in the earliest Sino-Japanese musical *MSS* (Fascicle 1, p.28). It appears frequently in *JCYR* and *SGYR* as a phrase-end marker. In transcription the sign is rotated through 90°, as here, and is usually (but not invariably) located over a barline. The sign appears to derive from a phrase-mark used in the punctuation of Chinese verse in print. It seems not to have a sound in Chinese. The term '*ichi*' comes from its resemblance to the numeral 'one', read as a cardinal number.

百 **O** These are signs for the bass-drumbeat *hyaku*, today executed as ♪♩. This method of execution, with a brief up-beat to the main beat, may reflect ancient practice. The circle form may be hollow, or solid and vermilion in colour.

. ₒ Intracolumnary, solid (or hollow) dots function as binary markers in the manuscript scores. Small solid dots (*kobyōshi*), written to the right of each column of tablature signs, mark successive beats in the structure of each binary unit, and thus of the measure – if the piece is measured. They do not appear on beats on which the bass-drumbeat falls.

✓ This sign – over a note in transcriptions from lute scores (*biwa* / *piba*) – shows that the string is to be plucked, exceptionally, with a retroflex stroke, the plucking finger moving upwards rather than downwards. In the early Japanese tradition (as opposed to that of Tang from the mid-eighth century onwards) the plectrum (*bachi* /*bo* 撥) will have been moved in the same sense as the finger when this sign was present in the score.

'A New "Prince of Luo [Lan]-ling" ' *Shin Raryō-ō / Xin Luolingwang / Xin Lanlingwang*

新 羅 陵 王 / 新 蘭 陵 王

or 'The Commanding Officer'[1]

團 長 樂

Tochōraku / Tuanzhang yue

The title and its significance
It seems certain that the adjective 'new' *shin/xin* 新 in this title qualifies the piece itself rather than the prince; just as the qualification 'new' was applied to a later version of 'Emptying the Cup', *Keibairaku/Qingbeiyue* 傾 盃 樂, to which danced the trained horses of the Xuanzong Emperor of Tang (712-56);[2] that is to say, the title is that of a later version of 'The Prince of Lanling'. The alternative title of 'The Commanding Officer' is surely an echo of the status of the original Prince of Lanling (Fascicle 5, p.2) who was an outstandingly great leader, worshipped by his men, as so plainly revealed in the moving biography in *Beishi*.

History of pieces of this, or related, title
In his *Tang xinong*, 'Plays & Performances of the Tang' 唐 戲 弄,[3] Ren Bantang 任 半 塘 alleges that Chinese tradition has no knowledge of specified 'old' and 'new' versions of the *Lanlingwang* piece. While this is true in the sense that 'new' does not seem to have been applied to any particular version in China, it is evident from the passage in *Bijimanzhi* (previously mentioned) (Fascicle 5, p.110) that two different versions, differing in modality and in structure, were known in the mid-twelfth century in Song China. Furthermore it was known that neither of these was the sixth-century original from Northern Qi. Although not described as such, therefore, the versions current in the twelfth century were certainly 'new' in relation to that original.

---

[1] The apparently nonsensical alternative title, 'Circular Senior' *Enchō-raku* 円 長 樂 has presumably arisen from confusion of 團 with 圓.
[2] See Gimm, 1966, pp.516ff.
[3] Ren, Bantang 1984, Shanghai guji chuban she chuban, p.622

Japanese sources indicate that the piece *Shin Raryō-ō* was already known in Japan at least by the early-ninth century, and both *JCYR* and *SGYR* record that, by Imperial Decree (of the Emperor Saga 嵯 峨, 809-23), it was conferred on the Household Troops Department of the Left (*Sahyōei-fu*, see p.4). *KKS* (6, p.115) appears to have omitted the all-important verb 'to give' 給 from the corresponding sentence in *its* account, but later adds [as a further, double-column note in *Nihon koten zenshū* (edition of 1928), written in smaller *kanji*]:

'It is said that, in the honourable period of *Kōnin* (810-23) there was an Imperial Decree that, at the end, the Household Troops of the Left emerged dancing, blowing [= playing] the Quick [of the suite].' 弘 仁 御 時 有 敕，終 左 兵 衛 舞 出 吹 急 云 。

Of great interest is the fact that follows from the decree, that this piece was felt to be a military piece, in character similar to the original *Lanlingwang ruzhen qu* (Fascicle 5, p.2); in that respect, it seems to have been regarded very differently from *Ryō-ō* itself. The latter had become an apotropaeic dance, overlaid with Buddhist associations and punning dragon-mask (Fascicle 5, pp.6-10). It is noteworthy that the period of this imperial gift to the Household Troops (of the Left presumably because it was a *Bugaku*-piece of the Left, belonging to the Tang-Music repertory) antedates the mission to Tang of 838 (Fascicle 1, p.13).

As Herbert (1979) established, ten embassies from Japan to China occurred during the seventh and eighth centuries. An earlier exchange of missions with the Sui Court had taken place in 607; but concentrated diplomatic activity between Japan and Tang was later conspicuous during two periods: 653-69 and 717-52. A number of these missions were mainly cultural in character. Such occurred in 630 and 653, and again in 701 (702 – according to Fujiie, 1988), under the Ambassador, Awata no Mabito, who (according to *Xin Tangshu XTS*) also headed a later embassy. One such mission, of great cultural importance, was that of 717 which included Abe no Nakamaro 阿 倍 仲 麻 呂 and Kibi no Makibi 吉 備 真 備. The former remained in China to the end of his life; but Kibi no Makibi returned to Japan in 734 and became Tutor to the future Empress Kōken. He went again to Tang with Chief Ambassador Fujiwara no Kiyokawa 藤 原 清 河 in 751 (752, Fujiie, 1988), returning in 753. The interest of Empress Kōken in *Ryō-ō* was described in Fascicle 5 (pp.12,13).

The Imperial Decree conferring the piece was promulgated at least ten years before Emperor Nimmyō 仁 明 came to the throne in 838, during whose reign a number of *Tōgaku* items were at least revised, and possibly even composed, since their titles do not occur in Tang lists. It is possible, then, that this piece was indeed an item from the *early* Tang repertory. This view is greatly strengthened by the analytical studies of N.J.N.. (See Appendix 5, p.233.)

The history of the piece is at first sight complicated by the existence of longer and shorter versions of the two movements, Broaching and Quick [no trace of a Prelude (if any such ever existed) survives], and by the evidence for the existence of a number of different traditions of descent. In prefatory comments and glosses to tablatures, reference to *Nishi-fu* and *Katsura-fu*, to [Toyohara no] Tokimoto, and to the *Wata-fu* (for details see later), imply connections with at least four manuscript traditions from the eleventh and twelfth centuries.

In the preface to the piece in *JCYR* and *SGYR*, it is explicit from the outset that Broaching (*Ha/Po*) and Quick (*Kyū/Ji*) were known to Moronaga in the twelfth century as pieces with 16 bass-drum beats – that is, in 16 measures. Nevertheless, *JCYR* furnishes only a version of the Broaching in eight measures; while *SGYR* supplies a primary version in 16 measures (at first sight quite different from that of *JCYR*), and a secondary version (*dō Ha / tong Po* 同 破) in eight measures, matching that in *JCYR*.

Again, *SGYR* marks the primary version of the Broaching (16 measures) as taken from the *Wata*-score (Fascicle 1, p.69, n.15), and so links this version with the eleventh-century musician, Minamoto no Yoriyoshi. Following the heading: 'Secondary Version, eight beats', *SGYR* adds the qualification: 'Version of a Tennōji musician' (see p.7).

IIPGS (*GKR*, 926) states that the 'maker' of *Shin Raryō-ō*, Monyō no Kimi[4] 門 陽 公, has not been traced. This is true also of the Tennōji musician, Ketsu no Kōjō (a number of other readings are possible), said to have recovered the Variant Broaching (as reported by *DNHS*).[5]

Prefatory Comments in the Manuscript Sources
KF/HSF/RK

'A New "Prince of Luo(Lan)ling" ': Old music. Also called 'The Commanding Officer'. To be used as the Quick of *Bairo* [a *Tōgaku* item in *Hyōjō*]. Broaching (slow). Three Sections [= times]. Bass-drumbeats of each Section, 16. Quick (fast). Four Sections [times], beats of each Section, 16. Some versions twelve beats. Recently often used. 新 羅 陵 王。 古 樂。 又 名 團 長 樂 。倍 臚 急 二 用 之。 破 延 ，三 帖 ，拍 子 帖 別 十 六 。急 早 ， 四 帖 拍 子 帖 別 十 六 或 説 十 二 ， 近 來 常 用 之。

(Note the use of 帖 *jō* as a 'time', rather than as a 'Section' – as in Fascicle 1, pp.65-82.)

[4] This could be a Chinese name: Men Yonggong – but rather improbably so.
[5] 347, 5. Again this might be a Chinese name: Que Gongzhen 闕 公 貞. Both Que and Men (n.4) are Chinese patronymics, but both names are unusual.

SSSTF

'A New "Prince of Luoling" ': Broaching, of bass-drumbeats, 16. Quick: of beats, 16. 新 羅 陵 王　破 拍 子 十 六　急 拍 子 十 六

JCYR

'A New "Prince of Luoling" ': one name is 'The Commanding Officer'. Broaching, beats 16; should be plucked [played] three times. In the last Section add beats. Quick, beats 16; should be played four times. In the last Section add beats. Total of beats [= measures] 112.

新 羅 陵 王 一ˋ 名 團 長 樂 破ˋ 拍 子 十 六 可 彈 三 反　終ˋ 帖 加
拍 子　急ˋ 拍 子 十 六 可 彈 四 反 終ˋ 帖 加 拍 子 合ˋ 拍 子　百 十 二

Nangū's *Horizontal Flute-Score*[6] states:
'Following the third Section of the Quick strike "three-times beats" '.
南ˋ 宮 橫 笛 譜 云 從 急 三 帖 打 三 度 拍 子

'In the honourable period of Kōnin [810-23], there was an Imperial Decree that this dance be given to the Household Troops Department of the Left [*Sahyōei-fu*].'
此ˋ 舞 弘 仁 御 時 有 敕 給 左 兵 衛 府

'In one variant, the Broaching has eight drumbeats; the Quick, twelve drumbeats. Middle-sized piece. Old music.'
一ˋ 説 破 拍 子 八　急ˋ 拍 子 十 二　中ˋ 曲　古ˋ 樂

'When the Tennōji [dancers] dance *Bairo*, they play the Broaching of this piece (in the eight-beat version) twice, and in the last time add beats.'
天ˋ 王 寺 舞 倍 臚 時 彈 當 曲 破 八 拍 子 説 二 反 終 帖 加 拍 子

SGYR

The preface is identical with that of *JCYR* but for three minor changes: 舞 with the ninth determinative: 人 (meaning 'dancer') for 舞 ('dance'), in paragraph 3; 倍 臚 之 舞 for 倍 臚, and 奏 for 彈, in paragraph 5. An upper-marginal gloss over the preface states:
'In the Quick of this piece, the bass-drumbeats are increased as in the Broaching of "Sogdians Drinking Wine" '. 此ˋ 曲 急 上 大 鼓 如 胡 飲 酒 破.
Regarding this phenomenon in *Koinju*, see Fascicle 4, **8,** p.3, and the associated score of the Broaching on p.7.

---

[6] Nangū Prince Sadayasu (see Fascicle 1, p.37, n.44).

4

BROACHING *Ha / Po* 破

SGYR: Of beats, 16. *Wata*-score version. 拍 子 十 六 綿 譜 説.

An upper marginal gloss above the beginning of the Broaching states:
'On the whole, the *Henfukō*-mode score of the *Nishi*-Master is the same as this
version' 西 師 返 風 香 調 譜 大 概 同 此 説。
  The gloss appears to argue persuasively for the age of the version of the
Broaching in sixteen measures, if a score in the archaic *Henfukō-chō* existed at
the date of this copy of *SGYR*. The *Henfukō-chō / Fan Fengxiang diao* 返 風 香
調 is a Mixo-Lydian modal octave on A (see Volume 7, Chapter 1, in
preparation). Its tuning is the fifteenth (in serial order) in *FBBF*[7], and its naming
implies a tuning of the lute strings: *A B e a*. The Nishi Master may be a reference
to Minamoto no Ken'en 源 賢 圓, pupil of Hakuga's second son, Minamoto no
Nobuaki 源 信 明, and founder of a lute school. Since the keys are different, the
statement presumably relates to identity in other respects.

Shin Raryō-ō, Broaching

SSSTF
[1] Intracolumnary binary markers absent throughout.

[7] Wolpert, 1977, pp.127, 131, 156-60

8 **O**hanjō

Half Section

VARIANT BROACHING (in *SGYR*) *dō Ha/tong Po* 同 破

JCYR (the only Broaching in *JCYR*): Of beats, eight. 拍 子 八

SGYR: Of beats, eight. Version of a Tennōji musician. 拍 子 八 天 王 寺 樂 人 說.

　(An upper marginal gloss notes: 'On the whole, the *Katsura*-score is the same as this version' 桂 譜 大 概 同 此 說.)[8]

---

[8] *Katsura-fu* (and *Nishi-fu*) were scores embodying the traditions of two schools.

JCYR

[1] 'As to the final notes on the [last] two *kakko* [beats], discard them and add the modified incipit (*kandō/huantou*). In this matter see *SGYR*' 終 詞 羯 鼓 二 去 之 加 換 頭 此 事 見 三 五 要 錄.

SGYR

[1] right: 一 説 'one version'

[2] left: measure 1, beat 8, and measure 2, beat 1, marked with hollow dots. Not understood.

[3] left: 'one version same as above' 一 説 同 上

[4] following the modified incipit read: 加 彈 之 'adding, play it'

QUICK	*Kyū /Ji* 急

JCYR	Quick 急

SGYR	Quick 急

An upper marginal gloss states: 'In this Quick, augment bass-drumbeats as in the Broaching of "Sogdians Drinking Wine"' 此 急 上 大 鼓 如 胡 飲 酒.

Shin Raryō-ō, Quick

KF/HSF/RK (Note different measure length in *SSSTF*)

[1] 'Play, continuing from the modified incipit.'

[2] 'Up to here, twelve [measures].'

[3] 'Follow this below in second time.'

JCYR

[1] right

[2] left

SGYR

[1] left 桂譜 '*Katsura* score'

[2] left

[3] right (flute gloss)

[4] left 一 説 'one version'

[5] left

[6] right (flute gloss)

10

Written-out repeat of Quick of *KF/HSF/RK* in twelve-bar form

Variant Quick *dō Kyū* /*tong Ji* 同 急

SGYR : 'Of beats, 12. In one version, beats six'
拍 子 十 二 　 一 説 拍 子 六.

Shin Raryō-ō (Variant Quick – *SGYR*)

(Variant Quick transcribed by L.E.R.P. *Music* of notes to variant transcribed by
R.F.W.) The reader is reminded that the lute is tuned *A d e a*, and only these
notes may occur as open-string sounds. *e* and *a* may also appear as stopped-string
sounds. Where repeated *e* or *a* occurs (stopped and open string in sequence – or
conversely), the stopped-string note is shown in score with stem directed
upwards, regardless of the position of this note-head on the stave.

SGYR

¹ left  'one version'

² left (flute gloss)

11

3 left		'In Tokimoto's version [Toyohara no Tokimoto, 1058-1123] [that which comes] below this [is to be played] twice 時 元 説 此 以 下 二 反 [making 16 measures].'
4 right (flute gloss)		
5 left		時 元 説 'Tokimoto's version' [This presumably implies that measure 11 is the same as measure 3, n.1.]

26 Piece[1]

'[Western] Liangzhou'

Sairyōshū or *Sairōshū* /(*Zui*) [*Xi*] *Liangzhou*

最 涼 州　　or　　[西] 涼 州

The title and its significance

There can be little doubt that the original title of this item was indeed 'Western Liangzhou' – geographically and historically a highly significant title – rather than 'The Very Cool Province' (as 最 涼 州 might be construed). The form of the title in Sino-Japanese may have arisen by substitution of one homophone for another: *sai* 最, for *sai* 西, because the lexigraph (涼, or written with the ice determinant, as in 冰) would be recognised (by a Japanese reader) in first place as an adjective, 'cool'. To qualify 'cool' by 'very' would seem more probable than to qualify 'West' or 'Western' in that way; and finally 'The Very Cool Province' would appear to make better sense than 'The Western Cool Province'. The existence in modern Japanese of compounds rhyming with *sairyō* (written with 最), compounds such as *sairyō* 最良 = 'best', 'ideal', and even *sairyōshū* 最 良 種 = 'best variety', suggests that the occurrence of *sai* in common expressions may have favoured substitution of 最 for 西. (S.J. has pointed out that a somewhat similar-sounding lexigraph not infrequently, but meaninglessly, begins titles in Chinese. This is the word 'intoxicated': 醉 *zui/sui, yo*. It often occurs at the beginning of Chinese 'song-labels' (*qupai* 曲 牌); for example: 'Drunken Great Peace' 醉 太 平; 'Drunken Brightness of Flowers' 醉 花 陽, etc. It is not the case, however, that *sai* 最 is a frequent first element in *Tōgaku* titles; and, in any case, the *on*-reading of 醉 is *sui* not *sai*.)

While there can be little uncertainty about the real geographical significance of the title *Sairyōshū* it is much more difficult to decide what is the relationship between this single musical movement, and specific musical items linked with the locality of Western Liangzhou; or what is the significance of the various alternative titles (see later). An alternative form for *ryō/liang*, namely 梁, the name of one of the Southern Dynasties (502-56), is recorded in *JCYR* and *SGYR*; but Xiliang 西 涼 was one of the group of 'Sixteen States' (*Shiliu guo* 十 六 國) that formed the Empire of Eastern Jin 東 晉 and endured in time from 304 to

---

[1] Departing from the practice adopted in Fascicle 4, the complete set of alternative titles shown by Hirade (1982; see Fascicle 4, p.xii) is not set out here, so as not to prejudice our argument. See p.17.

428[2]. Xiliang itself lasted as a state from 400 to 421, and its capital was Dunhuang 敦 煌 (later, in 405, Jiuquan 酒 泉).

The status of Province or Kingdom (*zhou*) was accorded both to 涼 and 梁; but the three-character group 'Xiliang zhou' can only refer to one of the Sixteen States, and to the first quarter of the fifth century, as also does the shorter name 'Xiliang' by itself. Its territory fell largely within the boundaries of today's Gansu Province and, as with the 'pan-handle' shape of the latter, its long and narrow outline was determined, presumably, by the Nanshan range of mountains running along the Northern border, and by the territory of non-Chinese peoples (non-漢 peoples), along the Southern border. Xiliangzhou was a principal corridor of contact with the oasës of the Turfan Depression (in particular with Kuchā), and it was the region of conflation of all the major Silk Roads, both those passing North of the Tianshan (天 山) range, and those lying to the South of the Himalaya. Through the territory of Western Liang passed important cultural influences, one of which, music, is noted in the 'Sui History' *Suishu* 隋 書[3]:

'The Xiliang repertory came into being at the end of the ascendency of the Fu clan, when Lü Guang[4] and Juqu Mengxun[5], having occupied Liangzhou, created it by modifying music of Kuchā. Its designation was: "The Qin/Han Performance"[6]. Emperor Taiwu of Wei then undertook pacification West of the [Yellow] River, obtained it, and called it "Music of Xiliang". Up to Wei [377-533] and [Later] Zhou [557-81] and thereafter, it was called: "The State Performance".'

　　西 涼 者，起 苻 氏 之 末，呂 光，沮 渠 蒙 遜 等，據 有 涼 州，變 龜 茲 聲 為 之，號 為 秦 漢 伎。魏 太 武 既 平 河 西 得 之，謂 之 西 涼 樂。至 魏，周 之 際。遂 謂 之 國 伎。今 曲 琵 琶，豎 頭 箜 篌 之 從，並 出 自 西 域，非 華 夏 舊 器。

2 Moule and Yetts, 1957, pp.35-51
3 15, p. 378; this chapter was completed in 656 (see Gimm, 1966, p.222).
4 Lü Guang became the Taizu Emperor of the Later Liang Dynasty in 386.
5 Juqu Mengxun became Prince Wuxuan 武 宣 王 of the Northern Liang Dynasty in 397.
6 The original significance of this binome: *Qin/Han* is obscure. A related term is *Qin/Han zi* 秦 漢 子, applied to the *piba*. Qin is an ancient name for Shaanxi Province, the region of Chinese territory on which Xiliang abutted. It was also the name of the dynasty that preceded the Han, and flourished from 255-09 BC (approximately). More than 30 years ago, Professor E.G. Pulleyblank suggested (see Picken, 1955, p.8) that the performance was so called because the performers were Chinese by birth though professionally engaged in territory previously outside metropolitan China. From the early texts that relate to the *piba* it is plain that some authors were at pains to suggest a Chinese origin for what was undoubtedly a foreign importation (Picken, 1955).
　　The term *ji* means a skill, talent, or ability; but it is clear that what is meant is an entire performance, involving a number of instrumentalists, singers and dancers: an 'act' or 'show', a 'performance', as we would understand it.

In the continuation, the passage implies that the Xiliang repertory was distinctive in content and in instrumentation. The text first reminds the reader that:

'As to the present-day families of bent-necked lutes and vertical angular harps[7], both emerged from countries bordering on Western China; these are not old instruments of China.' The passage then continues: 'Pieces of the same class as "New Tunes from Willow-Marsh" and "The Spiritual White Horse" arose among foreign tribes. Such songs of foreign tribes are not pieces handed down from Han and Wei [dynasties]. Consequently their instruments and melodies are not the same as those recorded by the scribes. 楊 澤 新 聲 ， 神 白 馬 之 類 ， 生 於 胡 戎 。 胡 戎 歌 非 漢 魏 遺 曲 ， 故 其 樂 器 聲 調 悉 與 書 史 不 同 。

Then comes a sequence of titles of song and dance pieces (not translated here); and finally a list of instruments:

'Their musical instruments include bells, lithophones, plectrum-plucked and finger-plucked zithers, horizontal angular harps, vertical angular harps, lutes, five-stringed [lutes]; free reed mouth-organs, vertical notched flutes, large double-reed cylindrically-bored pipes, long transverse flutes, small double-reed cylindrically-bored pipes, horizontal flutes; waisted drums, Qi drums[8], pole-borne drums; bronze cymbals [reading 鈸 for 拔]; conches. [In all] 19 kinds, constituting one Division. Of musicians, 27 men.'[9]

其 樂 器 有 鍾 ， 磬 ， 彈 箏 ， 搊 箏 ， 臥 箜 篌 ， 豎 箜 篌 ， 琵 琶 ， 五 弦 ， 笙 ， 簫 ， 大 篳 篥 ， 長 笛 ， 小 篳 篥 ， 橫 笛 ， 腰 鼓 ， 齊 鼓 ， 擔 鼓 ， 銅 拔 ， 貝 等 十 九 種 ， 為 一 部 。 工 二 十 七 人 。

As revealed by this passage from the *Sui History*, a principal source of cultural influences (including music) that impinged on Western Liangzhou was the oasis city-state of Kuchā, the inhabitants of which originally spoke an Indo-European language: Tocharian. Kuchā was one of the 36 States of the Western Region that bordered on China in the Han period. It was first besieged by the Chinese in 385 and became tributary to China during the Tang. It will be recalled (see Fascicle 5, p.1) that the mode-key group *Sada-chō*, to which *Sairyōshū* belongs, has been equated with the Kuchean mode: Sādhārita. This surely strengthens the view that the origin of the piece was connected in some way with Western Liangzhou.

It will also be recalled that the term 'Western Liang' has already appeared in this series in relation to the item 'One Time' (Fascicle 4, p.2); it was the third

[7] Literally 'erect-headed': *shutou* 豎 頭.
[8] The *Qigu* 齊 鼓 is described as like a lacquer cask (*qitong* 漆 桶; 3 litre capacity); more cryptically it is said to have a single, large head (membrane) disposed equally over the drum-face, 'like a musk-deer's navel' (*sheqi* 麝 臍) hence *qigu* 臍 鼓 = navel-drum – a pun on 齊 and 臍).
[9] Presumably more than one (of some instruments) participated in the ensemble.

tributary state, both in Gaozu's 'Nine Divisions' and in Taizong's 'Ten Divisions' of the Court Entertainment Music of the Tang. In each case, the term qualifies the word *ji* 伎: skill, craft, act, performance.

History of pieces of this, or related, title

The precise date of introduction of a *piece* entitled *Liangzhou* to the Chinese Court is linked with the military success of Guo Zhiyun (see later), Governor-General of the Liangzhou Commandery, and with the year 718; but Chinese interest in 'Xiliang Music' in general reaches back some centuries before the beginning of the Tang, as already shown by the passage from the *Sui History* previously cited. To the statement in that account that the said music was 'modified music of Kuchā', *Yuefu zalu* (*YFZL*) (890-900)[10] supplies the important further information that what was 'offered as tribute by the Liang Prefecture was originally in [the mode-key] *Zhenggongdiao* [and in suites of] larger and smaller sizes.' 涼 府 所 進 本 在 正 宮 調 大 遍 小 者。The stipulated mode, then, was Lydian (Picken, 1969, i, p.8), and in Tang practice the final will have been *D* – judging by Japanese survivals.

Yuefu shiji,[11] citing the lost *Yueyuan* 樂 苑 (post-Tang, but before *Yueshu* of 1101), states:

' "Liangzhou", a piece in the Lydian mode (*Gongdiao*); in the middle of the *Kaiyuan* [reign-period: 713-41] Guo Zhiyun, Governor-General of the Xiliang Prefecture, offered [it as tribute].' 涼 州 宮 調 曲 。 開 元 中,西 涼 府 都 督 郭 知 運 進。

'Liangzhou' pieces enjoyed enormous popularity in China, and this term even survived as a 'song-label' (*qupai* 曲 牌) in the great collections of songs compiled in the eighteenth century. In the body of Tang verse too, there are many 'Liangzhou' song-texts.

Other song-texts with 'Liangzhou' in their titles, by poets of the Tang, are preserved in *YFSJ*. Three of these by named authors, headed 'Liangzhou song-words' 涼 州 詞, are in quatrains of seven monosyllabic words to the line, rhyming *a a b a*. The authors are: Geng Wei 耿 湋 (*Jinshi* 進 士 in 762 – graduation-year), Zhang Ji 長 籍 (765-830) and Xue Feng 薛 逢 (*Jinshi* in 841). One text by Zhang Ji consists of three such quatrains, but each quatrain makes use of a different rhyme. The entire group of song-texts (some anonymous) is headed 'Liangzhou: 6 Items' 涼 州 [六 首]; but this tally is difficult to reconcile with the texts presented and incompletely numbered. Of the anonymous items, one (the third) is in four lines of five monosyllabic words, while the rest are in lines of seven. The entire group is preceded by a preface that cites both a passage

[10] *Yuefu zalu* (*YFZL*) (*Hubu* Section)
[11] *Yuefu shiji* (*YFSJ*) 79, p.1117

16

from the lost *Yueyuan* 樂 苑 (before 1101) and from *YFZL*. Lydian modes in three different keys are mentioned: *Zhenggongdiao* 正 宮 調 (on *E*), *Daodiao* [*Gong*] 道 調 [宮] (on *A*) and *Huangzhong Gongdiao* 黃 鍾 宮 調 (on *D*). The association of Liangzhou/Xiliangzhou music with the Lydian octave-species is evidently well established.

This preface also includes a reference to Guo Zhiyun, Governor General of the Xiliang Prefecture, as if the following song-texts imitated those originally linked with Guo's offering to the Tang Court in 718 (p.16). It is evident, however (see later), that none of these texts would fit the 'Western Liangzhou' melody as preserved in the *Tōgaku* manuscript sources. References to the plethora of 'Liangzhou' pieces recorded from Tang times onwards, in the Song, Yuan, Ming and Qing dynasties, are to be found in 'Dance in the Tang Period'[12]. It is evident that the term 'Liangzhou' was used to specify a style as well as a particular tune or song-label; and all the evidence suggests that a principal feature of this style was its Lydian modality: an octave-set with sharpened fourth and seventh.

While at first sight it would seem probable that the piece that survives in the *Tōgaku* manuscript repertory is that offered to the Tang Court in 718 by the Governor-General of Xiliang, there exists a further possibility, namely, that it is a vestige of 'Blessed Goodness', *Qingshanyue* 慶 善 樂, created when the Taizong Emperor of Tang (627-49) returned to his birthplace, the Palace of Blessed Goodness (Qingshan Gong 慶 善 宮), during an Imperial Progress[13] undertaken in 632.

While the manuscript tablatures, *JCYR* and *SGYR*, make no reference to any such association, *RMS* and *KKS* (6, p.115) and the later *RSCY* tablatures reveal an unexplained degree of prestige attaching to this item, in that it had been customary to use it exclusively on the occasion of private banquets for members of the Imperial Family of Japan. As far as these sources are concerned, the splendour of this association is unexplained. It would become understandable, however, if the Japanese were aware that, at a much earlier time, the piece was associated with Taizong's Imperial Progress.

Such awareness is explicit in the *ZKKS* account of *Sairyōshū* (*ZKKS* 3, p.156). This continuation of *KKS*, compiled either towards the end of the thirteenth century, or at the beginning of the fourteenth, states at the outset that the piece is of Tang date, either 'old' or 'new', and gives in sequence not merely the alternative titles 'Western-Liang Music' and 'Liangzhou', but also the titles (known from *JTS* and *XTS*): 'Music of the Blessed Goodness of Successful Completion', 'Music of Blessed Goodness', 'Dance of Nine Achievements', 'Nine Achievements' and 'Nine Achievements' Music'. The presence of these

---

[12] *Tangdai wudao* 唐 代 舞 蹈, Shanghai wenyi chuban she 1980, ed. Ouyang Yuqian 歐 陽 予 倩. See pp.122-4.
[13] *JTS* 28, 8, 1, p.1046; see later.

17

alternatives (noted by Hirade, 1982, p.527) implies that the Japanese were well aware of a possible connection with Taizong's Progress. This becomes the more probable when the text goes on to state that:

'This music is used at Imperial Private Banquets as *mairi onjō* [that is, as 'Entrance Music' on the occasion of such a banquet] some say.' 此 樂 內 宴，參 音 聲 用 之，或 云。

'In the reign of Emperor Saga [809-23], in the Fourth Year of Kōnin [813], First Month, 22nd Day, it was performed for the first time, having been obtained.' 嵯 峨 天 王 ノ 御 宇，弘 仁 四 年 正 月 二 十 二 日 始 被 行 之。

ZKKS continues to list occasions on which *Sairyōshū* was performed in association with Imperial Private Banquets up to 947, in the reign of Emperor Murakami 村 上 (946-67)[14]. The text also includes a passage based largely on *YFSJ*, as well as a passage from *XTS* (21, p.68). This latter is ascribed to *Tangshu* 唐 書, *Liyue zhi* 禮 樂 志. For Chinese, as for Japanese readers, the only *Tangshu* known, up to the beginning of the Song Dynasty, was what is now known as 'The Old Tang History', *Jiu Tangshu* 舊 唐 書.

It is evident, therefore, that the main Chinese historical sources, relating to Xiliang music and the 'Blessed Goodness Music', were known to the compiler of *ZKKS*. With all these references to performance (in *ZKKS*), beginning in 813, it is surely remarkable that *Kokonchōmonjū* (*KKCMJ*) does not even record the name of the piece in any of its forms. It is worthy of note that *ZKKS* states that the piece was performed for the first time in 813. This suggests that the actual date of transmission to Japan from China may have been shortly before 813, and certainly before the return of the Mission of 838 (of which Fujiwara no Sadatoshi was a member).

[S.J. continues to wish to temper the enthusiasm of L.E.R.P. that leads to identification of *Sairyōshū* with the *Qingshanyue* of Taizong's Progress in 632, and stresses the importance of giving weight to the great fame of the *piece* 'Liangzhou', presented as tribute to the Throne in the Kaiyuan reign-period (p.16). It became a *topos* for poets and later composers. Indeed, it is one of the most popular Chinese operatic song-labels, as shown by the contents of the great collectaneum: *Jiugong dacheng Nan Bei ci gongpu* 九 宮 大 成 南 北 詞 宮 譜 (1736-96), and by other sources. Song, Yuan, Ming and Qing sources all refer to a host of 'Liangzhou' pieces.]

Both *RMS* and *KKS* make plain, however, that the major concern of their respective authors, Ōga no Motomasa and Koma no Chikazane, was the history of *transmission* of the tradition of *performance in Japan* – not the history of the

---

[14] *Dainihonshi* (*DNHS*), reflecting conditions in the early nineteenth century, records performance of the piece at Private Banquets at that time also, adding (somewhat inadequately) 'in the long run it has proved popular' 蓋 有 所 受 也.

piece itself. The former will be set out in detail at a later stage (pp.25,26). A prior concern for us at this juncture is the origin and history in China of a piece plainly identified (in *KKS*) with *Sairyōshū*.

The momentous character of this identification was a chief reason for *not* exhibiting the full list of alternative titles at the outset, and for first making clear a seemingly more probable identification with an item of musical tribute offered to the Throne in the middle of the *Kaiyuan* Reign-Period (713-41 – say *c*.725). The later Japanese handbooks: *GKR* and *TGS*, give all the alternative titles; but only when these were found to be present already in *ZKKS*, together with a date of first performance in Japan, was it felt proper to give serious consideration to this identification.

A ninth-century Japanese list of Chinese books – to which[15] reference was made in Fascicle 3 (p.8) – reveals the presence of a copy of *The Six Boards of Administration of Great Tang*[16] (that is, The System of State Officials and their Duties). This compilation (still available in modern editions) bears the name of the Xuanzong Emperor and was begun in 731, completed in 738, and presented to the Throne in 739. In listing The Ten Divisions of Music-with-Dance, the said work includes 'the dance to the "Blessed Goodness Music" ':

'The First [Division] – called the Banquet-Music Performance – includes the dance to "Auspicious Clouds Music", the dance to the "Blessed Goodness Music", the dance to the "Destroying Formations Music" [and] the dance to the "In Accord with Heaven Music".'[17] 一 日 燕 樂 伎 有 景 雲 樂 之 舞 慶 善 樂 之 舞 破 陣 樂 之 舞 承 天 樂 之 舞.

Taizong died in 649, so that at least up to the time of presentation of [*D*]*TLD* to the Throne in 739 – a period of ninety years – 'The Blessed Goodness Music' was performed as an item of Banquet Music at the Tang Court. Its performance must have extended into the *Kaiyuan* reign-period of the Xuanzong Emperor; indeed it must still have been performed (on the basis of the relevant dates) when the 'Liangzhou' piece was offered as tribute by Guo Zhiyuan. It may be that performance continued at least to the date of abdication of Xuanzong in 756. This would mean that use of the music (*Sairyōshū*) by Emperor Saga in 813 might have occurred no more than 50 years after the death of Xuanzong in 762.

From references to *TD* in *JCYR* and *SGYR* it is certain that that work (*TD*) – completed in 801 or 803[18] – was known to the Japanese at an early date, even though its title does not occur in the ninth-century book list. In *TD*, Chapter 146

[15] *Nihon-koku genzaisho mokuroku* 日 本 國 現 在 書 目 錄. See the edition of Yashima Haruryō 矢 島 玄 亮 (1984), subtitled *Shūshō to kenkyū* 集 証 と 研 究, Kyūko sho-in 汲 古 書 院. The book list is believed to date from 891.
[16] [*Da*] *Tang liu dian (DTLD)* 大 唐 六 典 (completed in 738), compiled by Li Linfu 李 林 甫. Wenhai chuban she, Taipei, reprinted in 1962. See p.287. The text corrects a mis-writing of *zhen* 陣.
[17] See Fascicle 4, p.34.
[18] See Fascicle 3, p.8, n.13.

(one of seven devoted to music), important statements are made regarding both 'Xiliang Music' and the 'Blessed Goodness Music'. First, in relation to the modal category of 'Pure Music' (*Qingyue* 清 樂), it is stated that 'from the [Northern] Zhou and Sui [Dynasties] onwards, the Miscellaneous Pieces for Pipes and Strings, amounting to some hundreds of pieces, made much use of Xiliang music'. 自 周 隋 以 來 管 絃 雜 曲 將 數 百 曲 多 用 西 涼 樂 (146, p.761). Later, when discussing the Sitting & Standing Divisions of the Court musical ensembles, reference is made to a number of items from the entertainment-music repertory of the Tang Court:

'The "Glorious Imperium Music" is that which was made by Gaozong [650-83]. Of dancers there are 80 men [wearing] bird-caps [and] five-coloured, painted garments, as in the manner of the "Supreme Original Music" [or "First Full-Moon Music"] and the "Emperor's Birthday Music", when they sing of what has been restored by the King's Rule. From the "Music of Peace" onwards all [items] have mixed the great Thunder-Drum with the music of Kuchā. The sound causes [everything] to shake for a distance of 100 *li* [30 miles], and it is played standing. That "Music of Great Pacification" adds bronze gongs. Alone the "Blessed-Goodness Music" makes use of Xiliang music and is most serenely refined. Those three old dances: "Destroying Formations", "Supreme Original" and "Blessed-Goodness", all change their garments and caps; and [the musicians] join with bells and lithophones for sacrifices in the Suburban Temples. From the time when the Dowager Empress removed the Mandate of Heaven, these rites were forthwith abrogated. (From the *Anyue*-Class onwards, to be classed as the "Standing Performance".)' 光 聖 樂 高 宗 所 造 也 舞 者 八 十 人 鳥 冠 五 綵 畫 衣 兼 以 上 元 聖 壽 之 容 以 歌 王 業 所 興 自 安 樂 以 後 皆 雷 大 鼓 雜 龜 茲 樂 聲 振 百 里 並 立 奏 之 其 大 定 樂 加 金 鉦 唯 慶 善 樂 獨 用 西 涼 樂 最 為 閑 雅 其 舊 破 陣 上 元 慶 善 三 舞 皆 易 其 衣 冠 合 之 鐘 磬 以 饗 郊 廟 自 武 太 后 革 命 此 禮 遂 廢 (自 安 樂 部 為 之 立 部 伎) (146, pp.761,762)

[In connection with this use of the term 'Standing Performance', the distinction between the Sitting and Standing Divisions of the Palace musical ensembles seems to be first illustrated on a grave that dates from between 571 and 630. Exquisitely incised panels, on a gravestone in the form of a tortoise, show both Standing and Sitting Orchestras (each of eight players), as well as a group of six dancers, all performers being female. (See *Wenwu* 文 物, 1974, 9, pp.84-7)]

In Fascicle 3 (pp.4-8), it was argued that the Japanese must have had access to the first recension of what is known as *Tang Huiyao* (*THY*), since taboos on lexigraphs in Tang Imperial Names are respected in a lengthy quotation from *Huiyao* (*sic*) in a Japanese manuscript. This implies that a copy of the recension offered to the Throne in 801 was available in Japan, even though not listed in the ninth-century book list[19]. In the present *THY*, Taizong's Progress to the Palace of Blessed Goodness is described, and the text incorporates the emperor's song-words, written on that occasion.[20]

'In the sixth year of Zhen'guan [632], ninth month, twenty-ninth day, [the emperor] favoured The Palace of Blessed Goodness [with a visit] and banqueted attendant officials on the banks of the Waters of Wei[21]. That Palace, now, was the place where Taizong descended from Heaven to be born. The All-Highest composed a song-text with ten rhymes, as here quoted[22]: "Over the Mound of Shou" to "This Great-Wind Song".' [The song-text is translated in full later, p.36. After the song-words, *THY* continues]: 'He bestowed gifts on the local populace. [The occasion was] like to that when the Han emperor [Han Gaozu/Liu Bang 劉 邦 entertained the local elders, when he returned] to Yuan and [*his* birthplace] Bei [in 195 BC]. Thereupon the Rising & Retiring Officer, Lü Cai, making the song-words known to the Bureau of Music, had them prepared for winds and strings. Its title was: The Piece "Music of the Blessed Goodness of Meritorious Completion". Orders were given for eight rows of youths, all wearing *Jinde*-caps[23], and purple trouser-shirts, to do the "Dance of Nine Merits". Whenever there was a Winter-Solstice Banquet, or an occasion of great national blessing, it was performed in the Hall, in sequence with the "Dance of the Seven Virtues".' 貞 觀 六 年 九 月 二 十 九 日。幸 慶 善 宮。宴 從 臣 於 渭 濱。其 宮 即 太 宗 降 誕 之 所 。上 賦 詩 十 韻 云 。壽 邱… 此 大 風 詩。賞 賜 閭 里 。有 同 漢 之 宛 沛 焉。於 是 起 居 郎 呂 才。播 于 樂 府。被 之 管 絃。名 曰 功 成 慶 善 樂 之 曲。令 童 兒 八 佾。皆 冠 進 得 冠。紫 褲 [繻] 褶。為 九 功 之 舞。冬 至 享 讌。及 國 有 大 慶 與 七 德 之 舞 皆 進 於 庭。(33, p.614)

These passages from [D]*TLD*, *TD* and *THY*, indicate that the Japanese could have known of the existence of 'Blessed-Goodness Music', of its making use of music of Xiliang, of its association with Taizong's Progress to his birthplace in 632, and of the continuing performance of the piece, as an item in the repertory of Chinese Banquet Music-with-Dance, up to the beginning of the eighth century (witness *TD* and *THY*)[24].

The three Chinese sources thus far considered antedate the first presentation to the Throne of either 'The Old Tang History' (*Jiu Tangshu* 舊 唐 書) in 945, or

[19] See p.19.
[20] *THY* 33, p.614
[21] An important tributary of the Yellow River in Shaanxi (陝 西) Province.
[22] 云 signals a quotation.
[23] *TD* 57, p.329 describes *Jinde*-caps as decorated with nine gems or precious stones, white in colour and with gold ornaments.
[24] What effect the revolt of An Lushan 安 祿 山 had on the regularity of performance of the Banquet Music is not known, but it seems certain, from the fact that Fujiwara no Sadatoshi was reputedly able to obtain scores of so many items belonging to the Court repertory of the earlier Tang period, that scores at least survived.

'The New Tang History' (*Xin Tangshu* 新 唐 書) in 1061. Following the demonstration by Pulleyblank (1950) that, notwithstanding completion of *JTS* in 945, the basic annals of the earlier 'National History' (*Guoshi* 國 史) covering the period 618-759 were incorporated into *JTS*, it was observed (Picken, 1965), in regard to the four chapters of the 'Monograph on Music' (*Yinyuezhi* 音 樂 志) that, judging from dates in the text, later material was added to the ends of chapters rather than by interpolation. It was concluded that the bulk of *JTS*, Chapter 28 (with which we are chiefly concerned) probably dates from the eighth century, and was compiled at most within 150 years of the events described.

Twitchett (1992, pp.12-19) notes that both the section on Temple 'Music-with-Dance' (*Miaoyue* 廟 樂), and that on 'Banquet Music-with-Dance' (*Yanyue* 宴 樂), are very detailed down to the end of the Kaiyuan-period (741). This covers the period of particular interest to us, namely, the first third of the seventh century. Twitchett also suggests that Liu Kuang 劉 貺, probably born in the mid-680s, Chief Musician (*Xielü-lang* 協 律 郎) and appointed Director to the Office of Imperial Music in 721, may have been responsible for writing the monograph on music in the 'National History'.

There is, therefore, not even the gap of a century between the events of 632, now to be described, and their probable recording in the form in which we have them. Indeed, Twitchett has shown that the probable source of Liu Kuang's account was the wall inscription for the Director of the Imperial Music Office: *Taiyue ling biji* 太 樂 令 壁 記, composed by him most probably in 721, 90 years after Taizong's Progress in 632.

Both *JTS* and *XTS* describe the circumstances of the creation of this ballet-piece, 'The Blessed-Goodness Music-and-Dance'; its structural organisation; the number, sex, and age, of the dancers; their spatial distribution; their costume; and even the manner of the dance – all this in some detail, but with minor differences between the two accounts which, in the dates of their presentation to the Throne, are about a century apart. *JTS* (28, p.1046) states:

'In the sixth year [of Zhen'guan: 632] Taizong made an Imperial Progress to the Palace of Blessed Goodness, banqueted attendant officials on the bank of the Waters of Wei, and composed a song-text with ten [terminal] rhymes[25]. Now that Palace was the place where Taizong descended from Heaven to be born. Riding his chariot in the course of the Progress, each time he felt specially grateful for blessings received, he bestowed gifts on the local people. It resembled the actions of the Emperor of Han at Bei. Thereupon the Rising and Retiring Officer[26], Lü

---

[25] This expression: *shiyun* 十 韻, may at times be taken to mean ten poems with ten different rhymes. Taizong's surviving song-text exhibits ten open, rhyming syllables, all of which share the same terminal vowel. What was composed seems to have been a single song-text with ten rhymes.

[26] In the Tang, this officer had secretarial duties. At one time his functions related to visits at dawn by the emperor to the empress-dowager.

Cai, making the imperially composed song-words known to the Bureau of Music, had them prepared for winds and strings. Its title was: 'The Piece "Music of the Blessed Goodness of Meritorious Completion" '. Orders were given for eight rows of youths, all wearing *Jinde*-caps [see n.23] and purple trouser-shirts, to do "The Dance of Nine Merits". Whenever there was a Winter-Solstice Banquet or an occasion of great national blessing, it was performed in the Hall, in sequence with "The Dance of the Seven Virtues".'

We dispense with the Chinese text here, since the greater part of this passage is identical with the *THY* text, already translated, and probably accessible to the Japanese in the recension of 801/3. Later in the same chapter of *JTS*, the use of two items of Banquet Music-with-Dance as Refined Music-with-Dance (*Yayue*) is signalled by Imperial Decree in 665, during the reign of Gaozong (高 宗 650-83).

'For those Palace Instrumental Ensembles[27] that play in Suburban Temples and at Imperial Banquets, it is appropriate to use "The Music of Blessed Goodness of Meritorious Completion" for the Civil Dance. All wear shoes, hold pennants, are garbed in riding-breeches in the pattern of old-style clothes, and the youths are capped. For their Martial Dance, it is appropriate to use the music "Spiritual Merit Destroys the Formations". All wear armour and grasp halberds. Those men who hold banners also wear gold[28] armour. The number of men amounts in all to eight rows.' 其 郊 廟 享 宴 等 所 奏 宮 懸，文 舞 宜 用 功 成 慶 善 之 樂，皆 著 履 執 拂，依 舊 服 褲 褶，童 子 冠。其 武 舞 宜 用 神 功 破 陣 之 樂，皆 被 甲 持 戟，其 執 纛 之 人，亦 著 金 甲。人 數 並 依 八 佾。(28, p.1047)

Still later in the same chapter, in the course of a Memorial to the Throne presented in 677, the Assistant Senior Superintendant, Wei Wanshi 韋 萬 石, commenting on ritual music used in several different reign-periods of the early Tang, again records that: 'In accordance with an Imperial Edict of the Second Year of Linde, Tenth Month [665], respectfully received, the Civil Dance, being corrected, made use of the music of "Blessed Goodness of Meritorious Completion"; and the Martial Dance, being corrected, made use of the music "Spiritual Merit Destroys the Formations", both with changed instruments and costumes.' 奉 麟 德 二 年 十 月 敕，文 舞 改 用 功 成 慶 善 樂，武 舞 改 用 神 功 破 陣 樂，并 改 器 服 等。(28, p.1048)

Evidently, however, as the text goes on to say, these pieces were unsatisfactory for these purposes. Without stating the grounds for reverting to the use of other items in the repertory, it is certain that the two passages imply that both items were to be used as Refined Music in 665, when ritual occasions

---

[27] Literally 'suspended items' – that is, bell- and lithophone-chimes – used as a short-hand term for ritual, instrumental ensembles. See also Volume 7, Chapter 4, in preparation.
[28] Functional armour is unlikely to have been made from gold under any circumstances. Perhaps this costume-armour was of thin gilt-bronze.

23

required performance either of the Civil, or of the Martial Dance, or both. It is the case, however, that such items, even though adapted for use as Refined Music, continued to be used, in their original condition, as items in the repertory of the Banquet Music-and-Dance. This is evident from statements already examined from [D]TLD and TD, which together describe Court practice at least up to the beginning of the ninth century. In every instance the verbs in question are to be understood in the present tense.

That "The Blessed Goodness Music-and-Dance" came to be revised for ritual use will certainly have added to its prestige at the Tang Court. *JTS* (p.1049) states its dimensions, as well as those of *Pozhenyue* 破 陣 樂 and *Shangyuanyue* 上 元 樂. These three are the only pieces, originally in the Standing Division of the Banquet Music-with-Dance, ever to be revised for use as Refined Music. They are indeed the only *genuine Yayue* items ever to have been properly regarded as *Gagaku* in the entire *Tōgaku* repertory. All three are no longer performed, in either tradition, in Japan.

'As an item in the performance of the Standing Division, "The Destroying Formations Music" consists of 52 Sections [*bian* 遍; equivalent to *bian/pian* 偏 in other sources]; revised as Refined Music-with-Dance, it consists of two Sections only and is entitled "Seven Virtues". As an item in the performances of the Standing Division, "Blessed-Goodness Music" consists of seven Sections; revised as Refined Music, it consists of a single Section only and is entitled "Nine Merits". "The Supreme Original Dance" consists of 29 Sections; as nowadays used in the Refined Music, it is in no way reduced in length.'[29] 立 部 伎 內 破 陣 樂 五 十 二 遍，修 入 雅 樂，祇 有 兩 遍，名 曰 七 德。立 部 伎 內 慶 善 樂 七 遍，修 入 雅 樂，祇 有 一 遍，名 曰 九 功。上 元 舞 二 十 九 遍 ， 今 入 雅 樂 ， 一 無 所 減 。

XTS (p.469) notes: 'When the Dowager Empress Wu [took the Throne and][30] destroyed the Great Temple of the Tang, the "Seven Virtues" and "Nine Merits" dances were entirely lost; only their titles were preserved. Henceforth [for ritual purposes] only the Civil and Martial Dances of the Sui [dynasty] were again used.' 武 后 毀 唐 太 廟，七 德，九 功 之 舞 皆 亡，唯 其 名 存 。 自 後 復 用 隋 文 舞 ， 武 舞 而 已 。 (21, p.469)

This disappearance of the *dances* from use as Refined Music did not mean, however, that these items in their Banquet-Music form ceased to be part of *that* repertory, as made plain by [D]TLD and TD. The continued performance of the dance to the 'Destroying-Formations Music', and the dance to the 'Blessed-Goodness Music', after the abdication of Empress Wu in 705, is attested for 738 by [D]TLD, and for 801/803 by TD – performance, that is, as constituents of the Banquet Music-with-Dance.

---

[29] For detailed accounts of these three dances see Liu, 1987, pp.153-219.
[30] She did so (in 690) as 'Emperor' of a new 'Zhou' dynasty which lasted until 705.

A last comment from *JTS* tells us a little more about the performance of 'Blessed Goodness' on the occasion of Taizong's visit to his birthplace:

'Of dancers, 64 men, dressed in purple, with long sleeves, skirt and short jacket; black-varnished, dressed hair-do's; leather shoes. The dance-step was leisurely and slow, thus reflecting a blend of cultural refinement and virtue, as well as the Empire's being happily at peace.' 舞 者 六 十 四 人，衣 紫 大 袖 裙 襦，漆 髻 皮 履。舞 蹈 安 徐，以 象 文 德 洽 而 天 下 安 樂 也。(29, p.1060)

At a later stage, when the music of *Sairyōshū* has been presented, suggestions will be made regarding the possible significance of the terms for 'Sections', in *JTS* and *XTS* accounts (see p.45).

Taizong's Song-Text

The song-text by Taizong has been preserved, as has been seen in *THY* (p.21) and also in *YFSJ*[31], under the title: 'Song-words from the Tang, for the Music-with-Dance [Piece] "The Blessed Goodness of Meritorious Completion" (*Tang gongcheng qingshan yuewu ci* 唐 功 成 慶 善 樂 舞 辭). The preface to the poetic text cites *XTS* and *JTS* (as 'Tang History' and 'Old History' respectively; properly, of course, they are known today as 'New Tang History' and 'Old Tang History'). The poem itself (see our p.36) is one of which an emperor might well be proud: it fits the occasion perfectly in that, in 20 lines, it ranges over the entire history of China, places Taizong's birth in context, and finishes with a reference both to the feasting mentioned in historical accounts of his Progress, and to a much earlier and most famous song-and-dance banquet-piece, composed by the first emperor of Han.

The song-text is in 20 lines, each of five monosyllabic words, and every second line throughout rhymes: ab cb db eb etc., where b(s) are rhyming syllables. This implies that the song-text exhibits ten rhyming syllables: *shi yun* 十 韻 (as stated in *TD* and *JTS*). The piece preserved in the *Tōgaku* tablatures consists of 20 measures in 4/2 metre; and the tune can readily be adapted so as to fit an isometric, semantic, rhythmic pattern of | ♩ ♩ ♩♩♩ | as required by the verse.

The coincidences (if such they are) are surely so extensive as to justify further consideration of the piece as a survival from the seventh century.

Before examining prefaces to the tablature, and the music itself, one other historical matter must be examined, namely, the further history of the tradition of performance in Japan.

[31] 56, p.815

As has been shown (p.18), *ZKKS* records performances at the Imperial Court between 813 and 947. The two sources, *RMS* and *KKS*, however, reveal no knowledge of any particular occasion of performance before the twelfth century, and are chiefly concerned with (one might almost say 'disconcerted by') the fact that the piece was *not* transmitted to Ōga no Koresue 大 神 惟 季 (1026-94), but to his son, Motomasa (1079-1138)[32], author of *RMS*. According to *RMS*, the piece was conferred by Minamoto no Toshifusa (1035-1121), Lord Minister of the Left, on the fifth day of the seventh month in 1102. The source of the music itself, in a flute version, was none other than that Ō Kenmotsu, Minamoto no Yoriyoshi, so frequently named in connection with his *Wata-fu* [33], himself a pupil of Tamate or Kobe no Nobuchika 玉 手 / 戸 部 延 近 of the Yakushiji Temple 藥 師 寺.

The account in *KKS* (6, p.115) declares that the first recipient of the flute version was Koma no Yukitaka 犬白 行 高 (son-in-law of Koresue), who died in 1120 at the age of 59; but then Ō-tai (= Ō Kenmotsu), pupil of Nobuchika, was evidently the immediate and only source of the music, at a time when this item was unknown to the Court Musician Masanobu *Uta-no-suke* 正 延 雅 樂 允 (a rank equivalent to *Daihōgan*).

Again, in the account given in *KKS*, the patron seems to have been Minamoto no Masazane 源 雅 實 (1059-1127) of the first generation of the Tsuchimikado 土 御 門 family[34].

Both accounts establish a link with the Toyohara 豊 原 clan (Fascicle 1, pp.33-4): *RMS* states that Tokimitsu 時 光 (*c.* 1030) received the piece from Yoriyoshi, who taught The Lord Dainagon Tsuchimikado (probably Masazane is meant); while in *KKS* Tokimoto 時 元 (1058-1123), playing *shō*[35], performed the piece with Koma no Yukitaka. (Y.M. and L.E.R.P.)

No attempt will be made to translate either *RMS* or *KKS* passages as such; the identification of persons referred to by different titles, at different points in the narrative of the two texts, would require much space for elucidation, and serve no useful purpose. The point of historical importance that they appear jointly to confirm is: the occurrence of an interruption in the tradition of performance of the piece (as 'Entrance Music' *mairi-onjō* 参 音 聲 on the occasion of private banquets for the Imperial Family), an interruption that occurred between the middle of the tenth and the beginning of the twelfth centuries. This was indeed a time of extraordinary family or clan tension between

---

[32] This is made plain – as pointed out to L.E.R.P. by Y.M. – in the account available in *ZKKS*, pp.161-3.

[33] See Fascicle 1, p.69, n.15.

[34] There is a discrepancy in dates if one accepts Tsuchimikado Dainagon 大 內 言 as being Minamoto no (Tsuchimikado) Sadamichi.

[35] The locution *shōteki* 笙 笛 (as in the title *Shinsen shōteki-fu SSSTF*) is used.

Fujiwara regents (whose political power was declining), rising figures from the Minamoto clan, and the feuds of the Taira 平.

Prefatory Comments in the Manuscript Sources
KF/HSF/RK

'[Western] Liangzhou' (slow)
Old music. Should be played four times. Of beats, 20; in all 80. There are two traditions. There is no dance. In the third time, three-times beats are to be struck.
最 涼 洲 延 。 古 樂 。 可 吹 四 遍[36] 。 拍 子 二 十 合 八 十 。 有 二 傳[37] 。 三 帖 可 打 三 般[38] 拍 子

SSTF
'[Western] Liangzhou'
Of beats, 20
最 涼 洲 拍 子 二 十

JCYR
'[Western] Liangzhou' Upper marginal gloss: '*Ryūginshō* states there are two traditions: Okinaga michi-no-Sadahide; Kaki no michi Naru-ho [*sic*]'
最 涼 州 龍` 吟 抄 云 有 二 傳

臰	長	逍 ノ	貞	秀
オ	キ ナ	カ		
勝		ノ 道	成 ホ	
カ キ				

'For *ryō* [but with "ice" determinative rather than "water" – as here: 涼] some make *ryō* 梁 .
Of beats, 20. Should be played four times. Total beats, 80. In final time add beats.
Nangū's *Transverse Flute Score* states: "Strike three-times beats" (same as Tokimoto's mouth-organ score).
Middle-sized piece; old music (same as Nangū's score).'

涼` 或 作 梁 拍` 子 二 十 可` 彈 四 反 合` 拍 子 八 十 終` 帖 加 拍
子 南` 宮 橫 笛 譜 云 打 三 度 拍 子 (時` 元 [1058-1157] 笙 譜 同) 中` 曲

---

[36] Note the unusual equation (in this comment) of *hen* 遍 and *chō* 帖, where *hen* commonly means 'a time', and *chō* a differentiated sub-division of a musical unit or movement.
[37] This is a reference to traditions deriving from Katsu (or Kachi) no Michinari and Okinaga no Sadahide. See n.17, p.58.
[38] The use of this lexigraph *han /ban* 般, where *do /du* 度 is expected, is not understood.

古 樂 (南 宮 譜 同) [Brackets () mark parenthesis in manuscript in smaller lexigraphs]

SGYR: same as *JCYR* but for the absence of the upper marginal gloss.

RSCY: An upper marginal gloss refers to *Ryūginshō*, as in *JCYR*. The name Okinaga is written as in *JCYR*, with *michi* between naga and Sada, but without *katakana*-pronunciation signs, or particle *no*. 'Michinaru' is followed by *ko* 小. *RSCY* differs from *JCYR* in including (also specified as from *Ryūginshō*) a brief statement regarding the use of the piece as 'music' (*gaku-onjō* 樂 音 聲) for Private Banquets. Other details are as in *JCYR*.

Contrary to what is stated in the upper marginal gloss shown here (*JCYR*), these names do not occur in the passage on *Sairōshū* (reading of *RMS*) in *RMS* as at present constituted. *KKS* (*Nihonkoten zenshū* edn) shows them as Okinaga Sadahide and Katsumichi Naruhisa. *Dainihon-shi* shows them as in the facsimile printing of *KKS* (*NKZ* 1928): 息 長 貞 秀, 勝 道 成 久. *Katakana*-signs in *JCYR* show readings 'Okinaga' (*dakuten*, indicating voiced consonants, omitted) and 'Kaki'. As written in *JCYR*, however, the first name incorporates the honorific *michi-no* between patronymic and personal name.

It seems probable that the second of the two names is a corruption of Katsu no Michinaru. Both persons figure in the Postface to *HFF*. Katsu no Michinaru (see Fascicle 3, p.47 and n.4) is mentioned as having furnished a flute score with variants, used both by Prince Sadayasu, and by Hakuga (Marett, 1976, pp.11, 19), prior to the preparation of *HFF*. Michinaru himself was active in the first half of the ninth century. This implies that he may well have been in contact with court musicians who experienced the first performance of *Sairyōshū* as 'Entrance Music' in Japan in 813. Okinaga no Sadahide, mentioned in *HFF* as a master of the Tang flute, was perhaps a pupil of Katsu no Naonori 勝 尚 則, son of Michinaru. Alternatively he may have been a pupil of Heguri no Hideshige 平 群 秀 茂, who was probably active in the early tenth century. (For details see Marett, 1976.)

The presence of these two names is important evidence that the history of the piece in Japan, in a flute version, extends back into the first half of the ninth century. It is comforting to observe that the roles of Katsu no Michinaga and Okinaga no Sadahide in the history of the Tang-flute tradition in Japan, were first made plain, and set in their historical context, by a young scholar from New Zealand.

Sairyōshū '[Western] Liangzhou'

one time

SSSTF

[1] Intracolumnary, binary dots cease from here onwards.

[2] 'Variant has g" repeated' 説 十 十.

[3] *c♯'* shown unambiguously by tablature-sign: 工.

JCYR

[1] mordent supplied

[2] sharpening dot supplied

[3] mordent supplied

[4] (left) (gloss)

[5] mordent supplied

[6] slur supplied

[7] sharpening dot supplied

SGYR   一 説

[1] (right)   a variant

[2]   "   "

[3]   "   "

[4]   "   "

[5]   "   "

[6]   "   "

[SECONDARY VERSION (*dōkyoku/tongqu* 同 曲, *gakubyōshi* version; therefore not transcribed). See Fascicle 4, p.117]

Preliminary comments on the structure of the piece

While mouth-organ and lute tablatures display a piece in 20 measures without repeat, the zither version makes statements about 'times' at two points. The first occurs at the end of the twelfth measure: 'one time'; the second statement is marked at the end of measure 16: 'two times', but repetition is authorised only from measure 12 onwards. The effect of these statements is to yield, for zither also, a piece in 20 measures: [(4 x 3)+4 + 4], as stated in all four prefaces to the manuscripts transcribed: 'Of beats, 20' 拍 子 二 十. The piece then is 20 measures in tablature; with four times prescribed both for strings and for mouth-organ (*KF/HSF/RK*, p.27), a complete item of 80-measures duration would result. This latter mouth-organ score is alone in marking the piece as one to be played slowly. This is done by adding subscript 'lengthened' (*nobe/yan* 延), following the title. In the Japanese tradition that implies that the unit-beat is to be doubled in duration. *KF/HSF/RK* also states that there is no dance.

The handbooks afford no evidence that the *dance* of 'Blessed Goodness' was ever transmitted to Japan. For that matter, there is no evidence that the song-text of 'Blessed Goodness' was ever used (as *ei/yong* or *yun* 詠) in the Japanese context, and indeed it would have been quite inappropriate in a foreign context. Though the piece was already in use in Japan in the early-ninth century, as 'Entrance Music' for private banquets of the Imperial Family, Taizong's text does not appear in any Japanese source until the late-seventeenth century (*GKR*, 1690), though it may well have been available in printed form, in China itself, already in 801 (p.19). Of particular musical interest is the fact that, in this instance (unlike that in Fascicle 4, p.98), a structure in 20 measures does not result from repetition of a piece in ten measures.

As instances from *YFSJ* show, even in the Han, examples occur among the sub-urban (in the sense of extra-metropolitan) song-texts for sacrificial rites, of songs in 20 lines which consist of five quatrains. Examples are: 'Five Spirits'(*Wu shen* 五 神) and 'At Dawn atop the Dyke' (*Zhao long shou* 朝 隴 首) (*YFSJ* 1, p.8); both are song-texts in 20 lines of three monosyllabic words to the line.

The surviving song-text composed by the Taizong Emperor on the occasion of his visit to the Blessed-Goodness Palace in 632

In its notes on *Sairyōshū*, *GKR* (32, p.914) directs the reader to 'Collected Song-Texts of Old Music' (*Kogaku-shishū*古 樂 詩 集) but it seems probable, since a work of this title is unknown, that this term refers to *YFSJ*. *WXTK* and *TD* are also mentioned, somewhat vaguely. *THY* may well preserve the oldest version of Taizong's song-text, if this portion of the *THY*-text was already present in the *HY* of 801/803. The Chinese text reproduced in *GKR* is identical with the version in *YFSJ*, apart from a single graphic variant of 湄 in *GKR*; *YFSJ* gives the title as 'Song-Words from the Tang for the Music of the Blessed Goodness of

Meritorious Completion', with Taizong named as author. *GKR* gives name and title: 'The Taizong Emperor of Tang' 唐 太 宗 皇 帝; but *QTS* (incorporating the first eighteenth-century collection of Tang verse) gives the piece under the title: 'Progress to the Palace of Blessed Goodness [in the Prefecture] of Martial Merit' 幸 武 功 慶 善 宮. It is certain, however, as emerges in statements in *JTS* (and *XTS*), that the piece was a Civil Dance.

As shown (pp.21,22), the *THY* and *JTS* accounts specify that the verse had ten rhymes. The coincidence that a song-text in twenty lines, matching a musical piece in twenty measures, survives, is already remarkable; but the fact that, in the song-text, alternate lines rhyme (p.25), and that there are ten such rhyming, monosyllabic words (as reported in the sources), perhaps suggests that this is no coincidence. It suggests, rather, that *Sairyōshū* is indeed the surviving, single-movement version, of the 'Blessed-Goodness Dance', first taken into the Suburban Sacrificial Repertory in 665.

If indeed the descriptive comment 'ten rhymes' referred to the surviving song-words attributed to Taizong, the song-text shows us that the expression must have meant 'ten line-terminal rhyming syllables' in one poem, and not ten *different* rhymes in ten poems. Since *Sairyōshū* consists of 20 measures of eight beats, it would, as a tune, be obviously suited to a song-text in twenty lines, each of seven monosyllabic words; but previous examples (Fascicle 3, p.19, p.52) have illustrated how embellishment can be stripped from developed Chinese melodies to reveal a primary melodic core; and there is no difficulty in reducing a decorated melody in measures of eight beats to one suitable for a song-text in lines of 5 rather than lines of 7 monosyllabic words.

In view of the number of shorter items from the *Tōgaku* repertory in ten measures (or small multiples of ten) (see Fascicle 4, pp.29, 36, 41, 47, 54 and 98: 20 = 2 x 10) – their number increasing as this survey proceeds – it should be noticed that, from counts of numbers of lines in song-texts in *YFSJ*, in both ritual and secular repertories (as yet unpublished observations by L.E.R.P.), it is evident that, from the Han dynasty onwards, the frequency of occurrence of song-texts in ten lines (rather than eight, for example) increases. In the Tang period they are relatively frequent; but in earlier dynasties, though rare, they are not entirely absent. The dimensions of *Sairyōshū* (20 measures) indicate no more than that it is likely to be a tune of the Tang, rather than a tune from an earlier dynasty.

The song-text that now follows is set out, line by line, with translation, followed by transcription of the Chinese text into *pinyin* (the modern system of transliteration), underlaid by the Chinese original. A glance down the transcribed lines reveals the same rhyming vowel '-i' at the end of each second line (the first and last lines, of the first and last groups of four lines, also rhyme). In meaning, the poem traverses the whole of China's history, from its legendary beginning to Taizong's present, and to the precise occasion of the banquet with local officials.

Each group of four lines – each quatrain – covers a different period of activity. The first three bring us from remote pre-history to the state of pacification that prevailed in Taizong's reign; the remaining two quatrains are in the vivid autumnal present and the very occasion of the banquet itself. Looked at more closely, we see that the first three quatrains exhibit a measure of sub-division: the first brings us to Taizong's birth; the second takes us through a summary of steps in his establishing of the Imperium; the third looks in more detail at relationships with 'the Huns'. By Tang times the true Huns, the Xiongnu 匈 奴, had long since vacated their original homeland in the South-Eastern Gobi, in part having migrated to Bactria, being well established there by 128 BC; but the term was still used – as here by Taizong – for Turkic peoples beyond the Northern boundary of China.

Again, the last two quatrains, though linked, are different in content. In the fourth, Taizong is in State among his Officials, enjoying the Autumn scene; in the fifth, the harvest is achieved, the Lord has returned for the Harvest-Home, and he and his officials rejoice, as once did the villagers around the First Emperor of Han. It has already been shown that this 'semantic segmentation' of the text appears to be reflected in the musical structure of the piece.

The translation of Taizong's song-text which follows owes much to critical comments by Professor D.C. Twitchett (Princeton University); in particular, all identifications of locutions from 'The Book of Songs' are due to him. Professor Twitchett summarises the content of the five quatrains [(a) - (e)] – not, of course, separated in the original text – under the following illuminating headings:

(a) The Continuation of Royal Authority, Overriding Changes of Dynasty
(b) Our Imperial Achievements
(c) How Foreigners have Responded to Us
(d) Our Task is Done
(e) Celebration

Meaningful segmentation of the song-text is evidently correlated with the observed segmentation of the music into units of four measures:

(a)   Over the Mound of Shou[39] only old tracks
       Shou mou[40] wei jiu ji,
       壽 丘 / 某 唯 舊 跡，

[39] Shouqiu, in Qufu xian 曲 阜 縣, birth-place of the Yellow Emperor, where Shun made sundry implements. We are at the beginning of Chinese legendary history.
[40] Because of identity with the personal name of Confucius, *qiū* will have been read *mou*: 'a certain place'. *THY* reads 邱 for 丘 (an alternative).

Of the City of Feng[41] only former foundations
Feng yi nai qian ji.
酆 邑 乃 前 基 。

[But] We[42] are the Heir of successive Holy Kings
Yue yu cheng lei sheng,
粵 余 承 累 聖,

The Hanging Bow[43] likewise is in this place [That is: We have sons, and Heaven's Mandate will be sustained through Us.]
Xuan hu yi zai zi.
懸 弧 亦 在 茲 。

(b)   In younger years We met with Fortune's changes
Ruo ling feng yun gai,
弱 齡 逢 運 改 ,

We took up the sword, anxious to cure the ills of the age
Ti jian yu kuang shi.
提 劍 鬱 匡 時 。

At the head of Our army[44] the whole country[45] was settled
Zhi huiba huang ding,
指 麾 八 荒 定 ,

Winning over through gentleness the barbarians of the myriad states
Huai rou wan guo yi .
懷 柔 萬 國 夷 。

(c)   Scaling mountains some came to be received as guests
Ti shan xian[46] ru kuan,
梯 山 咸 入 款 ,

---

[41] Fengyi was the capital city of *Wen-wang* of the Zhou dynasty. The site is in modern Shaanxi Province, anciently the State of Chong 崇.
[42] This is the imperial 'We'. Taizong seems to embrace all the dynastic houses in a single, temporal continuity.
[43] It was customary to hang a bow to the left of the door when a son was born.
[44] Directing troops by signalling with flags.
[45] Literally 'the Eight Wastes'.
[46] *THY* and 'Complete Tang Poetry' (*Quan Tangshi* 全 唐 詩) read *xian* or *han* 咸 'together'; *YFSJ* has *sheng* 盛 'abundant'.

Riding the seas others have come to Us
Jia hai yi lai si.[47]
駕 海 亦 來 思。

A Xiongnu sovereign escorts Our tents in the field
Chanyu pei wu zhang
單 于 陪 武 帳，

One of his princes guards Our palace-eaves
Rizhu wei wenpi.
日 逐 衛 文 樨。[48]

(d)　From behind the screen, We pay our respects to the Four Peaks
Duan yi chao si yue,
端 辰 朝 四 岳。

Taking no action We entrust affairs to our officials
Wu wei ren bai si.
無 為 任 百 司。

The Frost-Festival illumines the Autumn scene
Shuangjie ming qiu jing,
霜 節 明 秋 景，

Thin ice congeals at water-margins
Qing bing jie shui mei.[49]
輕 冰 結 水 湄。

(e)　The bright yellows of Autumn[50] cover heights and lowlands
Yun huang bian yuan xi,
芸 黃 遍 原 隰，

---

[47] *laisi* is a locution probably taken from 'The Book of Songs' (*Shijing* 詩 經). It occurs in Mao nos. 167, 168, 171, 186, 190.
[48] *THY* 33, p.614 has *chi* 螭, reading 'our dragon-headed balustrade'. Court diarists stood beside these dragon heads when the court was in session; but this lexigraph no longer rhymes.
[49] *GKR* (*GKMR* p.974) uses an uncommon form of this lexigraph.
[50] *GKMR* has *yunxiang* 芸 香, a binome for the plant Rue: *Ruta graveolens* L. *YFSJ*, *THY* and *QTS* have *yunhuang* 芸 黃. This term, 'Rue-yellow', was used of fading leaves and flowers in general; the flowers of Rue are indeed deep yellow in colour. The line may refer, as does the preceding quatrain, to the coming of Autumn. Again there are *Shijing* references: *yunhuang* (Mao 214); *yuan xi* (Mao 163).

Of grains the full heads are stored high as hills high as cliffs
He ying ji jing di.[51]
禾 穎 積 京 坻

Together rejoicing We return to the homeland-banquet
Gong le huan xiang[52] *yan,*
共 樂 還 鄉 宴，

Enjoying this "Great Wind" song.
Huan ci [53] *Da Feng shi.* [54]
歡 此 大 風 詩。

The Ten Rhymes of Taizong's Song-Text

(sound-values from Karlgren, 1957; asterisks are used by K. to distinguish archaic values – *e.g.* those based on *Shijing* rhymes – from those of the dialect of Chang'an)

	Signature	Archaic / Ancient / Modern Pronunciations
基	**952 g.**	**ki̯əg / kji / ki*
茲	**966 b.**	**tsi̯əg / tsi / tsi*
時	**961 z.**	**di̯əg / zi / shi*
夷	**551 a.**	**di̯ər / i / yi*
思	**973 a.**	**si̯əg / si / si*
朡	**566 e'.**	**b'i̯ər / b'ji / p'i*

---

[51] *THY* reads 即 京 坻. For this use of *jing* see Mao 211.

[52] *GKMR* has 'tower' *qiao* 譙; but *xiang*, in the sense of homeland, makes much better sense; this is an occasion on which Taizong feasts with local officials at his birthplace. Wilhelm and Knechtges (1987, p.12) identify Qiao as Wugong 武 功, subject of another poem in 20 lines.

[53] *QTS* replaces 'this' *ci* 此 with 'compare' 比. One might perhaps think of construing in the sense of 'Enjoyment comparable with that of the "Great Wind" occasion' (see n. 53); but 'this' seems simpler and more natural.

[54] This is a reference to the song composed by Liu Bang 劉 邦, first Emperor of Han (Gaozu 高 祖, 207-195 BC). The song-words were composed, and the piece was danced, by Han Gaozu, and sung by 120 children, at a banquet at which he entertained the elders of his birthplace, Bei, in 195 BC (Sima Qian: *Shiji* 8, *Gaozu benji* 高 祖 本 紀, p.343).

司	**972 a.**	*$si̯əg$ / si / si
湄	**567 g.**	*$mi̯ər$ / mji / mei
坻	**590 l.**	*$d'i̯ər$ / d'i / ch'i
詩	**961 d'.**	*$śi̯əg$ / śi / shi

Recalling that Karlgren's 'Ancient Chinese' values (those between slashes – for example: / *kji* /) represent reconstructed sounds for the dialect of the Tang capital, Chang'an, in and about AD 600, this list shows that monosyllabic words at the end of every second line rhyme. All are open syllables sharing the same vowel 'i'.

A valuable independent study by Wilhelm and Knechtges (1987) – not seen until our translation (with commentary) was completed – examines the poetic output of the Taizong Emperor; it both translates and elucidates this song-text (1987, pp.10-12). These authors see the text as composed of ten couplets – as indeed it is. Its semantic segmentation into five quatrains is as evident, however, in their translation as in ours. The reader may care to compare the two. In some instances, differences are due to their acceptance of certain alternative versions of the text.

Professor Twitchett has drawn our attention to another song-text, in many respects similar, also composed by the Taizong Emperor during the Progress of 632. This is the piece entitled 'Martial Merit' (*Wugong* 武 功) .The title is the name of the Prefecture in which the Blessed-Goodness Palace was located. The text is again a poem in 20 lines of five monosyllabic words, with every second line rhyming throughout in what was, in Tang times, the same rhyme. In this instance, the rhyming syllable is a closed, nasal syllable. In Karlgren's orthography the successive rhyming syllables are: /dz'ung/, /tiung/, /kung/, /d'ung/, /kiung/, /p'iung/, /d'ung/, /k'ung/, /ɣung/ and /piung/. That is to say, the set rhymed in the sixth-century dialect of Chang'an. This song-text could have been sung to the *Sairyōshū* melody. It is to be noted that a third song-text that follows *Wugong* displays a different rhyme-system. It would seem that the two song-texts: *Qingshan-gong* and *Wugong*, were closely associated in the mind of their author.

The original modality of *Sairyōshū* and the argument for retaining certain ligatures when reducing the melody to fit Taizong's text

While Fujiwara no Moronaga's own introduction to pieces in the *Sada-chō* mode-key group of items would by itself encourage acceptance of the view that the original mode was Lydian (with sharpened fourth and seventh), the emphasis on the *Gongdiao* modal character of the music of Liangzhou (p.16) surely justifies restoration of those sharps – already shown in Moronaga's score, in accordance with his principle of transcription of items in the *Ichikotsu* – and *Sada*-mode groups. This has been done to the melodic line of this piece, as recorded in the mouth-organ version.

It has already been argued that any conflation of the four versions (two for mouth-organ, one for zither, one for lute) must be reduced, if a tune suitable for the syllabic singing of five, rather than seven, monosyllabic words to each eight-beat measure is to be recovered. In making such a reduction, it may further be argued that ligatures that incorporated the very characteristic sharpened fourth should be retained, since there can be no doubt that the Lydian character of the music of Liangzhou was one of its most striking features for Chinese ears in the Sui and early Tang. The reader may again be reminded that this was the sound of Sādhārita, the first Kuchean Mode, demonstrated by Zheng Yi (Volume 7, in preparation). According to the Sui account (p.14), the music of Liangzhou was modified music of Kuchā.

In order to produce a version of the conflation of this tune apt for singing Taizong's text, it has been decided: (1) to retain all instances of the tritone, *d* - *g♯* taken by leap; (2) to retain *f♯g♯* -ligatures, since it is *g♯* (not *f♯*) that is the auxiliary; and again (3), to retain descending *g♯f♯* -ligatures, where treatment of the *g♯* as an appoggiatura would lead to disappearance of a characteristic tritone leap in intermediate position in the measure.

Apart from these considerations, the reduction has been made as on previous occasions (Fascicle 3, p.19, p.52) save that, in the treatment of échappées, the first note has *not* been regarded as the original note of the undecorated melody when the first note is the sharpened fourth. To do otherwise would lead to the creation of measures that cadence on an auxiliary – on a *bian* 變.

Sairyōshū: Western Liangzhou

Conflation (N.J.N., p.139)

Song-line with text underlay (L.E.R.P.)

Shou mou wei jiu ji, Feng yi nai qian ji. Yue yu cheng lei sheng,

Xuan hu yi zai zi. Ruo ling feng yun gai, Ti jian yu kuang shi.

Zhi hui ba huang ding, Huai rou wan guo yi. Ti shan xian ru kuan,

Jia hai yi lai si. Chan - yu pei wu zhang, Ri - zhu wei wen-pi.

Duan yi chao si yue, Wu wei ren bai si. Shuang - jie ming qiu jing,

Qing bing jie shui mei. Yun huang bian yuan xi, He ying yi jing di.

Gong le huan xiang yan, Huan ci Da Feng shi.

The rhythm of each measure of the reduction is constant, reflecting the constant semantic rhythm of the text-lines of five monosyllabic words, save where a ligature that includes the sharpened fourth replaces the second minim of a measure. Each five-syllable line, in which a caesura follows the second syllable, may be held to consist of two hemistichs. The anapaestic rhythm of the second hemistich: | ♪♪♩|, is present, before reduction, in 7 out of 20 measures of the conflation. After reduction this rhythm is present in 17 of the 20 measures. Crotchets/quarter-notes are already available in the conflation, in place of a third minim/half-note in the 4/2 measures.

Since the monosyllable *mou* 某 (replacing *qiu* in the first line) is likely to have been pronounced with a rising inflection in pitch in the Tang as it is today, the ascending *f♯g♯*-ligature on this syllable is appropriate, as also on *líng* 齡 and *róu* 柔. This may be fortuitous, however, since elsewhere in the tune ligatures are not appropriate for the segmental tone of monosyllabic words, as pronounced today in 'ordinary speech'.

As a last comment on Taizong's song-text, it is to be noted that this semantic, rhythmic treatment of the five-syllable line is one widely popular in the construction of song-texts in the Tang. A survey of texts preserved in *YFSJ* has shown that at least 60 percent of all items labelled: *xing* 行 'to walk', are in lines of five syllables. Their rhythmic interpretation is usually the same as that shown for Taizong's lines, in accordance with their semantic rhythm. What can this term *xing* have signified as a label for a type of song-text?

An army on the march was referred to as *xing jun* 行 軍, and it is suggested that the term was originally applied to a small group of *rhythms* suitable for marching-songs. It is to be emphasised that the term *xing* occurs in modern use for processionals (*xingyue* 行 樂) in certain regional instrumental traditions. Although the alternative meaning of *xing*: 'a row', 'a series', might lead one to think of a suite-like, serial structure, the vast majority of *xing* are not subdivided into stanzas (*jie* 節 or *zhang* 章), marked in the course of the text. Clearly the *rhythm* of the reduced conflation is one well suited to marching, and much less boring than one consisting of four equal beats, fitting a text in lines of four monosyllabic words. Though not labelled *xing*, Taizong's text, in its slow ceremonial-march character, was appropriate to the sentiment of the words, and to an occasion when, surely, old soldiers were likely to be among his guests. This perception of the character of the piece is of course precisely compatible with the instruction *nobe/yan* 延, specified in the prefatory comment to the tablature in *KF/HSF/RK* (p.27).

A late medieval European melodic parallel to *Sairyōshū*

To anyone reared in the traditions of the Church of England and Anglican Churches overseas, or in other religious traditions in which hymn-singing is part of public worship, the first measure of *Sairyōshū* arrests attention because of its near identity with the first musical line of the tune 'Ravenshaw', commonly used for the hymn-text that begins: 'Lord, Thy Word abideth, And our footsteps guideth'.[55] The tune first appeared in English usage in *Hymns Ancient and Modern* (1875) and it is an abridgement (by the editor of that compilation, W.H. Monk) of a tune printed in 1531[56] in *Ein neu Gesengbuchlen* [ed. M.(Michael) Weisse].

Since there are those who criticise our use of the standard, functional names for the notes in heptatonic, diatonic note-sets, in our analyses of melodic structures of the Tang, it seems appropriate now to demonstrate how a late medieval European melody differs, in its unfolding, from 'Western Liangzhou', in spite of what might be described as an identity in incipit.

We owe to the late Father Rajeczky of the Musicological Institute of the Hungarian Academy of Sciences (Budapest) a yet earlier fifteenth-century version of the tune as it was in Hussite use.[57] While Weisse's version will have been sung (one may suppose) with the *b* flattened throughout (see Example 1), the Hussite version marks no flat. It is to be concluded that this melody was sung in the Lydian mode with *b*♮. The Latin text (of which the first two lines only are given by Weisse) is shown complete for the stanza in the Hussite version, and complete for the entire hymn in the *Gesangbuch* (1567) of J. Leisentrit.[58]

It seems possible that the various editors of the fifteenth and sixteenth centuries felt free to regard the melody as either Ionian or Lydian. What is striking about this hymn-tune, as compared with 'Western Liangzhou', is the restricted use of two phrase-finals only in the former: the fifth above (and the fourth below) the final, and the final itself. By contrast, 'Western Liangzhou' makes use of the sixth, the fifth, and the second above the final, as well as the final itself, as phrase-cadences. In other words, in the modal dynamics of *Sada-chō*, as exemplified in *Sairyōshū* – reflecting not merely those of the music of Liang, but also those of Kuchā – sub-mediant, dominant, super-final and final, all function as phrase-cadences. Furthermore, whereas in the Central-European tune the dominant functions as cadence twice as frequently as the final, in 'Western Liangzhou' the dominant is the least frequent, the sub-mediant, more frequent, and the final, the most frequent phrase-cadence.

A further marked difference exists in the use of the tritone in the Lydian versions of both these tunes. In the Hussite version of the European melody, the tritone is never taken by leap. In the conflated Lydian version of 'Western

---

[55] Words by Sir Henry Baker (H.W. Baker)

[56] Zum jungen Buntzel, 1531. The collection was reprinted in facsimile by K. Ameln (Kassel, 1957), and the tune appears on the page that follows that headed '*werdung Christi* A V'.

[57] Zdeněk, Nejedlý: *Dějiny husitského zpěvu* III (Prague, 1955: pp.222-3)

[58] See W. Bäumker: *Das katholische deutsche Kirchenlied in seinen Singweisen* (Freiburg i.B., 1886, I, 252, 1, No.7); reference from Dr Rajeczky.

Liangzhou', such a leap occurs four times, and it still appears three times even in the reduced version, prepared to fit the words of Taizong's song-text.

In the transcription of the melody (Example 1) from the original notation of Weisse, short vertical lines on the stave correspond to the punctuation of the Latin text. For the first stanza, the text itself has been completed (from the square bracket onwards), as in the Hussite and Leisentrit versions.

Example 1.

We see then how different the two melodies are, and how (in part) this difference is determined by the relative weight attached to the functions of different notes, in the different contexts of the two musical cultures. This is so, even though both melodies (in their Lydian versions) operate within the same heptatonic note-set (in terms of relative pitches). (See in this connection comparative studies of medieval Western melodies, and gamelan melodies, by Maceda, 1995, ii.)

The splendour of Taizong's opening, elegiac meditation on the waste of Shou has, perhaps, more in common with the *Affekt* of 'Hail to the Heavenly & Devoted Body of the Saints' than to the sixteenth-century's 'Through the disobedience of our father, Adam, we were damned unto eternity, no part of us was wholesome.' But such indeterminacy of musical *Affekt* is a not-unusual feature of musical expression, and of the musical experience in general.

Bian 遍 and *bian* 偏; and the abridgement of banquet-items transferred to ritual use

Attention has already been drawn (p.24) to the process of abridgement undertaken (according to *JTS* and *XTS*) in the revision of banquet entertainment items, on transfer to the ritual repertory for use in extra-metropolitan, sacrificial rites. This process is defined in terms of change in the number of constituent *biàn* 遍 / 偏 (both lexigraphs are read today in the same way and in the same segmental tone; alternatively, both may be aspirated: *piàn*).

The generalised meaning of syllables of this structure: "P-(W)-N", that is, syllables with a bilabial initial consonant, a medial vowel or semi-vowel, and a dental nasal final consonant (as summarised by Cooper, 1985, p.15) is 'pulling apart, breaking, dividing'. The primary meaning of the phonetic *bian* 扁 is closely connected with *pian* 篇: 'a leaf of a book, a section, a book'; 'a tablet of bamboo for writing on', and there can be no doubt that *JTS* and *XTS* are referring to 'sections' of a musical entity. What is unclear is the precise sense to be attached to the term in a musical context.

When *JTS* and *XTS* ascribe 52 *bian* to 'Destroying the Formations' as performed as an item of banquet entertainment music-with-dance, it is unlikely that this number refers to distinct 'movements' of a musical work as we would use that term. A hint of what the meaning may have been comes, perhaps, from the reference in *JTS* (p.1049) to 'The Supreme Original' in 29 *bian*, since *XTS* sets out the structure of this item of music-with-dance (*XTS*: p.468) as a list of twelve, two-lexigraph titles. In order to obtain 29 sections from a piece consisting of twelve named items, it would seem that certain items were either repeated in the course of performance, or composed of two or more sub-sections.

In the Japanese *Tōgaku* scores in various tablatures, a simple repeat is referred to as *hen*, where the lexigraph may be 返 or 遍; or it may be referred to as *jō* 帖 (which, it has been argued, is the same as Chinese *die/tie* 疊) or even 條 (reduced to its phonetic component), also *jō* – presumably a borrowed homophone, in its basic meaning of 'article' or 'item'. (The structural position in *Gyokuju goteika* is anomalous; see Fascicle 4, pp.134-5.)

Even Chinese texts occasionally equate *die* 疊 and *bian* 遍. This may occur when it is certain that neither can mean a simple repeat, a 'time'. Thus the preface to a suite in 11 *die* in the *Shuidiao* 水 調 mode (*YFSJ* 79, pp.1114-6) describes the structure as consisting of: Song (*ge* 歌) in five *die*, together with an Entering Broaching in six *die*. Each *die* has a song-text. The preface comments further on the feeling of resentment (*yuan* 怨) manifest in the tune for the fifth *die* of the Song (a quatrain in lines of five syllables to the line). In commenting on this particular piece (as the preface records), the Tang poet Bai Juyi 白 局 易 refers to 'the one five-word *bian* 遍' rather than *die*, as previously used in the preface.

From Japanese usage in the context of tablatures, it is plain that *jō* 帖 can be 'variants' rather than simple 'repeats' – as in the six Sections of the Broaching of *Ōdai-hajinraku* (Fascicle 1, pp.65-82; Fascicle 2, pp.77-9, 92, 93). On the other hand, the *jō* of *Gyokuju goteika* (Fascicle 3, pp.9,10) are simple repeats.

Even in the case of a Tang suite of standard 'Large-Piece' structure, in three main divisions: Prelude, Broaching, Quick, it is evident, counting every sub-division [as set out by Gimm (1966, pp.225-8)], that the total, theoretical number of *sections* (let us say: *bian*) might well amount to 14, even without repetition.

If, however, we think of *bian* ('sections') as being both repeats and/or variants, it becomes possible to imagine how such abridgements as reducing 'Destroying the Formations' from 52 to 2 *bian*, or reducing 'Blessed Goodness' (*JTS*) from 7 to 1 *bian*, might be carried out without entirely destroying the musical character of the original work.

From such a piece as 'Western Liangzhou'/'Blessed Goodness' a *senza-misura, tempo-giusto* Prelude could be devised (see the study of *Koinju* by N.J.N., Fascicle 5, pp.57-64). The piece itself would serve, in rhythmic terms, as a Broaching (in 4/2) but could be reduced to an Entering Broaching in 3/2 [as in the relationship between Stamping and Entering Broaching in *Shunnō-den* (Fascicle 2, pp.58-66)]. Repeats of these 'movements', together with variation, could readily bring the total of sections (*bian*) to seven.[59] Gimm (1966, p.228) noted that *die* are at times regarded as sub-divisions of *bian*, but elsewhere (as the passage from *YFSJ* 79 shows) *die* and *bian* are equated. Such uncertainties may make for wide fluctuations in the size of items as expressed in 'sections'.

A check (by N.J.N.) of numbers of sub-divisions, counting both Sections and repeats (taking the larger number of the latter if there is a choice) yielded the following numbers, in respect of the Large Pieces in *Ichikotsu-chō*: *Ōdai hajin-raku/Huang-di pozhenyue*, 17 sub-divisions; *Toraden/Tuanluanxuan*, 18 sub-divisions; *Shunnō-den/Chunying zhuan*, 20 sub-divisions.

Vagueness in the meaning of a musical, structural term, such as attaches to *bian*, may irritate; but it is not unique to this term and must be accepted as a consequence of the existence of a number of traditions, both changing traditions in time, and regionally different traditions. In the repertory of the seven-stringed zither, for example, *die* occurs in the title of a famous piece, played when friends are parting: 'Three Variants of "The Yang Pass" ' (*Yangguan san die* 陽 關 三 疊). The three *die* are three sections built on what may have been a Ming dynasty reminiscence of a much older song-melody. Incipit and refrain are repeated in each variant-presentation of the material, and a *Coda* in harmonics is added. Here *die* appears to be a restatement with variation.[60]

Yet again the term *nong* 弄 occurs in the title of another famous *qin*-composition: 'Three Playings (=Variants) of "Plum-Blossom" ' (*Meihua san nong* 梅 花 三 弄). The piece is constructed around three statements of a tune, said to derive from a flute melody of the fourth century. The three statements are varied *registrations* of the same tune, all in harmonics. The variation is in a sense minimal, since there is no change in embellishment (for example). As a result of changing the set of harmonics in which the tune is performed, there is change in overtone-content of individual notes (harmonics on *qin*-strings are not pure sine-waves!) and in the octave in which the tune is heard. *Nong* has the general meaning of 'play' or 'to play', in a playful sense. Again, here is a word of wide, and vague, significance and application, chosen for use in a technical sense, in musical (and for that matter, theatrical) contexts.

[59] Of the version in *XTS* in 50 *bian*, no more than that statement is known.
[60] A study of this piece by the late Professor Mitani will be found under the title: 'Some melodic features of Chinese qin music' in *Music and Tradition*, ed. D.R. Widdess and R.F. Wolpert, Cambridge University Press, 1981, pp.123-42.

It must not be forgotten that even the structure of the Large Piece itself is not named consistently in the same terms. *YFSJ* records a pre-Tang, tripartite musical structure consisting of *Yan* 豔, *Qu* 趨 and *Luan* 亂. The last term, it will be recalled, has already been discussed in connection with *Ranjō/Ranjo* (Fascicle 5, pp.27-31) in its meaning of *Coda*; and it is to be noted again that this term *Luan* occurs as late as the *Guangling san* zither suite in its later eighth-century version, in the binome *luansheng* 亂 聲 (see Fascicle 3, p.100).

'Spear-Play'
Rosō/Rōsō/Nongqiang   弄 槍
or
'Spear-Play Music'[1]
Rōsōraku/Nongqiang yue   弄 槍 樂

The title and its significance

The use of the verb 'to play with', 'to manifest' (the lexigraph originally displayed 'two hands' and 'jade') implies an exercise rather than a combat activity. The Chinese term *qiang* means primarily a sharp, pointed stick, and is also applied to the bamboo elements, sharpened to a point, that make up a bamboo fence. By extension it means a spear with a long shaft.

History of pieces of this, or related, title

The title does not occur in the Tang lists of entertainment music-with-dance (*JFJ, THY, JGL, YFZL*); and though many titles beginning with *nong* are listed in Ren Bantang (1984) this is not among them. An 'act' or 'performance', known as a 'Spear-Play Act', is described in *WXTK* (*c*.1308), as noted by *Gakukō-mokuroku* (*GKMR*), p.975: '*Wenxian-tongkao* states, in regard to "The Spear-Play Performance", that players without weapons [literally "naked"] carry a number of rings. A strong player stands several tens of paces away. Successively he pitches more than ten spears so that they pass through them [= the rings]. When finished, each has received his spear from the strong one.' 文 獻 通 考 曰，弄 槍 伎，蓋 工 裸 帶 數 環，捲 一 工 立 數 十 步 外 ， 連 擲 十 餘 槍 以 度 之，既 畢，乃 一 捲 授 其 槍 也 。 *GKMR* then adds 'it is also said that, in the Hundred Games of the Miscellaneous Music of the Song Dynasty, there was "Treading the Ball", "Kicking the Ball" and "Spear-Play". 又 曰 宋 朝 雜 樂 百 戲 ， 有 蹈 毬 蹴 毬 (踏) 弄 槍 。

For once, notwithstanding the absence of the title in Tang Chinese sources, *DNHS* gives a precise date for the appearance of the piece in Japan: 'In *Tempyō* 7 [735], in the reign of Emperor Shōmu, when the embassy sent to Tang returned to court [= to Japan], *Rōsō* was performed, namely this item.' 聖 武 帝 天 平 七 年 遺 唐 使 歸 朝 奏 弄[2] 槍 既 是 。 The year-date presumably relates to

---

[1] While 'music' (*raku/gaku/yue* 樂) is the final term in perhaps a majority of *Tōgaku* titles, and has (for that reason) not been translated previously, in this instance translation is appropriate, since the commoner form of the title consists of two lexigraphs only, without 'music'.
[2] A vulgar variant of *rō/nong* 'play' is used, composed of determinative 64 and, as phonetic, 'above' 上, over 'below' 下.

the return of the Mission that left for China in 733, of which one ship returned in 734, another in 736 (Fujiie, 1988, p.94).

While *JCYR* and *SGYR* speak of the relationship between music and dance, and state that the dancers decide the number of repetitions of the tune, *RMS* states there is no dance, *KKS*, that formerly there was a dance. *KF/HSF/RK*, however, states that the dance has become extinct. Whether or not the spear-throwing exercise was ever performed to music at the Japanese court seems doubtful.

Of great interest is the use in Buddhist ceremonies of the music that survived, as attested by *RMS*, *KKS* and *DNHS*. The first two of these sources state that it is to be used during the Flower-Offering in Memorial Services; while *DNHS* records that it was performed not only at Memorial Services associated with the Blessing of a Pagoda (*Keitō-hōe* 慶 塔 法 會), but also at all Freeing [of Birds] Ceremonies at the Temple of the War God (*Hachiman no hōjō-e* 八 幡 放 生 會). Emperor Suzaku 朱 雀 帝 (930-46) made use of it at *Sumō* Wrestling (*Sumō-setsu* 相 撲 節); and it was also employed as 'answering dance' (*tōbu* 答 舞) to 'The Prince of Qin Destroys the Formations' (*Shinnō-hajinraku* 秦 王 破 陣 樂) and also to the following answering dance: 'The Imperial Roebuck' (*Ōjo* 皇 獐).

Elsewhere unparalleled is the specified number of repeats of this tune (in 12 measures, each of 8 crotchet/quarter-note beats): up to 40 in Prince Sadayasu's early flute score (p.51); but the actual number depended on the dancers, we are told. Curiously, *KF/HSF/RK* gives the number as 47; but *KKS* (6, p.114, **20**) agrees with 40. At today's speed of performance, the tune would be played through once in 14 minutes. 40 repeats would yield a piece lasting for 560 minutes – that is 9 hrs 20 mins, assuming the tempo was constant. In the light of our transcriptions (p.52) and the conflation (p.145), a comfortable original pace may have been $\bullet$ = 96. This would imply one minute for a single time, and 40 mins for 40 times. Even 40 mins is long for a single tune to be repeated. However, as background music for ceremonies, such as the Freeing of Birds, such a duration may have been tolerable; but surely even 40 mins would be exceptionally long for the Flower-Offering. On the other hand, a faster pace ($\bullet$ > 96) might well be felt indecorous.

A last important historical association of this piece, recorded by *KKS* (5, p.94) is its connection with 'The Ten Heavens' or 'Ten *Devas*' (*Jūten-raku /* *Shitian yue* 十 天 樂) (p.81). This same source also states that, according to [Ue no] Mitsutoki [上] 光 時 (1087-1159), the character of the 'spear' used resembled that in the *Komagaku* piece: 'The Korean Halberd' (*Komaboko*) (*Koma* has the 'dog' determinative: 犬白 鋒. The Japanese lexigraph for *hoko/feng* uses the 'wood' 木 determinative.) The stave (*tō* or *sao* 桌) is said to be *c*.3.6 m. in length; the same character does not commonly have this meaning

49

in Chinese. The style of the dance resembled that of 'Great Peace' (*Taihei-raku/Taiping yue* 太 平 樂) – all this according to Mitsutoki: *Mitsutoki no setsu* 光 時 説 . Surprisingly – in view of the large number of repeats specified – *KF/HSF/RK* marks the piece as 'slow' ('delayed', 'lengthened', 'protracted' *nobe/yan* 延).

No performance of *Rōsō* is recorded in *KKCMJ*, but neither is any recorded for *Sairyōshū*, even though *ZKKS* makes plain that performance of the latter, on very special occasions, took place from 813 onwards. It may be that performance of *Rōsō,* either in circumstances of imperial familial intimacy, or on Buddhist ceremonial occasions, tended to fall outside the area of attention of Tachibana no Narisue 橘 成 季 , compiler of *KKCMJ*. *RMS* states that, not only was *Rosō* (spelling of *RMS*) 'an item performed in the music for the Great Buddhist Flower Memorial Service' 大 法 花 養 樂 に ナ る 物 也, but when *Jūtenraku* was not available, this was used. Nowadays, however, when *Jūtenraku* is done, it is said that this does not have the dance.' 十 天 樂 の な か り し 時 は こ れ を も ら い る, い ま の 世 十 天 樂 を す 。 さ れ ど 是 を も す ま い な し 。

HPGS (*GKR* 31, p.927) states: 'The piece *Rosō*'s sincerity has not been seen documented.' This is presumably a corruption of the standard encomium: 'does not have that which has been seen'; that is to say, its like has never been seen before - as affirmed by *ZKKS* in regard to *Anrakuen* (p.75). The text continues: 'Up to the time [concurrent with that] of [the 53rd Emperor, Junna 淳 和, posthumous name:] Ōto-ono 大 伴 [823-33], this dance was danced; [it] finally became extinct. The pictures of dancers of Tang [show] four men. The style resembles that of *Dances of the Right.* They wear a long outer robe; attached to the top of the cap (by binding with red braids) small bells are worn, as on Korean halberds. Grasping, brandishing and dragging [halberds] behind them, they dance it, etc., etc..'

弄 槍 曲 , 慥 無 書 見 [= 所 見 ?] ， 此 舞 至 于 大 伴 兼 時 舞 之 斷 絶 畢 。 唐 舞 圖 四 人 也 。 其 體 似 右 舞 ， 有 打 懸 以 赤 紐 結 付 冠 上 帶 鈸 如 犬白 [=*Koma*] 鋒 持 掉 曳 尻 舞 之 二 二 。

Prefaces from the manuscript sources

KF/HSF/RK

'Spear-Play' (slow). Old Music. Dance extinct. 47 times. Beats of each separate time, 12. A piece in the *Sada-chō* mode-key.

弄 槍 延 。 古 樂。絕 舞。四 十 七 條。拍 子 條 別 十 二。沙 汰
調 曲 也 。

SSSTF

'Spear-Play'. Of beats, 12. Old music.

弄 槍 拍 子 十 二　　古 樂

JCYR

'Spear-Play Music' Nangū's and Chōshūkyō's transverse flute score(s)[3] do not have the 'music' lexigraph.

南`宮 長 秋 卿 橫 笛 譜[4] 無 樂 字

Of beats, 12. Nangū's score says 40 times.

拍` 子 十 二　南[5] 宮 譜 云 [四 十][6] 帖

Each separate time, 12 beats.

[帖] 別 拍 子 十 二

But as to this dance, blow it following the dancers. The number of times is not fixed.

但 此 舞 隨 舞 吹 之　無[7] 定 數

Middle-sized piece. Old music.

中` 曲 古` 樂

---

[3] Note again close-coupling of names of Prince Sadayasu and Minamoto no Hiromasa in authorship of a transverse-flute score or scores.

[4] *SGYR* inserts particle ホ.

[5] *SGYR*: a large hollow dot precedes 'Nan-'.

[6] *SGYR*: '40' written in abbreviated form; repeat-sign duplicates *jō* 'time'.

[7] *SGYR*: 無 replaces Radicle 71. In *JCYR* too this substitution has been made, lacking Radicle 71.

Rōsōraku

JCYR

[1] (left) (gloss: ligature supplied)  一 説 'a variant'

[2] (right)  一 説 "

[3] (right)  一 説 "

[4] (left)  一 説 "

[5] (right)  一 説 "

[6] (left)  一 説 "

[7] (left)  一 説 "

[8] (right)  一 説 "

[9] sharpening dot, ligature and slur supplied

[10] (right) (gloss)  一 説 "

[11] (left)  一 説 "

SGYR

[1] (right)  'a variant'

[2] " "

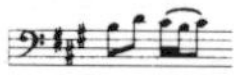

[3] " "

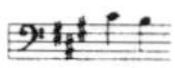

[4] " "

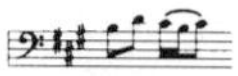

[5] (left) "

[6] (right) "

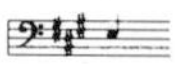

[7] " "

[8] (left) "

[9] " "

[10] (right) "

[11] " "

[12] " "

[13] Tablature sign: ㄱ deleted as error in *MS.* (匕 = 非), between *f♯* and *a*.

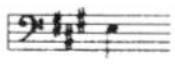

28 Suite[1]

'Bird(s) of the Qin[2] River'

Shingachō / Shūgachō / (Shibukawa-tori)[3] / Qinhe niao

沁[4] 河 鳥

The title and its significance

This again is a title unknown to the Tang lists. Of the history of the suite itself, all that is known derives from Japanese sources (see later); but the geographical reference in the title, amplified with such particularity by *JCYR* and *SGYR* (p.60), necessitates examination of the historical significance of this reference, before any consideration of the history of the suite itself.

Although Hirade (1982) chose to set the modern Japanese abbreviation of the first alternative in n.4 in first place, *JCYR* and *SGYR* correctly display 沁, once a tributary of the Yellow River (*Huanghe* 黃 河) in Shānxi Province (山 西)[5], a river referred to both as 'Qin Waters' (*Qinshui* 沁 水) and as 'Qin River' (*Qinhe* 沁 河). During the Sui dynasty (581-617), the Qin River was involved in the later phase of development and extension of a vast canal-system. The first phase involved another river 'Bian Waters' (*Bianshui* 汴 水), or 'Bian River' (*Bianhe* 汴 河), and its development as the 'Bian Canal' (*Bianqu* 汴 渠).

The detailed geography of these developments is probably impossible to determine with accuracy at this distance in time, (1) because of changes in the paths of water-courses over the centuries; (2) because of revision of the network in succeeding dynasties, in part occasioned by secular change in geographical features; (3) because of changes in place-names, or in the names of components of the canal system when what had been a river became a canal, for example. A major attempt at elucidation was made by Needham (1971)[6], and those interested in the Sui and other sources for the history of these developments will find these

---

[1] A Prelude is lost.
[2] The lexigraph is also read *shen* today in Chinese.
[3] Hirade's readings (1982).
[4] Graphic corruption in Japan of 沁 to 沚, yielding a reading *Shigachō/Zhihe niao,* was carried still further by substitution of an abbreviation of 澀 for 沚. In current Chinese, *zhi* 沚 is an islet in a stream; 澀 (*se* in Chinese) is 'rough' or 'astringent', as is the abbreviation (read *shibu* in Japanese). The Chinese original was undoubtedly 沁.
[5] Mathews' Chinese-English Dictionary (revised American Edition, Cambridge Mass., 1943) wrongly names the province as Shensi (= Shanxi, commonly written nowadays as Shaanxi 陝 西); but the basin of the Qin lay in the territory of today's Shansi (= Shanxi: 山 西) Province.
[6] IV, 3, pp.306ff

set out by Zhu Xie 朱 契 (1962)[7] ('Xie' should be preceded by the ninth determinative: 人).

What is quite certain is that the reference to Yang-*di* 煬 帝[8], second emperor of the dynasty, in the preface to *Shingachō*, in *JCYR* and *SGYR* (p.60), is appropriate, since it was during his reign (604 to 617 – when he was deposed), that these tremendous waterworks, involving both the Qin and the Bian Rivers, were undertaken. In the year of his enthronement, he announced his intention of founding a new capital at Luoyang 洛 陽 (Wright, 1978)[9]. As observed by Wright[10], 'the capital region was a food-deficit area', and it was towards securing 'resources of all the most productive land with the exception of Szechwan (which was linked to the capital by a well-established road)' that Yang-*di* extended the construction of a canal-network, begun in 584 by his father, Wen-*di* 文 帝 (reigned 581-604).

Yang-*di*'s first operations were directed to the canalised development of the Bian River. The new Bian Canal, completed in 605, ran parallel with, but South-West of, the ancient 'Wild Goose' (or merely 'vast') Canal: *Honggou* 鴻 溝 (the beginnings of which lay far back in the Fourth Century BC), later – and up to the end of the Sixth Century – known as the Bian Canal. This became silted up; and about AD 600, Yuwen Kai 宇 文 愷, Chief Engineer of the Sui, determined a new alignment, parallel to the 'Wild Goose Canal' – a new Bian Canal. This was completed in 605. For both Sui and Tang, this was 'The Grand Canal'[11]. Wright[12] translates a passage that describes the extraordinary pomp of Yang-*di*'s Progress, from his new capital of Luoyang to Jiangdu 江 都, his 'Yangzi Capital' – a stretch of water extending roughly between Luoyang and the great lake on the Huai River (*Huaihe* 淮 河), the *Hongze hu* 洪 澤 湖 a distance of more than 600 km.

In the 'Sui History'[13] statements are made that relate to the creation of 'The Through-Relief Canal' (*Tongji qu* 通 濟 渠) in 605; but details of this operation, in so far as they involved the Bian River, first appear in *Zizhi tongjian* 資 治 通 鑑 (*ZZTJ*)[14].

'In the first year of *Daye* [605], third month, 48th day of the cycle, he commanded the Secretary of State's Deputy of the Right, Huang Fuyi, to order more than a million persons, from all the Prefectures of Huaibei [Henan Province], to open up the *Tongji qu*: from Xiyuan, to lengthen the Gu and Luoshui to reach to the [Yellow] River; again from Banzhu, to lengthen the river

---

[7] pp.16,20
[8] Memorial name Yang, personal name Guang 廣; style A'ma 阿 孃.
[9] *The Sui Dynasty* (New York, 1978), p. 86
[10] p.178
[11] Needham, 1971, pp.307,308
[12] 1978, p.180
[13] 3, 煬 帝 本 紀; 24, 食 貨 志; see later. *Suishu* Zhonghua shuju edn (Beijing, 1973), p.63
[14] 180, 隋 紀, p.5618

to pass through Rongze and enter the Bian; also from East of Daliang, to lengthen the Bianshui, entering the Si, to reach the Huai...' 大 業 元 年 三 月 辛 亥，命 尚 書 右 丞 皇 甫 議 發 河 南，淮 北 郡 民 前 後 百 餘 萬，開 通 濟 渠。自 西 苑 引 穀，洛 水 達 於 河，復 自 板 渚 引 河 歷 榮 澤 入 汴，又 自 大 梁 之 東 引 汴 水 入 泗，達 於 淮...

The longer of the canal-developments, already mentioned when discussing the extension and canalisation of the Qin River (see previously), was (as Wright states[15]) the creation of the "Perpetual Relief Canal" (*Yongji qu* 永 濟 渠). The Sui History relates[16]:

'In the fourth year of *Daye* [608], Spring, first month, 42nd day of the cycle, an imperial mandate ordered men and women of all the Prefectures in Hebei – more than a million persons – to open up the "Perpetual Relief Canal", lengthening the Qinshui to the South to reach to the [Yellow] River, to the North, passing through Zhuo Prefecture.' 大 業 四 年 春 正 月 乙 巳，詔 發 河 北 諸 男 女 百 餘 萬 開 永 濟 渠，引 沁 水 南 達 于 河，北 通 涿 郡。

The Chinese sources clearly indicate the validity of the link between Yang-*di* of Sui and the 'making use of' or 'opening' of the Qin (and of the Bian) River, a link suggested in the preface to *Qinhe niao* both in *JCYR* and *SGYR*. That the piece was 'made' by Yang Guang 楊 廣 (known posthumously as Yang-*di*) as alleged in *DNHS* is perhaps unlikely, other than in the much qualified sense suggested in Fascicle 4 (p.33).

History of pieces of this, or related title

It is certain that this piece was in the repertory of the Japanese Court musicians at the time of the first Eye-Opening Ceremony at the Tōdaiji in 752. Furthermore it was classed as a 'middle-sized piece' (Volume 7, in preparation). The evidence comes not from the *Tōdaiji-yōroku*, but from the Shōsō-in's collection of inscribed items of apparel preserved from that occasion. Matsushima (1952, p.4) records the presence of a single, outer, cloth garment, inscribed: 'Tōji (=Tōdaiji), Tang Middle-Music, *Shingachō*, garment; *Tempyō-shōhō* fourth year [752], fourth month, ninth day' 唐 寺 唐 中 樂 沁 河 鳥 衫 天 平 勝 寶 四 年 四 月 九 日。 What 'middle-music' may have been will be discussed in Volume 7.

In relation to the age of this piece, it is perhaps significant that *JCYR* and *SGYR* class it as 'old music' (*kogaku* 古 樂). What 'old music' was is also to be discussed in Volume 7. It is certain that a tradition developed such that, in performance, 'old' pieces made use of the *ikko* 壹 鼓 (or 一 鼓) – the smallest size of hour-glass drum – rather than the *kakko*. *RMS*, however, having described use of *Shingachō* as a 'Way-Walking' (*michiyuki/xingdao* 行 道) in High

---

[15] p.179
[16] 3, 煬 帝 紀, p.70

Buddhist Memorial Services (*taihōe* 大 法 會) adds that, in accordance with this use, 'its sound is that both of "new" and "old" music (wormhole in MS obliterates remainder)' – this last is a comment in the text itself! The practical implication would seem to be that it was to be performed with *ikko* on religious occasions but otherwise with *kakko*.

KKS (6, p.113, **18**) records use of this piece in 864 by Jikaku-*taishi* (of the Nibu clan) in intoning the Name of the Buddha; and in 951 as Entrance Music for a private imperial banquet (cf. use of *Sairyōshū* for this purpose, p.18). *ZKKS* (3, p.165) notes that a flute score[17]: *Shinsen ryūginshō* 新 撰 龍 吟 抄, recorded that there was no dance for the Prelude, and this in spite of the fact that a score had existed. Prelude and dance had completely died out by the time *ZKKS* was compiled in the late-thirteenth century. The same text tells us that the Prelude consisted of 10 measures, and that the dances of Prelude and Broaching had only recently been lost.

It would seem probable that *Shingachō* was still a suite in two movements at the end of the thirteenth century, but already without dance. The text goes on to confirm that when this item was treated as 'new music', the musicians beat the *kakko*; when, however, it was treated as 'old music', the dancers slapped the *ikko* (presumably suspended round the neck; see Fascicle 4, p.62). *ZKKS* also elaborates the Jikaku-*taishi* story, stating that he went to Tang in 837. At the Zhulin, the voice of the Great Teacher being inadequate for the introduction to the 'Hail Amida' Prayers, this music, played by the flute, gave him support. The Great Teacher returned to Japan in 848 and transmitted this music by means of an ivory flute.

ZKKS is the first source to flesh out the bird (or birds) of the title with the name of a particular bird: *Reirichō* 令 利 鳥, the song of which is said to be 'the same' as this piece. The idiom in which this is expressed is striking: 'as to the sound of the aforementioned bird's singing, it is the same as this piece and so forth': 件 鳥 囀 音，此 曲 二 同 ト 云 … 。 Evidently, *ZKKS* did not know a bird of this name; and the text continues, asking whether this writing might be a mistake for *Sharichō* 舍 利 鳥 – the Mynah Bird. The Mynah Bird, however, is renowned for its powers of mimicking human speech, not for its distinctive, personal song; and no bird *Reirichō* is known to Morohashi's Dictionary or to the standard Chinese Zoological Dictionary: *Dongwuxue da cidian* 動 物 學 大 辭 典 (1932).

There is, however, a possibility that this unknown bird name arose from deformation of the name of a canal. The North-Western Canal of Yang-*di*'s development derived, in part, from the Qin River. While most commonly known as the 'Perpetual Relief Canal' (*Yongji qu* 永 濟 渠), this is occasionally referred

---

[17] Marett (1988, p.264) notes use of the title *Ryūginshō* for a late copy of *Chū Ōga ryūteki yōroku-fu* (colophon dated 1660).

to as the 'Perpetual Profit Canal' (*Yongli qu* 永 利 渠)[18]. This latter name could be read as '*Eiri* canal' in Sino-Japanese; in any case, however, this *Eiri* would have been a canal name, not a bird name.

Nevertheless, there is a canal name/bird name coincidence. As has been indicated, the 'new' Bian Canal replaced a forerunner of the Grand Canal, namely, the 'Wild-Goose Canal'. The bird referred to: *Hong* 鴻, is specifically *Anser segretum serrirostris*, the Eastern race of what is now known as *Anser fabalis serrirostris*, the Bean Goose. Even without the 'water'-determinative (水), *hong*, consisting of 工 and 鳥 (工鳥), meant (in Han times) 'a big and fat bird' (Karlgren, 1957, p.301, **l172** 1). When qualified by the water-determinative, it is the Bean Goose; but (as already mentioned, p.56) the word may also be used as a loan for 'vast': *hong* 洪.

A further passage, translated by Wright (1978, p.180), relates to the requisitioning of food associated with Yang-*di*'s creation of the *Tongji qu*: 'The common people sought out food with snare and net to such an extent that on land and waters, the birds and the beasts were almost extinguished...' ('Sui History' 24, pp.686,687 – Beijing 1973).

It is perhaps not unreasonable to suggest that the birds of the Qin River associated with Yang-*di*'s canal development, the birds that were economically the most important and seasonally the most conspicuous in their comings and goings, were the Bean Geese. They gave their name to a very ancient canal that became incorporated into developments undertaken in the time of that emperor: 'The Bean-Goose Waterway' (*Honggou* 鴻 溝).

[Letters from Mr Jeffery Boswall of the BBC Natural History Unit, Bristol (29 October, 1987), and from Mr Ron Kettle, National Sound Archive, British Library of Wildlife Sound, London (27 October, 1987), inform us that *Anser fabalis serrirostris* overwinters in China and breeds in Siberia (see C. Vaurie: *Birds of the Palearctic Fauna*, 2, p.101, 1965). The area of over-wintering is defined as extending 'from Korea south to the Red Basin of Szechwan, and Kwangtung in southwestern China'.]

---

[18] The 'Perpetual Relief Canal' is shown, for example, on a map in the *Lidai yudi yan'ge xian yaotu* 歷 代 輿 地 沿 革 險 要 圖 (1879), compiled by Yang Shoujing 楊 守 敬. The Section in question is *Sui dili zhitu* 隋 地 里 志 圖, and the precise reference is: 南 一 卷 中，中，二 十 六，二 十 七，永 濟 渠 。.

Prefaces to the sources in tablature

KF/HSF/RK

'Bird(s) of the Qin River'. Old music. Prelude: of drumbeats, 12. Emperor Yang of Sui made [it] in making use of the Zhi [= Qin] River. It is a *Sada-chō* piece. Dance extinct. Broaching: four times. Beats of separate times, 10. (*Shibu* – standing for the Japanese abbreviation of *se* 澀) 河 鳥。古 樂。序 拍 子 十。隋 楊 帝 用 *shibu* 河 作。沙 汰 調 曲 也。絕 舞。破 四 條 (abbreviated to righthand component) 拍 子 別 條 十 (The use of 楊 rather than 煬 may have arisen from confusion between the family name of the Sui dynasty and the posthumous title. This source uses the Japanese lexigraph *shibu* rather than Chinese *qin* 沁, on two occasions.)

SSSTF

'Bird(s) of the Qin River' Of beats, 10. 拍 子 十

JCYR

'Bird(s) of the Qin River'. Of '*Qin*' some make '*Shibu/Se*'. Prelude: of drumbeats, 10. There is no dance. The aforementioned Prelude is discontinued. Broaching: of beats, 10. The *Transverse Flute Score* of Nangū [Prince Sadayasu] states: Broaching is to be played five times, in all making 50 beats. In the fifth time, strike three-times beats. Middle-sized piece. Old Music. '*Days and Months of the Drunken Lord*' states that [the aforementioned piece was] used by the Emperor Yang of Sui in river-making. [A marginal note to the right records an error:] Note tentative correction: *Shibugawa/Sehe*.

　　沁 河 鳥 沁` 或 作 (*shibu*) 序` 拍 子 十 無` 舞 件 序 斷 了 破 拍 子 十 南` 宮 橫 笛 譜 云 破 可 吹 五 反 (*a*) 合 拍 子 五 十 五` 反 (*a*) 打 三 度 拍 子 中` 曲 古 樂 (*b*) 醉 卿 日 月 云 隋 煬 帝 用 于 河 作 [gloss to right of 河 作] 訂 (*shibu*) 河 亻 (= 意, as in 意 を)

SGYR twice uses 遍 for 反 (*a*); at (*b*) **O** (a large hollow dot) is inserted. The gloss – suggesting the abbreviation of 澀 as a possible alternative to 沁 – is absent from this MS.

An upper-marginal gloss is present in *SGYR*, absent in *JCYR*:
'Regarding the [placing of the] first [bass-]drumbeat there are two versions; one version has first drumbeat on the seventh beat; one version, on fifth beat.' (Note the evident counting of beats by *hyōshi/paizi* 拍 子, and the fact that the strings follow the first version; mouth-organ, the second. Furthermore it is evident that the Sino-Japanese freely dispenses with *dai/di* 第 as a qualifier for ordinal numerals: *go byōshi/wu paizi* 五 拍 子 can represent 'fifth beat' as well as 'five beats'.) 初 拍 子 有 兩 説 一 説 壹 鼓 七 拍 子 一 説 五 拍 子。

Shingachō

KF/HSF/RK

[1] (left) 'Blow continuing from modified incipit' 吹 續 喚 頭.

[2] *c#″* is shown unambiguously by a graphic variant of the mouth-organ tablature sign 美.

[3] *g#″* is shown unambiguously by mouth-organ tablature sign 工.

SSSTF

[1] (right) 'Join here in repeating' 付 反.

[2] as for *KF/HSF/RK*

[3]   "   "

JCYR   一 説 'a variant'

[1] (right)

[2] (left) gloss

[3] (right) gloss

                                     一 説   "

[4] (left)

SGYR   一 説 'a variant'

[1] (right)   "

[2]   "   "

桂 譜 Katsura-score

3 (left)

已 下 口 此 'from here on [same as? = 同] this'

4   'one variant same as preceding' 一 説 同 上.

Katsura-score

5 (left)
6 (right) gloss

7   "

'a variant'

8 (left)

9 (right)   'one variant same as preceding'

A striking feature of the opening of both primary versions for strings is the descending leap of a minor sixth, from the final to the mediant; and since *ZKKS* asserts that 'the sound of the song of the aforementioned bird is the same as this piece' (p.58), it seemed important to determine what sounds are made by a possible avian candidate for the role of 'bird of the Qin River', namely, by *Anser fabalis serrirostris*. An opening minor-sixth descent had not then been encountered in any other of the thirty-odd items that comprise the *Ichikotsu* and *Sada-chō* mode-key groups; and it was an obvious step to enquire whether any calls of the Bean Goose include such a musical feature. (The mouth-organs replace this descending minor sixth by an ascending major third, since the lower $f\sharp$ is not available in the mouth-organ scale.)

Through the kindness of Mr Ron Kettle, at that time Curator of the British Library of Wildlife Sounds (National Sound Archives, London), copies of tape-recordings of flock-calls made in Sweden, Finland and Lapland were obtained. A description (from the 1950's) notes that these are the 'least vocal of grey geese; calls are disyllabic, reedy, and bassoon-like, resembling lower notes of Pink-Footed Geese, *A. brachyrhynchus* (Scott and Boyd 1957)'.[19] Sonograms of the two types of flock-calls are there reproduced – I: "Ung-ank" made by Sture Palmér (Sveriges Radio, October 1966); and II: "bow-wow", by S. Wahlstrom, Sweden.

Both these types are to be heard in the recordings made available by Mr Kettle, with the qualification that the descent in pitch between 'ung' and 'ank' is an octave + a minor sixth (a compound sixth, or a thirteenth). Recently (3 March, 1992), Mr Richard Ranft, Curator, British Library of Wildlife Sounds, made for us a number of Sonograms at various speeds (and hence magnifications) from the previously mentioned Finnish recording, made in 1981. Examination of

[19] See *Handbook of the Birds of Europe the Middle East and North America: The Birds of the Western Palaearctic*, Stanley Cramp *Chief Editor*, Volume 1, Ostrich to Ducks, p.395.

Sonograms made with the birds flying as a flock suggests that the two notes of this call are, in fact, a male/female responsorial duet (private suggestion from Mr David Hindley, 1995) that enables members of a pair to remain in contact within the flock. Which bird is responsible for which note has not been determined by observation in the field, but it seems probable that the 'ung' vocalisation is that of the male.

The two sounds of the more striking of the two types of flock-call – the 'ung-ank' type – are heard, by a majority of listeners (whose musicality qualifies them to make such an identification) as a fall in pitch, between 'ung' and 'ank', amounting to a minor sixth – approximately $e\flat'$ to g. The change in octave is not always recognised; and this, of course, is not uncommon; judgement of the size of an interval between two consecutive sounds is for many listeners easier than that of the octave in which the interval lies. In two instances, listeners have perceived a component of higher pitch in 'ank'; but musicians usually hear the minor sixth. This difference in perception is due to the acoustic complexity of the second component. Qualitatively, the two sounds are very different, to the ear as well as to the Sonograph. The 'ung' has a bassoon-like quality; and its Sonogram reveals a 'musical sound' with harmonics displayed as well-defined frequencies.

Measurements made on Sonograms from Mr Ranft (by Dr C.J. Adkins, Cavendish Laboratory, Cambridge) and on narrow-band spectrograms of the whole call (by kindness of Professor C.J. Darwin, Dean of The School of Biological Sciences, University of Sussex) have shown the fundamental frequency of 'ung' to lie at about $e\flat'''$ (if c' is *Middle C*). A Sonogram of a single call showed a first harmonic of about 620 Hz. In the narrow-band spectrogram the fundamental frequency of 'ung' in another call was about 613 Hz. The second harmonic of the fundamental frequency was shown by both procedures as 390 Hz. The fundamental frequency of 195 Hz is not present, however, but pitch-perception does not require that the fundamental be perceptible. This last point had been emphasised by Dr Ian Cross (Faculty of Music, University of Cambridge). The perceived pitch of the second syllable of the call, at the distance of an octave and a minor sixth below the first, is 'virtual' rather than 'real', a phenomenon from the realm of psychoacoustics.

A further aspect of the 'ung+ank' call was already apparent from the first Sonogram published by Palmér, namely that the first element is somewhat longer than the second. Very roughly, his figure suggests that from the beginning of 'ung' to the beginning of 'ank' the time-interval is about 0.6 sec., while 'ank' lasts about 0.2 sec..

If the perceived fall of a minor sixth + an octave, between 'ung' and 'ank' in this particular flock-call (as opposed to the 'bow-wow' type), is strikingly reminiscent of the opening of the two string versions of the piece, 'Bird(s) of the Qin River', the observed greater duration of 'ung' (+ the time interval between 'ung' and 'ank') as compared with the duration of 'ank', appears to approximate to what is represented in the upper marginal gloss, present in *SGYR* but absent in *JCYR*. In the transcription, both string versions have been written so as to follow the first version specified in this gloss. (The mouth-organ tablatures show no knowledge of this metrical variant.) For the mouth-organ, the first drumbeat falls on the fifth beat of a standard eight-beat measure. For the strings, the piece opens with an anacrusis (on the final) of minim duration, so that the first drumbeat falls on the seventh beat of an eight-beat measure that follows the anacrusis.

Because of the scaling of the mouth-organ, a descending minor sixth opening, with fall from final to mediant, is necessarily inverted to a rising major third by a performer who wishes to take advantage of the sonority of the cluster-chord on the lowest *D* in the scale.

The first variant shown in *JCYR* (note 1), gives a rising major third (as for mouth-organ), but the initial final (*D*) is – in effect – lengthened to a dotted quarter-note/crotchet, so that the rhythmic effect still resembles, in its temporal characteristics, what happens in the 'ung-ank' call.

In the light of these observations, it seems to us not impossible that the opening of the piece 'Bird(s) of the Qin River', with its falling octave + minor sixth, was intended as a contrafactum of the hypothesised duet of the more striking of the two flock-calls of the Bean Goose, the bird that will have made so notable an addition to the protein supply necessary for sustenance of inhabitants of Yang-*di*'s new capital.

It is surely remarkable that the pitches of the call, recorded from this species more than a thousand years after that emperor's day, are so close to the absolute pitch of the opening minor sixth of the bird call, as transcribed today; but then, we know that the frequency of *A* in the instrumental ensembles of the Tang scarcely differed from today's Concert Pitch (see Volume 7, Chapter 6 – in preparation).

Preliminary comments on the structure of the piece

ZKKS records that the lost Prelude consisted of 10 beats (= measures); *KF/HSF/RK* states 12; again, *ZKKS* records that the Broaching consists of 12 – 'or some say 10' – beats with a varied incipit (*kandō/huantou* 換 頭) of one measure. In specifying incipit lengths, the mouth-organ scores differ from the string scores, and the length of the incipit differs between *JCYR* and *SGYR*. These discrepancies, in so far as they concern the Broaching, are possibly related to the question of where the first drumbeat falls, as set out in the upper marginal gloss in *SGYR*.

It is suggested that the simplest, and most straightforward, interpretation of the gloss would be that, in one version of the piece – a piece in measures of eight throughout – the principal drumstroke falls on the seventh and penultimate beat of each measure throughout. In the alternative version, it falls in the more usual position, on the fifth beat throughout. It may be recalled that, in the Stamping of *Shunnōden* (Fascicle 2, pp.58-61), the drumstroke falls on the seventh beat; by contrast, all the items in 4/2-metre in Fascicle 4 (for example) show the drumstroke on the fifth beat. If we accept this suggestion as the meaning of the upper marginal gloss, we might assume the existence of a version, such as the mouth-organ manuscripts offer, but with the drumbeat on beat 7 throughout, as implied by the alternative specified in the gloss.

There is, however, at least one other possible interpretation of the words: 'first drumbeat on beat 7'. As the tablatures of *JCYR* and *SGYR* show, the prolongation sign (引|) that follows the first note (a simultaneous octave in *JCYR*) seems to imply a doubling of its duration from quarter-note/crotchet to half-note/minim. If we begin to count beats from this lengthened first note, the first measure would consist of ten beats; but if we regard the placing of the drumbeat as marking the seventh beat of an eight-beat measure, the piece might be re-barred smoothly until the end of an eighth measure. At that point, however, the whole-note/semibreve *b* would need to be halved, so as to fit the new metrical sub-division, and there would be difficulty again in measure 10. This suggests that a rational re-barring of the piece as we have it, supposing that the first measure *begins* with a half-note/minim, is not possible. It seems reasonable, then, to regard the minim as an anacrusis.

A resemblance exists between the rhythm of variant 1 of *JCYR* and what the strings offer in the primary version (signalled by the upper-marginal gloss in *SGYR*), with the final (*D*) longer than the mediant (*F♯*); but the overall time-scale is changed: halved in the former. In *SGYR* (first version) the effect is again a prolongation of the opening final, *D*; the mediant (reinforced by a mordent) is shortened to a quaver/eighth-note.

While the first four measures (amounting to an ABCD-structure) are pentatonic in *KF/HSF/RK* – apart from a *c♯* in measure 3 – *SSSTF* is hexatonic and quasi-Mixo-Lydian (with *c♮*) until reaching this same point in measure 3. Measures 5 to 7, with *c♯* and *g♯* in *KF/HSF/RK*, and *c♮*, *c♯*, and *g♯*, in *SSSTF*, are to some extent Lydian in character, as the *Sada-chō* mode-key is said to have been. The cadence on the sub-mediant, *b*, in measure 8, would be more appropriate, however, in a five-note *Gongdiao* context; and the cadence in measure 10 is Mixo-Lydian in both mouth-organ versions. Unlike others of the *Sada-chō* items, no instance of a tritone leap in either direction occurs in *Shingachō* even when the key signature is changed to one of three sharps. Such a change is probably justified, however, for all the *Sada-chō* pieces, in view of Moronaga's prefatory comment on the characteristics of that mode, and the statements made in Chinese sources regarding the *Gongdiao* character (that is, Lydian in heptatonic form) of the music from Western Liang.

The uncertainty regarding length, revealed in the statement '10 or 12 measures' in some sources, may have arisen from alternative inclusion or exclusion of the two-measure variant-incipit in the total count of measures.

'Introit to "Perfect Virtue" '

Ittokuen, Itokuen, Ichitokuen / Yide yan

壹 / 一 德 鹽

The title and its significance (both in this and the following item, Japanese sources use an abbreviated form of the Chinese lexigraph *yan* 鹽.)
The meaning of this title remains uncertain. The phrase: *Yide* occurs in the *Guanzi* book ('Master Guan' 管 子 – late fourth-century BC) with the meaning of 'a kind of excellent virtue': 'Worthies of the Empire especially excel in a refined kind of excellent virtue' 天 下 之 賢 人 也 ， 猶 尚 精 一 德。[1]
The word *en/yan* means 'salt'; but it has been suggested (*DNHS*, p.223) that the term (written either way) has been substituted for a homophone: 豔 (also written 艶 or 鹽). 鹽 (Karlgren **609 n** * *i ä m* / yen) is regarded as a loan for 'beautiful' 豔 (Karlgren **1247 a - b** *i ä m*-/yen). 鹽 seems to have developed from the compound (Karlgren **609 a - b**), consisting of 'man' 人, 'eye' 臣, and 'vessel' 皿, meaning 'to see oneself reflected in a bowl of water'. The same lexigraph (read *yan*) was also the name of a suite-movement in Han times.[2] *YFSJ* (26, p.377) states that the Large Piece (*daqu* 大 曲) comprised *Yan, Qi* (Karlgren **3 m** **d'i a/ d'i e/* ch' ï 'to run') and *Luan* (Fascicle 5, p.27). The position occupied by *Yan* in this triplet of terms leads one to suppose that the movement may have had some introductory or preludial function.

Many years ago now, when work on the transcription of Jiang Kui's secular songs was in progress (Picken, 1966, p.143), Arthur Waley suggested that the word *yan* (written in its 'salt' form) and used as a component in a title: 'The Yellow Emperor's *Yan*' was a substitute for yet another word: *yin* 引, originally meaning 'to draw a bow', but (by meaning-extension) coming to signify 'to lead' or 'to guide' (Karlgren **371 a** **d i ĕ n / i ĕ n:/* yin). The early Tang pronunciations of 豔 (Karlgren **1247 a - b**) and 引, *i ä m* and *i e n:*, respectively, were therefore similar and their interchange becomes plausible. Hence our use of the translation 'Introit'.

Two titles that include 鹽 occur in *JFJ*[3]. Any link between the two is doubtful; but both are constructed as is title **28**. *DNHS* too notes the presence of

[1] *Zhongwen ciyuan* 中 文 辭 源 1980, p.0007
[2] See Yang Yinliu, 1980, pp.115-20, for Han suite-form.
[3] See *Jiaofangji qianding* 1974, pp.94,159.

the somewhat similar title: *Yidou yan* 一 斗 鹽 (in its Japanese *on*-reading: *Itoen*), but doubts that the two are the same piece. *Dou* (Karlgren **116 a** **tu/təu:*/tou) is the name of two Chinese zodiacal constellations: the Northern *dou* (seven stars in Ursa Major – the Great Bear or Dipper), and the Southern *dou* (six stars in Sagittarius). Since worship is addressed to 'The Spirit-Lord of the Northern *Dou*', it would have been gratifying if *Yide yan* and *Yidou yan* could have been equated.

However, *de* 德 (Karlgren **919 k** **tək / tək /* tê) is phonetically far removed from *dou* in its sound-history. 'The Great Bear's Introit' has a good ring to it; but historical phonetics exclude that possibility, as does also the construction *yidou*. Indeed, for this title 'A Peck of Salt' seems to be the most natural reading.

A second title in *JFJ* (p.106), constructed in parallel fashion, is 'A Pinch of Salt' (*Yi'nie yan* 一 捻 鹽); but again there is no reason to suppose that *yan*, in this context, is a musical movement.

In support of Waley's suggestion that 鹽 stands for 引, a third title in *JFJ* is *Zhezhi yin* 柘 枝 引. As described by Twitchett and Christie (1959, p.177), the *Zhezhi* ('Thorn-Branch' dance) was performed by two dancers, or two rows of dancers, each responding to the movements of the other. The binome *Zhezhi* also occurs in the list of Large Pieces in *JFJ*, but no musical trace survives in the *Tōgaku* repertory. In his note on the title *Zhezhi*, Ren Bantang (1974, p.120) suggests that *yin* here signified the Free Prelude (*Sanxu* 散 序) of a Large Piece, since *Zhezhi* is indeed also listed as a Large Piece in *JFJ*. He is plainly reluctant, however, to accept that *yin* 引 has this meaning in titles of items of lesser standing. [*Yin* is still a common movement-title in traditional Chinese music, both in the *guqin* repertory, and in that of instrumental ensembles – as in *yintou* 引 頭 (Jones, 1995, p.317).]

History of pieces of this, or related title

Little is recorded in the sources regarding the history of this piece, and what there is carries little weight. *RMS* and *KKS* have nothing to say regarding history; *WMRJS* gives the title only under the *Sada-chō* heading; *KKCMJ* does not mention it. *ZKKS* (3, p.167) states that the piece was made by Mishima Buzō 三 島 武 藏, but adds that it is also said to have been made by Yang Lifu 陽 例 夫 (or Litian 例 天) and was 'music for the ascension to the throne of the Prince of Han' 漢 王 御 即 位 ノ 樂. Gaozu 高 祖, founder of the House of Han, originally Liu Bang 劉 邦, was known as Han-*wang* – 'Prince of Han' – during the period 206-03 BC, though his reign is counted from 207 or 206 BC. The same text also observes that 'nowadays' – that is, presumably, in the mid-thirteenth century – 'it is used in welcoming officiating priests, making incantations, or offering petitions, etc.; also, it is said to be played at dance performances at the "Eternal Bliss Assembly" on the 16th day.' 近 來 導 師 咒

願 等 ノ 迎 二 用 之 又 云, 常 樂 會 十 六 日 舞 奏 マイラスル 二 吹
之 。 *DNHS* repeats most of these points, adding only that the preludial *yan* was a
type of song from Chu 楚. This association may have arisen because the *yan* was
part of a Large Piece; and the Han Emperor, Wu-*di*, had a passion for the music
of that state, as made explicit in *YFSJ* (see Volume 7, in preparation).

As with *Shingachō* (p.57,58), we have a piece linked – for no explicit reason
– with Buddhist ceremonial. As with *Sairyōshū*, though no Palace entertainment
performances are recorded in *KKCMJ*, but performances as private Entrance
Music are recorded in *ZKKS*, this last records performances of *Ittokuen* during
Buddhist ceremonies. *ZKKS* qualifies his statement, however, by adding the
phrase: 'furthermore, it is said' or 'in addition it is said' (*mata-i* 又 云), as if the
author were reporting a matter of hearsay rather than first-hand knowledge.

In addition to the association with the first emperor of Han, *ZKKS* reports
attribution of the piece to a certain Ondō or Otowarabe/Yintong 音 童 'Sound-
Boy' – also credited with the composition of *Anrakuen* (p.75). Under the latter
heading, this composer or adapter is said to have exercised his abilities for the
benefit of an emperor of Tang.

ZKKS describes the piece as being both 'old' and 'new' music, both as
'small' and 'middle-sized', both as 'Tang' and as 'Japanese' (*Wa* 和).

In view of the relationship between *Ittokuen* and *Anrakuen* (see later), and
the evidence *either* that the latter was developed by a process of reduction from
the former *or* conversely, the suggestion that *Anrakuen* was composed pursuant
to an imperial decree when a Tang emperor was enthroned, is perhaps justifiable.
This is, of course, a matter of speculation only; but the quality of the music, and
the prestige of the item as evinced by use, suggest that this may at one time have
been a piece of some standing in the repertory. If so, it would be understandable
that a Tang-Chinese copyist would have been cautious about revealing the august
function it had once discharged.

No fewer than five binomial names of reign periods in the Tang had *toku/de*
德 as second component, including the first such period: *Wude* 武 德 'Martial
Virtue', decreed on the First Day of the Second Month in the Year 618 (see
Fascicle 4, pp.106-11). Gaozu (personal name Shude 叔 德) was enthroned on
the 18th Day of the Sixth Month of that same Year. (As work proceeds in our
study of the *Tōgaku* repertory, evidence of the presence of items from the earlier
rather than the later Tang increases.)

Prefatory comments in the manuscript sources

KF/HSF/RK

'Introit to "Perfect Virtue" ' Slow. Old music. Four times; beats of each time: 14.
There is no dance. 壹 德 鹽 延 古 樂。四 條 拍 子 條 別 十 四。無 舞

SSSTF

'Introit to "Perfect Virtue" ' Of beats, 14. 一 德 鹽 拍 子 十 四

JCYR (see also *RSCY*)

'Introit to "Perfect Virtue" ' Slow. Of beats, 14. One variant, 10 beats. Small
piece. Old music. There is no dance. 壹 德 鹽 延 拍 子 十 四 一 説 拍
子 十 小 曲 古 樂 無 舞.

SGYR (as *JCYR*, but without mention of a ten-measure variant)

Ittokuen

70

71

KF/HSF/RK

[1] *g#″* and *c#″* unambiguously shown by tablature signs 美 and 工.

SSSTF

[1] (as for *KF/HSF/RK*)

[2] natural note *c‴*, shown unambiguously by tablature sign 比.

JCYR

[1] (left) (flute-gloss)

[2]   ″   ″

[3]   ″   ″

[4]   ″   ″

[5] ligature supplied

[6] (left) (flute-gloss)

[7] (right)

巾 為 斗 絲竹 譜
'Silk and Bamboo Score'

SGYR

[1] (right)

桂 譜: 已 下 同
Katsura Score: 'from here onwards the same'

[2] (left) (flute-gloss)

[3] 'One variant same as preceding' 一 説 同 上.

Preliminary comments on the structure of the piece

Plainly, the alternative lengths of the piece – 14 or 10 measures – are due merely
to whether the repeat of the end of the first four measures (of eight beats) is
observed or not. The Lydian character of the tune is explicit in the unambiguous

mouth-organ tablatures (*SSSTF*, however, once exhibits a *C'''* appoggiatura); tritone leaps from beat 4 to 5 in measure 1, and from beat 8 in measure 8 to beat 1 in measure 9, are conspicuous features. If repeated crotchets/quarter-notes are regarded as minims/half-notes, the piece exhibits a number of measures isorhythmic in structure: ‖: ♩ ♩♩♩ ♩♩ :‖. At a relatively slow speed, this imparts strength and forward impetus to the tune. Unusually, *f♯* functions as cadence at the end of two measures in the second half of the piece. Without *JCYR*'s *ichi* (—)-marking at the end of measure 10, the emphatic cadence on *f♯* (at the end of measure 11) would lead one to think of the second half as consisting of two groups of three measures. It almost looks as if Moronaga himself was in two minds about the phrasing, since a further *ichi*-sign is inserted at the end of measure 11. This irregularity does nothing to impair the flow of the piece, however; indeed *that* is strengthened by the partial repetition of measure 12 as measure 13. The cadences in measures 4 (8) and 14 are unusually emphatic.

Our observations (in Fascicles 1-5 and Volume 6) on the construction of items that may have been composed in Japan, suggest that *Ittokuen* is unlikely to have been composed by a Japanese, notwithstanding the attribution to an otherwise unknown – unknown to us! – Mishima Buzō who may have been no more than a reviser or arranger of a pre-existent piece. The pronouncedly Lydian character of the piece would seem to qualify it as being an item under the modal influence of the Xiliangzhou tradition (see p.16). That it could be a piece of Han date appears improbable, at least in its present form, not merely because of the centuries' gap between Han and Tang, but also because it is perhaps unlikely that Han musical taste would have tolerated so thoroughgoing a heptatonic melody as this. The tritone leaps in the mouth-organ versions are such as occur in Zhu Xi's ritual tunes in the *Huangzhong-qing* mode (Picken, 1956, pp.152-6); those six tunes, attributed at least to the Kaiyuan 開 元 period (713-42), would appear to have been made under the influence of the musical taste of Liangzhou.

ZKKS makes an important observation, not as yet considered, relating to structure: 'Its *sahō* is like that of *Anrakuen* 其 作 法 安 樂 鹽 ノ ゴ ト ツ.' In modern Japanese, the term *sahō* has come to be used exclusively in the sense of 'manners', 'etiquette', 'decorum', 'propriety'; but in Chinese, *zuofa* 作 法 still means a 'work-plan' or 'process'; and the primary meaning of the two lexigraphs is 'plan, or method, of making or composing'.

Inspection of the conflations (N.J.N.) of *Ittokuen* and *Anrakuen* (pp.157,162) shows that the latter might be regarded as an abbreviated version of the former, a version in which the dimensions are reduced from 14 (or 10) to 12 (or 8) measures; a version in which (accepting the larger dimensions of both) 9 occurrences of *g♯* have been reduced to 3, and 4 occurrences of *c♯* to 2. As a result, there are no tritone leaps in *Anrakuen*; but this latter retains, unchanged, measures 3 and 4 (7 and 8) and 13 and 14, of *Ittokuen*.

Alternatively, of course, it might be argued that *Ittokuen* is a version of an earlier *Anrakuen*, already expanded (by Chinese musicians) to make a more attractive Lydian version, in keeping with the musical taste of eighth-century China.

'Introit to "Peace-Music" ' (='Introit to *Amma*')

Anrakuen/Anyue yan

安 樂 鹽

The title and its significance

The significance of this title in Heian times is revealed by comments in *WMRJS* and *ZKKS*, as well as in the prefaces to tablatures in *JCYR*, *SGYR* and *RSCY*. In isolation, some connection with the music of An State (*An'guo* 安 國), or even with the piece: 'Young Gentleman An' (*An gongzi* 安 公 子) might be posited. An'guo (Fascicle 4, 1987, p.33) comprised the territory of Parthia, including modern Bokhara, and was the seventh among the Nine Classes of Music cultivated at the Chinese Court during the Sui dynasty (581-618)(*TD* 146, p.762; Fascicle 4, p.33). This music (Class *An'guo*) was retained as the first category of music in the Standing Class of the Banquet Music as organised in 642.

Both these possibilities are ruled out, however, by the interpretation 'Introit to *Amma*'. Authority for this interpretation rests in the first place on the smallest source systematically used by us when beginning any enquiry into the history of items from the *Tōgaku* repertory. The entry in *WMRJS* is of lapidary succinctness, with the title itself shortened to 'Introit to *An*' (安 鹽); this heading precedes the statement: 'Tune for when *An* emerge' 安 出 時 音 聲. *JCYR* and *SGYR*, both give an expanded version of this statement:

'Nowadays when commoners [are about to] emerge [to perform] *Amma*, first do this tune.' 世 俗 出 安 摩 時 先 為 此 音 聲。 Both scores state that this instruction derives from the *Transverse-Flute Score* (921) of Prince Sadayasu (Nangū; 870-924). *ZKKS* amplifies the statement somewhat by indicating that this was still a valid instruction in the mid-thirteenth century, almost a century after the death of Moronaga:

'The Nangū score states: "When commoners nowadays emerge [to perform] *Amma*, first do this tune".' 南 宮 譜 云 ， 世 俗 現 出 安 摩 之 時 先 為 此 音 聲 。 'Commoners' presumably refers to dancers and musicians without rank, according to the system instituted in 702 during the Taihō reign-period (701-03).

Whatever may have been the origin of this piece (*Anrakuen*), its function and meaning for Court musicians and dancers seem plain from these several statements, all saying much the same thing, at greater or lesser length: *An* was understood not as linked in any way with 'An'guo' or with that 'Young

Gentleman', but as an abbreviation of the title *An-ma* (*Amma*) (Fascicle 5, 1990, p.24), and the complete title, *Anrakuen*, signified an introduction to the music and dance of *Amma*.

History of pieces of this, or related title

Our earliest Japanese sources of information – Moronaga's prefaces in *JCYR* and *SGYR* – offer no hint as to the source of the piece itself. The passages (*JCYR*, *SGYR*) that end with 'tune' (*onjō/yinsheng* 音 聲) continue ambiguously:

'The sincerity that comes from this has not [previously] been seen' – that is to say, the sincerity is incomparable. 其 由 慥 無 所 見。 (*ZKKS* 3, p.166, changes *yori/you* 由 to *kyoku/qu* 曲, 'from' to 'piece', yielding the reading: 'The sincerity of this piece'.) For 'sincerity' we may well substitute – as for Latin *sinceritas* – 'purity', 'genuineness', 'integrity'.

This statement is surely an extraordinary one to be made so emphatically. *ZKKS* records, precisely, a glorious occasional performance:

'On the day of the Ceremony of Eternal Bliss, play it before *Amma*. When the one who performs the dance advances, there are special features about his steps. Now as to this piece, following Imperial Decree, Yintong/Ontō made it in the honourable time of an Emperor of Tang.' 常 樂 會 ノ 日 ， 安 摩 以 前 ニ 吹 之，舞 奏 ラ 進 ス ， 委 細 彼 段 ニ ア リ，抑 此 曲 ， 唐 帝 ノ 御 時，依 敕 音 童 作 之 。 *HPGS* (p.927) gives the name of the maker as Yinchong or Yinzhong (音 重; see also p.69). *DNHS* offers no suggestions regarding composition; nor is there for this piece (unlike *Ittokuen*) any suggestion of Japanese creation.

As has been seen, the *Anrakuen* tune is clearly related to *Ittokuen* (the previous item: **29**), but shorter. In **29** (p.73), it was suggested that shortening of *Ittokuen* to make *Anrakuen* is more probable than the converse; but expansion and 'Lydianisation' of *Anrakuen* to produce *Ittokuen* is also a possibility, in particular when one recalls the existence of the Class *Anraku/Anyue* during the Sui and early Tang dynasties. *TD* twice tells us something of the character of the *Anyue*. From the manner of listing of the Nine Classes of the Court Music of Sui (*TD* 146, p.762), it is plain that the seventh class was the music of An State; and in the listing of the Ten Classes (from 642), the first is that of *Anyue*. That this **29**: *Anyue* ('An-Music' or 'Peace-Music') was the music of An State seems doubtful in the light of statements about music, as recorded in the Tang. The longer statement (*TD* 146, p.761) alleges:

'The "Peace-Music" is that which was made after Qi was pacified [by force of arms] by the [Northern] Zhou. Since the rows [of dancers] in a square resembled the walls of a city, in Zhou times it was called "City-Dance". Of dancers there were 80 men. From carved wood they made masking dog snouts. They wore pendant gold ornaments on their ears, [with] cotton-thread making

76

hair, [with] painted jackets and leather caps. The manner in which dance-steps were made was like in character to those of Qiang foreigners.' 安 樂 後 周 武 平 齊 所 作 也 行 列 方 正 象 城 郭 周 代 謂 之 城 舞。 舞 者 八 十 人 刻 木 為 狗 喙 戴 耳 以 金 飾 之 垂 線 為 髮 畫 襖 皮 帽。 舞 蹈 姿 制 猶 作 羌 胡 狀。

It is important to note that Du You, author of *TD*, is referring to the Northern Zhou, even though he might appear to be referring to what are known as the 'Later Zhou' (*Hou* Zhou); but the Later Zhou were not established as a dynasty until the mid-tenth century. Also, he refers to Qi. Northern Zhou survived as a dynasty from 557 until 581; and Qi came to an end in 577.

The number of dancers specified in this passage from *TD* (80) is even larger than for an ordinary imperial occasion (8 rows of 8 dancers); the reference to a square formation would have applied, however, to any court-ritual dance.

It seems not impossible, then, that this *Anrakuen* was derived from the *Anyue* dance-with-music created perhaps in 577, and retained as the first item of the Banquet Music of the Tang (Standing Division). By 642, when the Ten Classes were established, Taizong's reign was at its mid-point. We know, from *Sairyōshū*, that the use of Xiliangzhou music, with its characteristic Lydian modality, was popular at the Chinese Court. Might we then (as an alternative to what was first proposed in relation to item **29**: *Ittokuen*) regard **30**: *Anrakuen* rather as a fragment of an earlier, more nearly pentatonic version of *Anyue*? *Ittokuen* might then derive from a more up-to-date, Lydianised version of *Anyue*.

Regarding the description of the costume and properties of the dancers of *Anyue* in the Banquet Music, and the relationship to dances of the Qiang (suggested in *TD*), it is not at first sight obvious why the 'Peace-Music' of Taizong should have characteristics linking it with a Tibeto-Burman people of Western China. Is it possible that this was a symbolic pacification of the Qiang (by Taizong) that was equated with the pacification of Northern Qi by the Northern Zhou, some 50 years or so before the time of Taizong?

Provisionally, it is suggested that *Anrakuen* (like *Ittokuen*) is an adaptation of an early Tang 'Peace-Music' item (*Anyue*). *Anrakuen* and *Ittokuen* would then derive from two Tang-Chinese versions of the same piece: *Anyue*, originally composed in the sixth century. It is striking that *ZKKS* refers to 'special steps' associated with *Anrakuen*, just as *TD* refers to dance-steps 'like those of the Qiang'.

Prefatory comments in the sources
KF/HSF/RK

'Introit to "Peace-Music".' Slow. Old music. Four times. Beats of separate times, 12. There is no dance. 安 樂 鹽 延 。古 樂 。四 條 拍 子 條 別 十 二。無 舞

SSSTF

'Introit to "Peace-Music".' Of beats, 12. Old music. 安 樂 鹽　 拍 子 十 二 古 樂

JCYR

'Introit to "Peace-Music" '. Of beats, 12. Small piece. Old music. There is no dance. Nangū's *Transverse-Flute Score* states: When commoners emerge for *Amma*, first do this tune. The sincerity that comes from this has never been heard [before]. 安 樂 鹽。拍 子 十 二 小 曲 古 樂 無 舞 南 宮 橫 笛 譜 云 世 俗 出 安 摩 時 先 為 此 音 聲 其 由 慥 無 聞 (所 イ) 見 。 A correction is marked beside the last four lexigraphs: 'heard'(聞) is changed to 'seen'(見). The last sentence then reads (literally): 'The sincerity that comes from this has never been seen before.'

SGYR has correctly 無 所 見 (literally: 'has not what seen'). Note that *ZKKS* replaces 'from' (由 *yori/yu*) by 'piece' (曲 *kyoku/qu*) leading to the reading: 'this piece's sincerity'.

Anrakuen

78

JCYR

[1] (left)(flute-gloss)

[2] (right)(gloss)

SGYR   桂 譜 'Katsura-score'

[1] (right)

[2] (left)   (forward plucked)

[3] 'One variant same as preceding' 一 説 同 上

[4] (lcft)   (forward plucked)

Preliminary comments on the structure of the piece

A curious feature of the description of the piece in *ZKKS* is the ambiguous statement: 'first beat, 5; from then onwards, 8; slow.' 初 拍 子 五 下 八 延 。 Remembering that the term *hyōshi* 拍 子 means, primarily, the bass-drumbeat, and secondarily, a measure in which that drumbeat falls, it seems likely that this statement signifies that the first drumbeat falls in the fifth *measure*. Each measure of the repeat, however, will receive a drumbeat, and the series will continue through a further four measures to the end of the piece, making eight beats in all. It will be noted that an upper marginal gloss in *SGYR* said something very similar in regard to item **28** (p.55).

The scores for mouth-organ, zither and lute offer no support for there being only five beats in the first measure, but eight in all subsequent measures. Whatever the significance of this percussion pattern other similar instances have been recorded, in the course of Fascicles 1 to 5, where the *taiko* does not begin to sound until some measures after the piece has begun.

31 Piece

'Ten Devas'

Jūtenraku / Shitian yue

十 天 樂

The title and its significance

That this title must mean 'Ten Devas', rather than 'Ten Heavens' has already been argued in Fascicle 3 (1985, p.33, n.13). This interpretation is supported (as suggested there) by the appearance of ten Bodhisattvas holding flower offerings, fire-vomiting serpents, etc. while the music of 'Ten Devas' was played (see Fascicle 3). This is described as occurring during a performance of *Karyōbin*, which performance, from details in the prefaces to that piece in *JCYR* and *SGYR*, can only have been the reconsecration (in 861) of the gigantic bronze image of the Buddha of the Tōdaiji, or a ceremony of comparable magnitude. (See also translations of these prefaces and that of *RSCY*, examined in relation to 'Bodhisattvas', Fascicle 4, 1987, pp.66-8.)

In Chinese Buddhism, 'heaven' (*ten/tian* 天) may occasionally stand for the heavens; but more commonly it refers to a spirit, a celestial being, one who has advanced beyond the ten stages of ascent of the Bodhisattvas but is not as yet a Buddha. A particular category of 'Ten Devas' does not appear in the dictionary of Soothill and Hodous. 'Twelve Devas' are a feature of the pantheon of the 'True Words' (*Shingon* 貞 言) sect of Japanese Buddhism; but there are no grounds for supposing that the Ten Devas of our title indicate *Shingon* overtones in relation to this piece. The link with a specific dance scenario, however, is explicit.

History of pieces of this, or related, title

Though regarding the piece as 'old music', the prefaces in *JCYR* and *SGYR* (p.83) cite a statement by Prince Sadayasu in his *Transverse-Flute Score* of 921: 'This is that which was made by the Flute-Master, Tsuneyo no Otouo [the reading: "Tsuneyo" is taken from *ZKKS*] at the time of a ceremony in the Preaching-Hall of Tōdaiji.' His testimony establishes that the piece was certainly known in the early-tenth century. *RMS* too records its creation and performance at the Tōdaiji, but names no composer, adding that records should be examined (to determine the facts). The devas are described as 'descending', encouraging one to imagine, perhaps, a spectacular descent from the height of the lofty chasm of the Great Hall where the Buddha now presides.

WMRJS records that: 'a tradition among old folk (*kōrōden*) relates that this is what was made and respectfully offered at the time of a ceremony in the Preaching-Hall of Tōdaiji, by the Flute-Master Tsuneyo no Otouo.' 十 天 樂 古 老 傳 云 東 大 寺 講 堂 會 之 時 笛 師 常 世 第 魚 奉 所 造 也。

Both *HPGS* (p.928) and *ZKKS* (3, p.167) expand these statements. The former attributes composition to the reign of Emperor Shōmu (724-48); but the latter, while agreeing that the composer was Tsuneyo no Otouo, does not accept as proven that this occurred in that reign. Both link first performance with the Tōdaiji, and both refer to the Preaching-Hall, adding (however) that the occasion was (in the Buddhist sense) a day of Pūjā, when offerings of all kinds are made to the Buddha. Quite specifically, both state:

'Of Devas, ten men descend' – 'from the Void' (in *ZKKS*) – 'to be revealed before the Buddha, offering flowers' – in *HPGS*. The latter source continues:

'Therefore a new piece was made, so that it might be played. By imperial decree, the Flute Master, Tsuneyo no Otouo [here written 乙 魚] made it, calling it "Ten Devas Music", etc., etc.. (Was this Otouo under the honourable roof of the Household Troops in the time of Emperor Shōmu? This has not yet been examined, etc., etc.)' 故 有 作 新 曲 可 奏 之 敕 笛 師 常 世 乙 魚 作 之，名 之 十 天 樂 云 云 (乙 魚 當 于 近 御 宇 聖 武 帝 世 相 違 乎，未 詳 之 云 云). *ZKKS* (p.168) asks:

'Is it beyond doubt that Tsuneyo no Otouo was a man of Shōmu's reign?' 但 常 世 乙 魚 ハ 聖 武 ノ 御 時 ノ 人 ニ ア ラ サ ル 歟。

Finally *ZKKS* considers possible dates:

'The date of that Preaching-Hall Ceremony has not been investigated. There was a Making of Offerings in the Preaching-Hall in Jōwa 5 [838]. Enchō 5 [927], sixth month, sixteenth day [was another day when] there was a Preaching-Hall Ceremony.' 彼 講 堂 會，年 紀 不 審，講 堂 供 養 ハ，承 和 五 年 メ リ，講 堂 會，延 長 五 年 六 月 十 六 日 也… Plainly, since this latter date is later than the death of Prince Sadayasu in 924 (see p.81), 'Ten Devas' must have been composed prior to the latter ceremony.

If, as the colophon to *HFF* states (see Volume 7, Chapter 1 – in preparation), Tsuneyo no Otouo was a pupil of Ōto no Kiyogami – the seventh in sequence – it is surely unlikely (for the following reasons) that he could have been 'under the roof of the Household Troops' in the time of Emperor Shōmu (724-48). In the same colophon it is stated that the Teacher of Kiyogami's Flute Teacher taught in the reign of the Kōken 孝 謙 Empress (749-58). That is to say, not one, but two generations of teachers must have elapsed from the time of the Kōken Empress till Kiyogami acquired a flute teacher. The date of Kiyogami's birth is unknown (see again Volume 7, Chapter 1); if, however, he were in his twenties when being taught – a generation later than the time of the Empress – he would have been perhaps 58, when he set out (never to return) with the Mission to Tang of 838. In the period 724-48, Tsuneyo no Otouo would surely have been too young to have been a pupil of Kiyogami.

Prefatory comments in the manuscript sources

KF/HSF/RK

'Ten Devas': (Slow). Old music. Of beats, 8. A *Sada-chō* piece. There is no dance. 十 天 樂 延 。 古 樂 。拍 子 八。沙 汰 調 曲 也 。 無 舞 。

SSSTF

'Ten Devas': Of beats, eight. Old music. 十 天 樂　拍 子 八　古 樂

JCYR , SGYR, RSCY

'Ten Devas': Of beats, eight. Middle-sized piece. Old music. There is no dance. Southern Palace's *Transverse-Flute Score* states: 'This is that which was made by the Flute-Master, Tsuneyo no Otouo, at the time of a Preaching-Hall Ceremony at the Tōdaiji.' 十 天 樂　拍 子 八　中 曲　古 樂　無 舞　南 宮 横 笛 譜 云 此 東 大 寺 講 堂 會 笛 師 常 世 ノ 弟 魚 所 作 也 。

Jūtenraku

JCYR

¹ sharpening dot supplied

² (left)(gloss)   *ligature supplied

一 説
'a variant'

³ (right)

⁴ ligature supplied

⁵ (right)   一 説

⁶ sharpening dot supplied

SGYR

¹ (left)   綿 譜 'Wata-score'

² (right)   一 説

3   "   一 説

Preliminary comments on the structure of the piece

It is perhaps surprising that the prefatory comments in *KF/HSF/RK* emphasise the *Sada-chō* character of this piece, when both mouth-organ scores show neither *c* nor *g* as sharpened: five occurrences of *c* and two of *g*. Furthermore, there is no instance of a leap from *d* to *g* (or conversely) such as might once have been a tritone. *ZKKS* suggests it may be both 'old' and 'new', thereby justifying alternative use of *ikko* and *kakko* drums in performance. Unquestionably, the piece was in existence at the time of the reconsecration of the Great Buddha of the Tōdaiji in 861. The tune could readily be converted to a purely pentatonic *Gongdiao* condition; in which form it would be taken for a Chinese tune. In spite of its relatively late appearance in the sources, *Jūtenraku* may be a fragment of a forgotten Tang piece, revived and modified by that Flute Master of uncertain *floruit*.

Appendix 1
Conflations and Analyses (N.J.N.)

Preamble

Those who have followed analytical and critical expositions of items from the
Tang-music repertory in Fascicles 1 to 5, cannot have failed to notice that the
scales of melodies transcribed from primary mouth-organ sources differ from the
scales of those transcribed from primary zither and lute sources. The four
principal manuscripts – the basis of this study – are totally independent of each
other in origin and tradition; but the two mouth-organ scores adhere consistently
to the Mixo-Lydian type of scale: *D E F♯ G A B C*, while the two string-scores of
Fujiwara no Moronaga adhere equally consistently to the Lydian scale-type: *D E
F♯ G♯ A B C♯*. The former is the *Shangdiao* scale-pattern in the mode-key on *D*: in
Chinese terms, the first inversion of a fundamental, heptatonic, *Gongdiao* scale
on *C* – (*Shang* being the second note of the *Gongdiao*-set). The other is the basic,
heptatonic *Gongdiao* scale itself, but pitched on *D*. There is ample proof, in all
that has gone before, that almost every movement throughout the entire sequence
of items transcribed in *Music from the Tang Court* presents four versions of that
same movement, aurally and visibly identified in the common title. The scale
difference does not reduce the validity of this statement.

In analytical commentaries that follow in this volume, it has been useful on
occasion to compare tunes as whole units or in parts, in aligned comparative
tables, in order to clarify points of technical and musical interest. This kind of
example has proved both practicable and enlightening, ever since the first
expository studies of *Ōdai-hajinraku* were undertaken in Fascicle 2.

The same practice is continued here in Volume 6, with the first published
transcriptions of eight items in the Sino-Japanese *Sada* mode, treated by
Moronaga as a sub-category of the *Ichikotsu* mode, the modal class to which all
items in Fascicles 1-4 belong. Analysis and technical scrutiny of the following
Sada pieces has inevitably necessitated further comparative illustrations; the
validity of simultaneous comparisons of tunes in both scales is not thereby
impaired. Recognition of scale differences, imposed and authenticated by the
earliest sources of the Tang Music in tablature in Japan, has been acknowledged
and consistently displayed by the editorial policy adopted in the series: *Music
from the Tang Court*.

All conflations and analyses of pieces classed in *Ichikotsu-chō* have
consistently been presented in the Mixo-Lydian-type scale that applies to most
critical comment on them. All conflations with commentaries, relating to items
classed as *Sada-chō* are here presented in the Lydian-type scale, the scale that
Moronaga associated with music of Kuchā (Fascicle 5, p.xiii). It is not explicitly

stated by him, however, that all *Sada-chō* items derived from the Kuchean repertory.

In the Tang-Music repertory as it survives in the Japanese sources, scalar discrepancies between items in the common mode-key on *D* in no way challenge the validity of the music, or the nature and operation of the musical language. Tonal perspectives may interest the modern listener, who may subjectively prefer a tune in one or other scalar form; but for the Japanese who saved, and protected, extant sources from a thousand years ago, the two structural forms of scale co-existed, flourished and were played by ear in these scalar conditions for a least some hundreds of years. The evidence for this assertion is still enshrined – one is tempted to say 'petrified' – in contemporary performance practices of Tang Music in Japan: *Tōgaku*.

24. Piece: **The Prince of Lanling** (*Ryō-ō/Ling-wang* 陵 王)

Free Prelude	(p.88)
Wild Prelude	(p.103)
Entering Broaching	(p.113)
Amma	(p.119)

The Free Prelude: *Ranjo* (Fascicle 5, p.14)

Conflation

Descriptions of *Ryō-ō* in Chinese and Japanese sources are many and varied, as the historical exposition of this Suite in Fascicle 5 demonstrates. From the seventh century onwards, accounts of the piece survive, in terms increasingly coloured by the posthumous reputation of the protagonist, General Changgong of Northern Qi, known as 'Prince of Lanling'. [In Fascicle 5, it seemed appropriate to translate his title of '*wang*' as 'King' – the usual interpretation; but for him – as for the youthful Taizong, in the early seventh century – it is more appropriate to use the lesser title: 'Prince', 'Prince of the Orchidaceous Grave-Mound' and 'Prince of Qin' respectively (L.E.R.P.)]

Changgong was a leader of exceptional physical bearing, loved by his men, fearless in battle, and heroic in the face of adversity. Raised to the highest honours in victory, he was later brought down, victim of intrigue, jealousy and political misfortune. Disgraced in death, Changgong lived again in history, with all the qualities of greatness and national heroism reserved for legendary super-men of all time.

A musical representation, most commonly known in Japan as *Ryō-ō*, undoubtedly enjoyed a wide reputation and popularity over many centuries. To the present day the single movement, Entering Broaching, is danced at the Court, and most particularly at the Kasuga Shrine in Nara. The Court Repertory also includes a second and separate piece of related title: *Shin Raryō-ō* ('A New "Prince of Lanling" ', see this volume, p.1), which testifies to a re-birth in China of interest in the Prince's story. It too is a military suite, probably of later composition than the item discussed here and in Fascicle 5 (see also App.5).

The popularity and longevity of *Ryō-ō* may have been sustained by the acquisition of extra-musical associations (see Fascicle 5), as much as by an entertaining combination of music and dance. Representing the brave facial features and bearing of the hero, the discipline of military gesture, and the natural order of the universe, as reflected in Confucian, Daoist and Buddhist world views, the dances and their choreography must have offered attractions independent of that of the music – which alone concerns us here.

In Heian times, *Ryō-ō* included more movements than those that survive in tablature today. Of the four complete movements still to be seen in tablature, all presumably danced in Japan at some stage, only one – the Entering Broaching – was ever danced (we may be certain) in the Tang capital. In order of performance, movements that survive are *Ranjo* or *Ranjō* ('Free Prelude' or 'Free Tune'), *Kōjo* ('Wild Prelude'), *Juha* ('Entering Broaching'), and *Amma* ('Mother Durga'). For convenience in the following comments and analysis, the first movement will be referred to as *Ranjo*, Free Prelude.

The version of the *Ranjo* to be justified is hardly a 'conflation' in the same sense as those of preceding items from the repertory. In four flute versions of the melody, as preserved in tablatures in the (comparatively late) Ōga-family manuscript tradition, the earliest manuscript may date from 1330 (Marett, 1988). L.E.R.P. has recorded their minor differences in transcription (Fascicle 5, p.14), and firmly established the continuity of the melodic line, through all four versions, as secure, continuous and complete. What appears on p.91 is a slightly edited and simplified version of the transcription previously published. Only minor revision has been necessary to obtain a useful study version of the Free Prelude, a version in keeping with the standard of conflations provided (since 1981) in *Music from the Tang Court*. Such differences as exist between manuscripts are few and inconsequential.

The total length in transcription is 120 beats: music for a dance performance that consists of the first 112 beats repeated several times from the beginning, and concluding with 8 additional beats (113-20), to be played at the end of the last repeat, confirming cadence and mode.

The transcription exhibits considerable repetition, as if, at one time, the piece were divided into two equal parts: the first, ending on the sixth of the mode-key, *b*; the second, repeating much of the first part, and concluding on the mode-final, *d*. The first part runs smoothly to a defined central point, where *b* is prolonged and emphasised. This has been taken as the median cadence – beat 56 of the transcription – the only point at which a binary division is feasible.

In the present revision, the second, detached quarter-note, *b* (beats 57-8 of the transcription) has been discarded as a copyist's error; and beats 55-8 have been reduced to a single cadence note of the value of one half-note, thus matching the cadence values of the two last phrases. The first part of the present version of the Free Prelude (of 56 beats) finishes with a half-note that replaces the two detached quarter-notes and rests.

After a linking passage, the second part of the transcription repeats the first part, with small changes, from beat 67 onwards. Referring to the numbering of beats of the edited version below – now called the 'conflation' – beats 17-31 of the first section are seen to be slightly varied and extended in repeated form (beats 65-87) in the second part of the conflation, but without beats 23-4. These two beats have been retained as beats 75-6 of the conflation. Beats 33-50 follow (as beats 89-106), with beats 47-8 (not repeated in the transcription) restored to their context, as beats 103-4. The amended Free Prelude now consists of two equal parts, each of 56 unit beats, and cadencing on *b* and *d* respectively – in all, 112 beats. The last repeat amounts to a total of 120 beats, including the additional cadence on the mode-final. For convenience, the conflation has been numbered *above* the notes in binary beats, *below* the notes in pairs of quarter-note unit-beats.

For the conflation of the Free Prelude, a basic standard of notation has been adopted. Quarter-notes and eighth-notes are the norm. Extrinsic decoration by flute players, as written down in the fourteenth-century tablatures, has been omitted, resulting in a simpler version suitable for analysis. Study of ornamental practices of performers towards the end of the Kamakura period, in so far as these relate to the binary-beat principle, has over the years made possible the preparation of acceptable *basic* versions of items from the *Tōgaku* repertory. Which of two consecutive notes within one binary beat is primary may need to be decided; for example, where two notes, the first of which is metrically stronger than the second, sound within the value of a half-note, a quarter-note, and even an eighth-note. In practical terms, the decision usually rests on whether the two notes move conjunctly or disjunctly, within a simple note value. If movement between two notes is conjunct, the second of the two notes is likely to be primary; if disjunct, the first will probably be primary. The conflation is a version of the transcriptions, reconciled for technical analysis. The natural condition of the melody is preserved; nothing essential has been stripped away. Only occasionally in these pages will a basic version be drawn into discussion for further detailed consideration.

In support of the above principles of reduction, Fascicle 3 offered two complete versions of *Ōdai hajin-raku*, 'The Emperor Destroys the Formations'. The first is a transcription (L.E.R.P.) from the flute score *Kaichū-fu* (1095?), while beneath it for comparison is the conflation (N.J.N.) of the same suite (Fascicle 2, pp.76-9), arranged from the earliest, primary, mouth-organ and string sources (*c*.1172-1302) transcribed in Fascicle 1 (pp.40-81). The confrontation is revealing in several ways, not only because the two versions, from independent sources, compare favourably, but more particularly because the *Kaichū-fu* version, with several kinds of embellishments, appears (by comparison) to be underpinned by the basic conflation. On the above premises, the reduction of decorated versions of *Tōgaku* compositions to simpler versions has merit for historical and clinical study. In this series the purpose of such reduction has been solely for the sake of analysis of technical procedures, and for investigation of the basic elements of musical language, as moulded by the creative imagination of Tang musicians. Further observations on the development of decorative devices, in the performance of Tang melodies in Japan, have been made by Marett (1985, 1986).

Example 1. *Ryō-ō*: conflation of the *Ranjo*, Free Prelude

Analysis

Ryō-ō is unique in several ways. The description in Fascicle 5 notes a collection of movements of various kinds. By the twelfth century, a full performance ostensibly included pieces of diverse titles and styles, in prescribed sequence, with consecutive repetitions of movements along the way, and repetitions of earlier movements recalled at later stages. By late Heian times, a full performance, with dance-spectacle, must have been an extravaganza of music, colour, choreography, and symbolic representation; altogether an entertainment of substantial duration and significance.

In China, only one of these movements, the Entering Broaching, is known for certain to have been danced at court. When *Ryō-ō* was danced in Japan at the consecration of the great Tōdaiji Temple at Nara in 752, no mention was made (in records of the occasion) of the performance of a Free Prelude (or Free Tune of some kind) by way of introduction to the Entering Broaching. The records of that Temple reveal, however, that a Free Tune (a *Ranjō*) was danced in advance of a sequence of music-with-dance events that led to an early-evening performance of *Ryō-ō* on the fourteenth day of the third month in the year 861, when reconsecration occurred (see Fascicle 5, p.15, column 2). The practice of using a Free Tune was therefore known in Japan in the ninth century; but there is no evidence that the records of the Tōdaiji on that occasion refer to the Free Tune of *Ryō-ō*.

By Moronaga's time (late-twelfth century), all the additional movements were known to him – at least by name, as his preface to the piece shows. The present analysis is confined to the four complete movements transcribed in Fascicle 5: the Free Prelude, the Wild Prelude, the Entering Broaching, and *Amma*, conflations of which are provided. The mode throughout is *Sada-chō*, and the scale of the mode-key is the Lydian octave-species on *D*.

This Free Prelude is one of the more novel features of the suite. L.E.R.P. has shown (Fascicle 5, pp.27-31) that the Chinese reading of the characters for 'Ranjo' had no other meaning in Tang China than 'coda-tune' or 'closing-tune'; they were never used in China for an opening movement. In Japan, however, Free Prelude and Free Tune were titles of certain types of composition, played *before* certain categories of music ('New' or 'Old', for example) or *before* certain types of composition – a 'Large Piece', for example. Furthermore, and peculiar to this item, the Free Prelude of *Ryō-ō* is not one of several retained in the 'modern' *Tōgaku* repertory for introducing large pieces in this mode-key. This Free Prelude is specifically the Free Prelude of *Ryō-ō*, the first movement in the suite-like sequence, and is so acknowledged by Toyohara no Toshiaki in *KF/HSF/RK*, and by Fujiwara no Moronaga in *JCYR*. In support of this position, Moronaga cites the long-lost flute score (920-1) of Prince Sadayasu (also known as Ribu-ō and Nangū): 'First play the Free Prelude' (Fascicle 5, p.12). For the Japanese, the Free Prelude must have been a special part of the suite. Its primary position, introducing both mode and suite at some length, and immediately preceding the arcane representations of the Wild Prelude, corroborates its importance to the whole composition.

The Free Prelude appears to exist and function on two modal levels; but no description of the piece in these terms has been found in a Japanese historical source (nor, of course, in any Chinese source). Although there is no written precedent for such a musical structure, the description rests on the principal structural division of the piece into two halves, Part 1 and Part 2, and on themselves sub-dividing into two lesser parts, A and B, each sub-division operating independently of the other. Their respective independence is manifest in that the lesser parts A and B (and A' and B') display their own melodic formulae and scale patterns, and bear the same contrasting relationship to each other in each half of the melody, Parts 1 and 2.

The octave-species of the complete Free Prelude, the Lydian octave-species on *D*, is the scale of the *Sada* modal sub-group to which all the movements of *Ryō-ō* belong, including the seemingly independent diversions of the secondary sections: B and B'. In this composition, then, two different 'aspects' or 'perspectives' of the mode are evident – terms first used in *Tōgaku*-analysis in Fascicle 2, pp.89-91; and these aspects function independently, according to the area of the scale on which each sub-division of the melody – A or B – concentrates.

The form of the Free Prelude, with its broad structural sections, substantiates the continuity and correlation between the two halves, Part 1 and Part 2.

Table 1. Free Prelude: ground-form and structure

Part 1.　　Part 2.
‖:A - B ‖ b - A' - B' - a :‖ a' ‖

A & B, and A' & B', are sub-divisions of the two halves, Part 1 and Part 2; b is a short transition or link derived from B, and a is a codetta derived from A but attached to B'. a', acting as coda played after the last time through, is the conclusive, mode-final cadence relating to a, the codetta. With reference to the numbering of unit-beats (quarter-notes) in the conflation, the binary plan becomes clearer when the accompanying details are added.

Table 2. The Free Prelude: analytical Table

___

Part 1.

A	beats 1-31	= 31 beats duration
B	" 32-56	= 25 " "

Summary, A + B:	beats 1-56	= 56 beats duration

Part 2.

b, transition	beats 57-64	= 8 beats duration
A'	" 65-87	= 23 " "
B'	" 88-106	= 19 " "
a, codetta	" 107-12	= 6 " "

Summary, b+A'+B'+a:	beats 57-112	= 56 beats duration

a', coda	beats 113-20	= 8 beats duration

Parts 1 + 2 + a'	beats 1-120	= 120 beats duration

For more detailed analysis of the Free Prelude, application of the weighted-scale procedure is useful. Since the standard unit of time measurement is the quarter-note, the total time duration of each pitch of the scale in a stipulated length of melody can readily be determined. The number of occurrences of each pitch can also be counted, as can the number of times each pitch functions as first or last member of a structural period. The total figures collected for each note, and assembled in scalar sequence, furnish a statement in numerical terms of the anatomy of the melodic specimen under investigation. Applied to the separate halves of the Free Prelude, a weighted-scale, made up from totals of time durations and occurrences of each note, and of the times each note sounds as first and last of principal divisions (in this instance, the two halves) yields the following results.

Table 3. Free Prelude: weighted-scales of each half of the melody

___

		e	$f\sharp$	$g\sharp$	a	b	$c\sharp$	d
Part 1	Beats 1-56	13.5	15	22	20.5	24	3.5	21.5
Part 2	Beats 57-112	7	12	23.5	22.5	30.5	10.5	17

Since each half of the Free Prelude shares similar melodic materials and structures, there is no great difference between the linear statements of numerical data; but the relationship between individual notes is unexpected. First, the same four notes, *g♯ - a - b - d*, combine to contribute three-quarters of the musical effect of the tune (73 percent in the first half, and 76 in the second); secondly, the sixth of the scale unquestionably upstages the mode-final – more so in the second half; thirdly, even the fourth of the scale – in the tradition of Han China no more than an auxiliary to the fifth (the dominant) – asserts itself *versus the final*; fourthly, the tonal weight of this Prelude is concentrated around the dominant and its closest neighbours; and fifthly, because of the preceding concentration, the basic, pentatonic structure – comparatively weak with respect to the second and third notes of the scale – finds the mode-final also weak. Ultimately, the position of the mode-final is partly redressed by the addition of the coda, a'. With a' added, the weight of the note, *d*, is improved; but so also is that of *g♯* and *a*.

Although both halves of the melody are broadly similar, some interesting observations have emerged from application of the weighted-scale procedure.

The movement may be approached in another way, however, namely, by comparison of the data of all the A sections: A, A', and a, with those of all the B sections: B, b and B'. On this basis, application of the same weighting method yields a rather different set of figures:

Table 4. Free Prelude: summary of weighted-scale data of A-related and B-related sections

	e	*f♯*	*g♯*	*a*	*b*	*c♯*	*d*
Part 1, Sections A (beats 1-31), A' (beats 65-87), and a (107-112)	17.5	13	-	41.5	20	3.5	36.5
Part 2 Sections B (beats 32-56), b (57-64), and B' (88-106)	3	14	45.5	1.5	32.5	10.5	2

The A sections use the *Gongdiao* pentatonic scale on *d* in a manner recognizable in terms of *Tōgaku*-analysis to date. Although the third of the scale (*f♯*) is comparatively light in its weighting, the auxiliary notes are silent or minimal; the mode-final and the dominant are strong in these parts of the tune. The conflation shows *d'- a'- d''- a''* to be the axis of these sections. By contrast, the B sections almost dispense with the *Gongdiao* pentatonic scale on *d* and its dominant-mode-

95

final relationship, concentrating (surprisingly) on *b* and *g♯*, with *f♯* and *c♯* enclosing them as a block of four notes: a third enclosed in a fifth.

In the A sections, the dominant and final make up 59 percent of the total weight, while the sixth of the scale (the fourth is silent) amounts to 15 percent. In the B sections, by contrast, *d* and *a* amount to 3 percent of the total weight, and *g♯* and *b* amount to 72 percent. *This* summary of weighted-scale data discloses not the affinity between the A and B sub-divisions, but their profound diversity. Where A gives way to B, *g♯* substitutes for *a* and assumes immediate self-importance; from this point (beats 31-2) onwards, the dominant and final are not heard again until the move back to A (as A') is negotiated through a brief transition, b (beats 57-64), where *g♯* and *c♯* surrender their acquired status when return to *Gongdiao* modality is foreshadowed. Similar tonal manipulation is repeated in Part 2 when A' moves into B' (beats 87-8), and when the necessary mode-final cadence brings Part 2 to a close (beats 106-12).

The form of the Free Prelude is dictated by the diversity of a few melodic formulae, or note patterns, and the scales they contrive. Its peculiarity is that the A and B sections exist in disparate groups of patterns contained in the single octave-series on *d*. Each section is aurally identified, accordingly, in its own note patterns and underlying scale formation. For this reason, the A and B sections of the Free Prelude cannot be subjected to the same kind of comparative through-analysis, shown to be practicable for most other *Tōgaku* items. A and B have nothing in common, and have no parallel in alignment.

Example 2. Free Prelude: aligned analysis in Parts and sectional groups
A Sections

B Sections

(Part 1 – unit beats 32-56; Part 2 – beats 57-64, and 88-106)

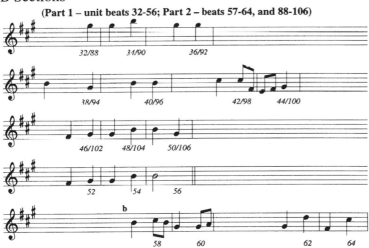

Compared with other movements of the repertory, the physical attributes of the Free Prelude are less typical. The materials of the A and B sections have no natural connections. It is appropriate to enquire, therefore, whether they belong to the familiar language of *Tōgaku* encountered in previous items.

In this regard, the cadences at the ends of the two main sections of the melody invite attention. Defined in time, rhythm and position, they serve unmistakably as functional landmarks in their different contexts. The first cadence formula (beats 51-56), integral to the B material, has never occurred before in this repertory – that is to say it has not occurred as a *full* cadence on the sixth of the scale, formed from the notes *f♯* - *g♯* - *b*, in the mode-key on *d*. Intermediate cadences on the sixth occur, but only one other movement (see later *Sairyōshū*) reaches the sixth precisely in this way. In most circumstances one accepts degrees of flexibility in repetitions of melodic formulae; inflexible rigidity is neither required nor expected in a developed folk tradition. In this movement, however, the melody insists on three occurrences (without variation) of this progression (beats 45-9, 51-6 and 101-5). Such repetition endorses its authenticity in this particular context. When a selection of passages is lined up beneath it (see Example 3), the halfway cadence of the Free Prelude illustrates its independence of other cadential progressions to the sixth of the scale.

The difference in scale formations of the various examples does not invalidate comparison of the *Ryō-ō* melodies with others in the mode. It will be remembered that, throughout the *Tōgaku* analyses, the melodies recorded in the string and wind sources are versions of the same melodies, regardless of their separate, lineal allegiances to the Mixo-Lydian, or Lydian, octave-species. Nowhere in a composition in this mode-key, is a median cadence found at the halfway point on the sixth of the scale, nor indeed at the end of the first part of a binary movement. *Hokuteiraku* (Fascicle 4, pp.22-6) may be an exception, where the fourteen measures divide into two-measure phrases after the second, fourth, sixth and eighth measures. In the sixth measure, there is a cadence on the sixth of the scale; but the pattern is not that of the Free Prelude. Opinions may differ on whether the cadence from *Hokuteiraku* is a binary division-marker; but there can be no doubt that only the Free Prelude exhibits the step from the third of the scale, followed by the direct leap to cadence on the sixth. The fact that the *Shunnō-den* example moves a step further to cadence on the sub-final disqualifies it from consideration here, although it includes the three notes: *f♯* - *g♯* - *b*.

Example 3. Free Prelude: the first cadence, compared with other cadence-forms on *b* in the same mode-key

Checking back to the conflation of the Free Prelude, one is reminded that, for the most part, the B sections are centred on the two notes in question: *g♯* and *b*. They are the novelty of the first cadence formula; and they occupy much of the listener's attention in the B and B' sections. Against other cadences on the sixth of the scale, it is the strong insistence on the fourth that renders the formula – and indeed the B sections – such an oddity among the company of tunes already encountered. Heretofore, cadences on the sixth came from the third of the scale, directly or indirectly; the third/sixth relationship is strong in this musical language. Regular cadence patterns from other items are these (Example 4); and standard cadences rising and falling to *b'* in this mode-key are recognisable variants of them.

99

Example 4. Standard cadence patterns to the sixth of the scale, in the mode-key on *d*

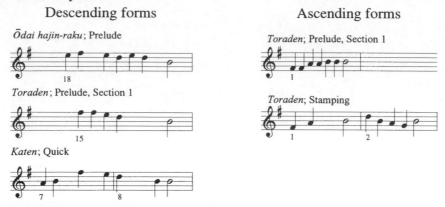

Descending forms

Ōdai hajin-raku; Prelude

Toraden; Prelude, Section 1

Katen; Quick

Ascending forms

Toraden; Prelude, Section 1

Toraden; Stamping

The concluding cadences of the Free Prelude also differ from those of *Tōgaku*-titles in the same mode. Final cadences are usually definitive and positive, longer pieces taking more time for concluding statements, shorter pieces making the point effectively and concisely within their means. By way of example, the Prelude of *Ōdai hajin-raku* (Fascicle 2, pp.76-7), one of the largest single movements in this mode, spreads the preparation for its formal conclusion over 32 beats (drumbeat periods 28-9). Then, in period 30, the final period, only two pitches are sounded, *e* and *d*, the mode-final taking eight of the twelve beats of the period.

Example 5. *Ōdai hajin-raku*; Prelude, drumbeat periods 28-30

Two pieces nearer in length to the Free Prelude of *Ryō-ō* are *Ka-kyokushi* (128 beats in 16 measures) and *Hokuteiraku* (112 beats in 14 measures) (Fascicle 5, pp.65 and 67 respectively). Both tunes require two measures (16 beats) for the preparation and statement of their final cadences and, like the extended Prelude of *Ōdai hajin-raku*, preparation and statement are calculated for modal and musical effect. Aligning the cadences from the three pieces, Example 6 shows their efficient preparation and timing, and the similarity of phraseology in the closing stages of Tang tunes in this mode.

Example 6. Final cadence passages of three *Tōgaku* items in the mode-key on *d*

The preceding examples speak for themselves in terms of inherent craft and appreciation of the movement of musical sound through time, relative to the energy that activates it, and the function intended. The two final cadences of the Free Prelude, however, are less successful in these respects. Barely invoking the familiar patterns of the standard samples (Example 7), they fall on the ear without warning, bringing the music to an abrupt halt. The dominant-triadic structure just prior to the ultimate mode-final in cadence position (beats 107-9), is strangely at odds with established mode-final cadence formulae. The following comparative table assembles mode-final cadences from various items, regardless of their position in whole melodies; only one (*Tori*, Quick: Fascicle 3, pp.43-5) is the end of a movement. The bounds of variation are stretched by the Free Prelude patterns.

Example 7. Comparison of mode-final cadence forms: the Free Prelude, and nine cadences from other items

Analysis of the Free Prelude has yielded some unexpected results. The heterogeneity of the A and B sections varies, and contrasts elements of interest which (in this instance) support the length of the piece and challenge conventions of style. Moreover, the dissimilarity between sub-divisions, identified in unrelated, formulaic materials and opposing modal perspectives, is exploited.

The same features occur in close proximity, but not in literal repetition, in each binary division. Earlier, when the formal procedure of the movement was being introduced, it was said that the Free Prelude 'exists and functions on two modal levels', even though no historical sources draw attention to any such phenomenon. Further consideration has endorsed this approach.

Two levels of activity exist simultaneously in the scale of the one mode, in the mode-key on *d*. The A sections operate in a *Gongdiao* pentatonic structure: *d - e - f♯ - a - b*, the B sections, in another *Gongdiao* pentatonic structure: *e - f♯ - g♯ - b - c♯*; the formulaic vocabulary of both sections is comprised within the *Sada-chō* heptatonic scale: *d - e - f♯ - g♯ - a - b - c♯ - d'*. The explanation is reasonable in the light of Moronaga's description of the *Sada-chō* heptatonic scale as a Lydian-type octave-series (a *Gongdiao* series) transposed one tone down from its original pitch on *E* [accepting *D* as the final of the entire modal system (Fascicle 5, pp.xii, xiii)]. However the Free Prelude was composed, the music would not have been thought of in this way at the time.

Nevertheless, what was done intuitively can be described – and perhaps explained – long after the tune has lost currency. The *heptatonic Gongdiao* octave-series in the mode-key on *D* includes two, *Gong-pentatonic* structures, the primary one on *d*, and a secondary one on *e*, each a transposition of the other. The Free Prelude takes advantage of this fact, thereby assuming an identity which may be shared with several other tunes belonging to the *Sada-chō* modal sub-group.

Kōjo, Wild Prelude

Conflation
Primary materials of the Wild Prelude in tablature are few – almost entirely confined to two comparatively late sources (Fascicle 5, pp.16,17). It is fortunate that they contain both substantial written material, as well as the tablatures from which to fashion a reconstruction of the movement. Both manuscripts record the whole of the Wild Prelude in variant forms, including (in the case of the copied version in *SGYR*) sporadic addenda, written beside the columns in tablature, or pasted in as labels, addenda that record scraps of information relating to other known (or amended) renditions. From a much later source only the first section of the Wild Prelude was transcribed (5, p.17); but this neither conflicts with earlier versions nor adds further information. Its supporting evidence is acknowledged.

Like the Free Prelude, the scale of the Wild Prelude is the Lydian octave-species with *d* as final, and the piece is classed in the *Sada* mode. There are eight divisions or Sections to the Wild Prelude, of which only the even-numbered members finish on the mode-final. In attempting to blend the transcriptions into a summary, single-stave statement, problems raised by the independence of the versions had to be confronted, if reconciliation was to be achieved.

Transcription from *SGYR* (copy of 1328) raises questions relative to a practical realization. As pointed out (Fascicle 5, p.20): 'The paucity of intra-columnary dots makes rhythmisation more than usually uncertain'. Streams of stemless closed note heads spaced along the staves, with some pitches slurred in two- and three-note groups without beat-dots, hint at an outline of melody when comparison of sources is required; but time, and particularly rhythm, are basic to the musical form and character of a melody, more basic than a close comparability of tablatures between several versions. The attempted alignment of the two major sources in transcription (5, pp.17-20) was helpful, by way of suggested correlations; but there were no easy solutions in respect of the Wild Prelude.

While preparing a conflation, and attempting to reconcile primary sources and secondary notations – differing as they do in numbers and pitches of notes, and in feasible durations and rhythmic values – all the transcribed material has received equal consideration. Critical decisions were difficult to make, the more so when varied forms of passages cited earlier in the composition returned in later Sections, with further discrepancies similar to, but not identical with, those of the first encounter. Nevertheless, while preparing a conflation representing its sources and traditions, a rational attitude has prevailed; the end-result is functionally acceptable and in keeping with its genre.

The Wild Prelude consists of eight, unmeasured and unequal Sections, marked off by a single drum-stroke, sounding with the last cadential note in each Section. In devising the conflation, two elements of the transcriptions have been watched closely: the *tei* – ⊤ – signs in *SGYR*, and the positions of binary-beat dots in *RTHKF*. The *tei* are marked in the conflation, but the irregularly placed dots required constant attention. Time and rhythm had to be convincingly decided from two not entirely trustworthy versions, and the binary-beat principle had to be maintained. The following comments explain the conflation.

First Section: the first phrase is close to the *RTHKF* and *SGYR* versions. After *tei*, the second part of the conflation picks up at the third binary beat in *RTHKF*, returning to the notes of *SGYR* after its third binary marker.

Second Section: in comparison with the lute score, the flute version appears to have been abbreviated, and attention is called to a passage in the footnote (Fascicle 5, *RTHKF*, n.1, p.17), the contents of which bear some resemblance to the version of *SGYR* at the comparable place, thus providing the pattern wherewith to fill the lacuna in the flute version. With minor adaptations, the conflation reflects the material from both primary versions.

Third Section: as both sources repeat their versions of the First Section, the conflation of the First Section is repeated as the Third Section.

Fourth Section: both versions somewhat resemble those of the Second Section. Differences are: that the time-values of *RTHKF* are changed; the amount of repetition in *SGYR* is reduced; and the *tei*-sign has been omitted. If, hypothetically, one reads the slurred groups of *SGYR* note heads in the Second Section as single-beat units, and equal to one unslurred note head – a view not necessarily substantiated at the present time – the Second Section would number 21 beats and 30 beats, in *RTHKF* and *SGYR* respectively, without any adaptation of the *RTHKF* footnote 1.

By contrast, if the primary versions of the Fourth Section are considered as they stand, and under the same metrical considerations, each would number 22 beats. It is reasonable to suggest that, by the end of the Kamakura period, retardation in *Tōgaku* performance had brought about a shortening of this Section; and that the flute and lute traditions had adopted length reductions independently. Each of the four transcribed versions, two of each Section, is complete in itself. In the light of the probability that Second and Fourth Sections were once the same, the problem in conflation is one of reconciliation and adaptation.

Although copyists of each manuscript will have been independent, even ignorant of each other, it is well to remember that there were only forty years between the writing or copying of the two scores. In the light of late-thirteenth and early-fourteenth century practice, a rationalised conflation might exclude the *RTHKF* footnote from consideration, and offer an adequately representative working version of the Second and Fourth Sections, each of about 22 beats duration. However, editorial policy in this series has maintained a strong commitment to reconstruction of the music as closely as possible to standards of the Tang, and (to some extent) of the neo-Tang fluorescence in Japan. For this reason, the longer conflation offered here (30 beats) may be closer to the earlier, historical period, and hence more suitable as a reconstruction of both Sections.

Fifth Section: The first six beats of both versions appear again in later Sections: in the Sixth Section, towards the middle of the second part in *SGYR*, and in the Eighth Section, in both versions, as beats 1-6. The choice between $f\sharp$ and $g\sharp$ in these passages favours the latter note, and is adopted here. In the Fifth Section, repetitions of note patterns occur, both before and after *tei*-signs where it is difficult to align the sources convincingly. From the *tei*-sign onwards, the continuous passage of the lute version is accepted; following this, the flute version completes the Section, in keeping with the beat-dots in *RTHKF*, and note heads of *SGYR*.

Sixth Section: *SGYR* has been followed for the first eight beats, while the continuation combines both versions up to the *tei*-sign. The second part then repeats the *SGYR* note pattern and continues to the end, drawing equally on both sources.

Seventh Section: The intracolumnary dots in the first part are faulty in both sources; but if the first two binary-dots of *SGYR* are moved forwards or backwards by one beat, the sequence of notes and durations is feasible.

Eighth Section: here *RTHKF* is satisfactory in its present form. Noting the absence from *SGYR* of an intermediate *tei*-sign, the passage that follows *tei* in the Seventh Section is almost the same as a passage in the Eighth Section. In fact, beats 15-32 of the former are repeated, slightly varied, in beats 7-24 of the latter. Now, as *tei* in the Seventh Section occurs after the eighteenth beat, the appropriate structural position for *tei* in the Eighth Section would be after the tenth beat. It has, therefore, been added at this point.

Attention may be drawn to the median cadences of the conflations, occurring at the intermediate *tei*-signs of *SGYR*. In the absence of definitive durational and rhythmic indications throughout transcriptions of the lute versions, there can be no certainty that the standard rhythm, commonly found at cadences in many *Tōgaku* items, prevails in the Wild Prelude. The most usual cadence forms require three beats at least: the second half of a binary beat (in these transcriptions one quarter-note, or two eighth-notes) leading to a full binary beat for the cadence note itself. This note is usually one half-note/minim, but may sometimes be two quarter-notes, or one quarter-note and two eighth-notes where the cadence has acquired embellishment, or some kind of in-filling.

In *RTHKF* the final cadence patterns of each section – where *SGYR* has a second *tei*-marking – cover two whole binary beats, the second of which is, without exception, one plain half-note. Also invariably, in the flute versions, the penultimate binary beat consists of two quarter-notes, the first note of which descends by one degree, except in the First and Third Sections (the same), where the descent is one of two degrees, but not to the cadence note of the mode-final. The second note of the penultimate binary beat anticipates the actual cadence note, prior to its repetition (with inevitable stress) as the first beat of the next, and last, binary-beat of the Section. For the lute version, no useful comment on cadence rhythms can be offered.

In passages relative to the intermediate *tei*-markings of *SGYR* then, it will be found that the flute versions, in their source condition, are not compatible in time or rhythm, nor secure in pitch, as compared with similar passages in the lute versions. The possibility of stretching the musical time (and consequent rhythms) of intermediate cadence forms, to achieve conformity with more established cadence rhythms (in *Ōdai hajin-raku* for instance), has been resisted. Half-note

106

values at intermediate cadences, or *tei*-signs, do not occur. The Sectional cadences and drumbeats of the Wild Prelude, therefore, mark off the eight, major, structural divisions of the movement, while the span of melody throughout each Section continues, in terms of its patterned texture and inherent phrasing.

Example 8. Conflation of the Wild Prelude (see next page)

Analysis

Like the Broaching of *Ōdai hajin-raku*, the Wild Prelude of *Ryō-ō* is a movement consisting of a fixed number of detached, self-contained Sections, all composed of plain and varied repetitions of shared materials. The conflation of the Broaching of the former (Fascicle 2, pp.92-3) shows the formal structure of each Section to be similar, and the formulaic materials to be widely shared. Without repeating analytical details of the Broaching, the common identity of Sections is palpable: Sections 1 and 2; Sections 2 and 4; in the final drum-beat periods of four of the six Sections; and to greater or lesser degrees in other portions of various Sections. Other previously noted movements in similar Sections are: the Prelude of *Toraden* (Fascicle 2, pp.18-35 and conflations in Fascicle 3, pp.78-9); and *Gyokuju goteika* (Fascicle 3, pp.12-17, and Fascicle 4, pp,134-5) where, in both instances, repetitions of the tune are Sections of the movement.

The eight Sections of the Wild Prelude belong closely to each other in musical language and melodic style; but their individual lengths and binary divisions vary, as do the cadence notes, marked in the conflations according to the *tei*-signs from *SGYR* (Fascicle 5, pp.17-20). All Sections of the Wild Prelude include two cadence markings, with the exception of Sections 4 and 8, where *tei*-signs occur only after the last notes. Since the conflation of Section 4 is a variant of Section 2, a first *tei* in Section 4 is marked in agreement with 2. Similarly, a *tei*-sign has been supplied in Section 8, where the central passages of Section 7 are repeated. In the flute and lute scores, Sections conclude with drumbeats, consistently indicated by *hyaku*-signs (百), in the manner of Moronaga's string scores. Lacking *tei*-signs, the flute scores display the same final drum-beat signs, save in Sections 5, 7 and 8. Table 5 lists the number of beats in each Section, together with cadence notes, and shows the varied organization and orderly sequence of events as they occur throughout the movement as a whole.

Example 8. Conflation of the Wild Prelude

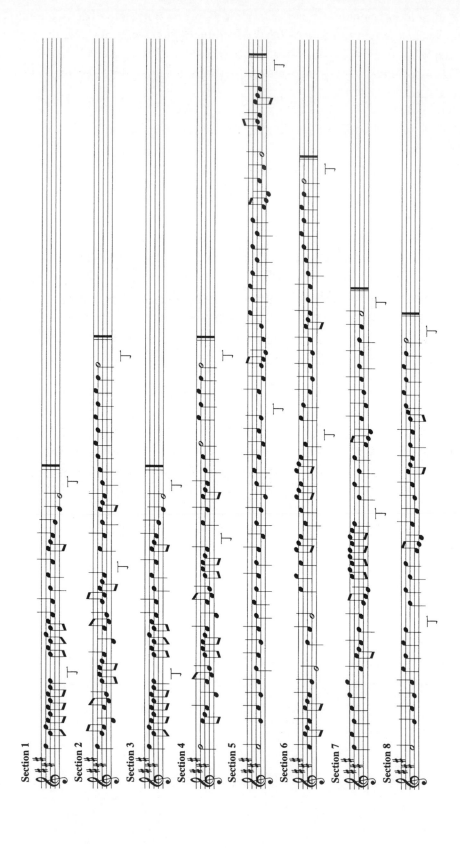

Table 5. The Wild Prelude: Table of numbers of beats,
and principal cadence notes, in each Section

First Section:	6 + 14	= 20 beats;	cadences on	b and e
Second Section:	14 + 16	= 30 "	"	a and d
Third Section:	6 + 14	= 20 "	"	b and e
Fourth Section:	16 + 14	= 30 "	"	a and d
Fifth Section:	26 + 26	= 52 "	"	$g\sharp$ and a
Sixth Section:	18 + 26	= 44 "	"	$c\sharp$ and d
Seventh Section:	18 + 16	= 34 "	"	d and a
Eighth Section:	10 + 22	= 32 "	"	d and d

The first two Sections of the Wild Prelude are repeated as Sections 3 and 4, save that the *SGYR* score of Section 4 omits repetition of the central sub-phrase of Section 2, and the *tei*-sign that follows it. In the conflation of Section 4, both omissions have been restored, for practical and analytical purposes. The remaining discrepancies between conflations and sources attempt to reconcile flute versions with the lute version. The latter is a late-Kamakura addition to *SGYR*; unfortunately, the tablature lacks reliable information on durations and rhythm.

Pairing of consecutive Sections in the first half of the Wild Prelude suggests that the original condition of the complete movement may have been along those lines throughout. The final cadence notes of the four pairs of Sections support this idea; and there are patterns in the sequence of cadence notes that balance in paired Sections, and complement an extended movement. The latter four Sections, however, indulge in lengthy periphrases, having moved from the more contained musical style of the first four Sections. In addition, a bold departure from traditional Chinese modal convention is manifested, in that the intermediate cadence notes of Sections 5 and 6 – the *bian* 變 notes (auxiliaries) of the pentatonic *Gongdiao* scale in the mode-key on D – are notes least expected to occupy prominent positions and responsibilities in music of this genre (though previous analyses have shown that this does sometimes occur).

In pursuit of further analysis, there are several paths that one might follow. In this instance, the binary principle that underlies the musical language of the Tang inheritance is particularly strong; and the Wild Prelude is an apt example of its validity and strength. The binary principle, evident here down to the smallest metrical unit, is sustained throughout the composition as a whole. Melodies of even numbers of binary beats are formed into two-part Sections; the Sections themselves are apparently grouped in complementary pairs of binary Sections; and these pairs of pairs make up two major components of the total: Sections

109

1 - 4 and 5 - 8, in which all cadence passages of the even-numbered Sections share the same melody; the quarter- and half-way divisions of the movement are thus closed with the same long passages of definitive, mode-final statements.

The following Example discloses a skilled dependence on formula and repetition that renders comprehensible and orderly what otherwise in this genre might appear irresolute and tortuous. The length of each excerpt, compared with that of its complete Section, is large: in the first two entries, much more than three-quarters of the total numbers of beats of their Sections.

Example 9. The Wild Prelude: congruity of closing phrases of Sections 2, 4, 6 and 8

In the course of discussing the form of the Free Prelude, attention was drawn to the prominence of the third, fourth and sixth of the scale in the B-related sections of the melody (pp.95-8). Sharp contrast was pointed out between the A sections with their conventional formulae in the basic *Gong* pentatonic scale on final, *d*, and the B sections with other formulae, drawn from a secondary, *Gong* pentatonic scale on the super-final, *e*. Each group of materials, both accommodated within the one modal (Lydian-type) heptatonic scale on *d*, focuses on a particular selection of notes of the scale, thus presenting opposing – or at least, different – perspectives on the mode. Something similar, but less extreme, is disclosed in the Wild Prelude, where the mode-final disappears, for appreciable stretches of time, having been displaced by groups of note patterns and cadence formulae that imply the function of the dominant as tonal centre.

It is the size of the Wild Prelude, and the nature of the extended phrases of the later Sections, that bring about a certain modal ambivalence. Although not strong enough to conflict with the ultimate authority of the final (in the hierarchy of notes), the dominant challenges it for comparatively long periods of time. A listing of intermediate and final cadence notes in pairs of Sections illustrates the internal sequence of events, and the design of the Wild Prelude as a whole.

Table 6. The Wild Prelude: order of cadence notes in paired sections

Sections 1 and 2	*b*,	*e*,	*a*,	*d*;	50 beats
Sections 3 and 4	*b*,	*e*,	*a*,	*d*;	50 beats
Sections 5 and 6	*g♯*,	*a*,	*c♯*,	*d*;	96 beats
Sections 7 and 8	*d*,	*a*,	*d*,	*d*;	66 beats

Impressions of alternating modal perspectives come to the fore in Sections 5 and 6 where, as previously indicated, emphasis is placed on the action of the two auxiliary notes of the modal scale as intermediate cadence notes. These are curious gestures compared with the familiar cadence-note choices of genuine *Tōgaku* items known to have come from the Tang capital; but modal flexibility in the Wild Prelude is suggested soon after the beginning, indeed as early as Section 1, where the second cadence appears with the same striking effect as intermediate cadences on the super-final in periods 4 and 7 of the First Section of the Prelude of *Toraden* (Fascicle 3, p.70); this same passage from Section 1 of the Wild Prelude is repeated in Section 3. Section 5 – consisting of 52 beats – fails to sound the final of the mode until beat 34, and dispenses with it entirely after beat 44. The dominant opening, the cadences on *g♯* and *a*, and the fleeting appearance of the mode-final hold the Section to a dominant-centred perspective on the scale. Section 6 (44 beats) continues in the same scale, with the mode-final being sounded once on beat 26, but not again until the cadence formula is introduced at the end. In Section 7 the pendulum swings more freely between the two centres of attraction, and a more equitable balance is restored in Section 8.

Illustrations of modal behaviour of the formulaic vocabulary are usefully compared in a first analysis of the Wild Prelude. Aligned passages from various Sections quickly display the individual – and perhaps competing – strengths of dominant and mode-final concentrations. They also reveal the amount of material shared around the principal tonal areas. At present, it is enough to align Sections 5-8 in one example. They flow, one after the other, as though Section 5 were a main source, generating and filling out its subsidiaries. The shorter Sections, 1 and 3, appear to maintain a degree of independence; but the notes of their second phrases are to be found in the first parts of Sections 5, 6 and 7. Similarly, the distinctive formula of the first parts of Sections 2 and 4 is present in variant forms in the second parts of Sections 5-8.

Example 10. The Wild Prelude: aligned analysis of Sections 5-8

Finally, if the mode-final cadence-passages are removed from the four even-numbered Sections in Example 8, what remains amounts to almost three-quarters of the movement in the power of the dominant – a well-sustained orientation indeed, maintained at the expense of the mode-final, the appearances of which are restricted to passing references and occasional reminders of its existence. The significance of consecutive, paired couplings of Sections, is demonstrable in the recurring mode-final definitions that conclude the even-numbered Sections. These are the cornerstones of the composition; they hold together a somewhat loose and rambling piece. In this condition, nevertheless, it served its purpose (as history avers), accompanying ritual dance and silent recitation, throughout many generations.

Conflation

Descriptive writing about *Ryō-ō*, in Chinese and Japanese historical sources relating to social and cultural history, attests persistent interest in this movement throughout the centuries (Fascicle 5, pp.1-25). The Entering Broaching is still danced and played by Japanese Court Musicians in public recitals, both at home and abroad. The movement retains popularity and prestige above that of many other *Tōgaku* items, on account of: the solemnity of the music as now played; the gesture, mime and costume colour of the protagonist; the bizarre mask with its dragon crest; and the memory of heroic military achievement.

Now, for the very first time in these fascicles, the nature and practice of the *Sada*-mode (*Sada-chō*) in China receives our attention. This is the first movement, out of the quasi-suite that once constituted *Ryō-ō*, of which we can be certain (a) that it is a Tang composition, and (b) that it illustrates what Tang musicians understood by the modal name: *Shatuo-diao*. The items in this mode-key constitute a small group of eight titles (twelve movements in all) immediately linked by Moronaga with the class of *Ichikotsu-chō* – presumably because the Lydian octave-set of these pieces was that of his hypothesised, perfect version of the modal characteristics of this class; even so, he must have been aware that the original modality of the equivalent *Yuediao* was Mixo-Lydian, not Lydian (see Preamble, pp.86,87), as the *shō/sheng* mouth-organ tablatures, as well as Chinese historical sources, show.

The contents of Fascicles 5 and 6, of which *Ryō-ō* is first on the list, are classed by Moronaga in the *Sada* mode (Fascicle 5, pp.xii,xiii, gives his description of the mode). In his distinguishing of the mode, Moronaga draws on the text *Huiyao* (801 or 803), to explain that *Sada-chō* is a basic *Gongdiao* (Lydian) scale on the second degree (*taizoku/taicu* 簇) of the basic scale. From the sources available, L.E.R.P. concluded that Moronaga 'knew this to be a Lydian octave-series', and that, by his time, it had become a transposed mode: 'transposed a tone down from its original pitch on *E* (accepting *D* as the final of the entire modal system).'

No detailed introduction to the Entering Broaching is necessary, beyond noting that the two auxiliaries in the scale of this mode-key are *g♯* and *c♯*, and that the mouth-organ scores, throughout the *Sada-chō* pieces, sometimes show these two notes raised. It seems possible that, already in China, some of these items were becoming more Mixo-Lydian than Lydian in character. Comparatively unimportant discrepancies between transcribed wind and string versions are to be seen in measures 5, 7, 9, 12 and 15, of the Entering Broaching (Fascicle 5, pp.21-3).

Example 11. *Ryō-ō*: Conflation of the Entering Broaching

The Entering Broaching of *Ryō-ō* returns to the style and structure of *Tōgaku* movements known to have been received from China by the Japanese, and retained as their own. The sixteen measures divide into two equal parts, subdividing again into quarters.

Although the title 'Broaching'(*Ha/Po* 破) has occurred a number of times in this series, there have been only two previous instances of the term 'Entering Broaching'. No attempt has yet been made to distinguish between 'Broaching' and 'Entering Broaching' as formal categories of movements. This may become possible when a larger proportion of the Tang repertory has been examined.

The first use of the term in the series occurs in the Large Piece: *Toraden* (Fascicle 2, pp.36-8; Fascicle 3, p.72). Counting Prelude and Middle Prelude as separate movements, the Entering Broaching is the third movement of five, and consists of nine measures of three binary beats each, followed by open (or unmeasured) binary-beat periods in the manner of a Prelude, with a final cadence at the sixteenth drumbeat. Later in the suite the same Entering Broaching was to be played as a final movement, there titled 'Quick'.

The second occurrence of the term is as the fourth movement of six in another Large Piece: *Shunnō-den* (Fascicle 2, pp.64-6; Fascicle 3, p.76). In sixteen measures of three binary beats throughout, it too is repeated at the end of the suite as a 'Quick'.

Unlike the two pieces just recalled, the Entering Broaching of *Ryō-ō* consists of sixteen regular measures of *four* binary beats each. This is typical of the time measurement of movements called simply 'Broaching', as in *Katen* (Fascicle 3, pp.23-4); *Tori* (Fascicle 3, p.39); *Kaibairaku* (Fascicle 3, pp.49-50); and *Bosatsu* (Fascicle 4, pp.71-3).

114

Two Broachings outside the quadruple standard are: (1) the Broaching in six Sections of *Ōdai hajin-raku* (Fascicle 1, pp.65-82; Fascicle 2, pp.77-9), the first four Sections of which are mostly in twenty measures of three binary beats, while the remaining two Sections consist of twenty, short, irregular periods, of two, three, and four binary beats; (2) the Broaching of *Koinju* (Fascicle 4, p.7), in fourteen measures of strict duple time. As already acknowledged, no secure basis has yet been established on which to determine 'normal' forms and functions of movements called 'Broaching' or 'Entering Broaching'.

The Entering Broaching of *Ryō-ō* consists of four equal parts, with *ichi-*signs by Moronaga following the second and tenth measures, and following the third binary-beat of the eighth and sixteenth measures. The halfway point, *Hanjō* is signalled following the third binary beat of the eighth measure. Structural and textural analysis of the melody produces very interesting features: measures 1 and 2 generate measures 3-4 and 12; measures 4-8 repeat in measures 12-16; and measures 9-11 reflect measures 5-6 and 13-14. The sixteen measures of the complete melody appear to be indebted to measures 1-2 and 5-8.

Example 12. The Entering Broaching: aligned analysis

Analysis brings to view several characteristic features of the melody. First: observe measures 8 and 16. The link at the Half-Section (*Hanjō*) (measure 8), and the varied incipit (*Kandō*) (measure 16) that follows the end – constituting the fourth binary beats of both these measures – are typical 'fillers', to be found in certain tunes that, in recital or concert, repeat themselves in rotation as parts of a single performance. (For the term *Hanjō* see Fascicle 1, p.19. Examples of *Kandō*, both brief and extended, are first shown on p.61, Fascicle 2.) *KF/HSF/RK* and *SSSTF* prescribe repetition of the Entering Broaching in performance. The varied rhythms of the cadence measures of the conflation (all present in the transcriptions – Fascicle 5, pp.21-3) may well represent later Japanese versions of the same tune, rather than earlier Chinese ones. The *Kandō* add their small weight to this view. Indeed, the character of the two *Kandō*-beats resembles that of other cadence measures in this piece, where what (possibly) were once held, or repeated, notes in earlier versions (for example, as retained in measure 10), have subsequently been filled out, in measures 2, 4, 6, 8, 12, 14 and 16. In the following review of the sub-phrase structure implicit in the melody, reduced versions of the cadence formulae of even-numbered measures are tabled. A feasible sequence of measures in cadence rhythms emerges.

Example 13. The Entering Broaching: hypothetical, reduced versions of even-numbered cadential measures

A literal listing of cadence notes occurring in the conflation touches on their functions and musicality in context; for comparison, the order of cadence notes in the conflation is displayed here (Table 7) above the order of cadence notes in the reduced measures shown in Example 13. The influence of Japanese instrumental performance practices over several centuries has probably contributed to the not insignificant differences.

Table 7. The Entering Broaching: Comparative Table of Cadence Notes of Two-Measure Sub-Phrases

Cadence notes of even-numbered measures of the conflation,	*d,*	*c♯,*	*a,*	*d,* | *a,*	*c♯,*	*a,*	*d.*
Cadence notes of the same measures as shown in Example 13,	*d,*	*a,*	*e,*	*d,* | *a,*	*a,*	*e,*	*d.*

The modality of the Entering Broaching lies close to the surface. The four-measure, four-phrase structure needs no explanation. The first and third phrases are dominant-centred; and notwithstanding the sub-final cadence note, there can be no doubt about the tonal centre of the second phrase. By applying the weighted-scale procedure, more information on modal action and reaction can be elicited. The data are expressed here in the mouth-organ scale of the conflation. Cadence notes are underlined.

Table 8. The Entering Broaching: Weighted-Scales
from the Four Phrases of the Conflation

		a	*b*	*c♯*	*d*	*e*	*f♯*	*g♯*
Measures	1-4	19	23	<u>25.5</u>	7	-	-	2.5
	5-8	19.5	13.5	-	<u>23.5</u>	10	12	5.5
	9-12	25	13	<u>6</u>	3	9.5	8.5	12
	13-16	17.5	13	-	<u>24.5</u>	8.5	12	5.5
Measures	1-16	81	62.5	31.5	<u>58</u>	28	32.5	25.5

In the first phrase there are just three important notes, and the mode-final is not one of them. To the ear, the dominant is strong; but it only rates third place after *b* and *c♯* – the latter being an auxiliary note of the scale. The upper tetrachord of the octave-species is the working material of the first phrase. In the second phrase, while the dominant remains at its previous level, the mode-final comes into its own. The scale of this phrase is the *Gongdiao* pentatonic scale, with the hierarchy of notes functioning in the traditional manner. From strongest to weakest, the order of notes is *d*, *a*, *b*, *f♯* and *e*. Of the auxiliary (*bian*) notes in measures 5-8, *g♯* makes the least contribution, and *c♯* does not appear – an interesting reversal of the role of the sub-final in the first phrase.

In the third phrase we are in dominant territory again. This time the dominant is the note of most weight, and its immediately adjacent notes support it, *g♯* and *b*, being nearest in weight but only half its value, and therefore not close enough to contend with it. The mode-final is again very weak; even the auxiliaries score four times (*g♯*) and twice (*c♯*) as much as the mode-final. The fourth phrase is almost identical with the second. The *Gongdiao* re-asserts itself; the auxiliaries are subdued; and the mode-final is well on top in the end.

In review, the first three movements of *Ryō-ō* are extraordinarily interesting. The *modus operandi* of the Free Prelude is an ABA'B' form, with a cadence tagged on at the end – a peremptory and last-minute reminder of the mode-final, silent throughout the 24 beats of B' until this moment, when the only cadential statement on the mode-final in the entire composition is thrust forward. Contrast between the A and B sections is sharp, changes in modal perspective seemingly capricious. In the Free Prelude, formulaic repetition and developing length of composition appear to be seeking conciliation as the millennium neared its end. A problem now confronting Japanese musicians was that natural musical invention was reaching out beyond the long established bounds of traditional modal composition. The question taxing the musical imagination, therefore, was how to mount the burgeoning creativity into suitably compatible time-frames, while tonal and scalar materials remained behind, enslaved by out-worn theories and practices. It will be remembered that note patterns of the Free Prelude are few.

In this regard, the Wild Prelude expresses itself more ingenuously. The tonal centres exploited therein are the closest: a mode-final and its dominant, and they share the total duration of the piece, establishing themselves without conflict. Having time and space in which to manoeuvre, they have equal opportunity to assert themselves without (in the end) unduly disturbing a simple, compatible relationship. The Free Prelude is abnormal, certainly unconventional, while the Wild Prelude is stylistically conventional and conservative, a relic of a distant past, perhaps.

By comparison, the Entering Broaching is slightly longer than the Free Prelude, and half the length of the Wild Prelude; and it moves forward steadily from first to last. It has an educated order and balance about itself, both in, and between, its various components, qualities recognised aurally and technically. Together, the three movements stretch our knowledge of modal procedures and practices beyond what has been discovered and discussed hitherto in studies of the Entertainment Music of the Tang.

Retiring Music: *Amma*

The enigma of *Amma* lies in its origin and transmission, not in the tune from the manuscripts of *COGRTYF* and *RTYF*, dating from 1330 to 1688. Drawn from the same sources as the Free Prelude, the transcription (Fascicle 5, pp.25-7) shows a complete melody in the same flute style. In the case of *Amma*, the text of the transcription is essentially the same as that of the Tenri *MS*. In making the conflation (it is very close to the text of the transcription), the same guidelines have been followed as in conflating the Free Prelude. Notation is mostly in quarter-notes and eighth-notes, without rests; *ichi*-signs have been completed regularly in binary beats, on the basis that 36 of those provided are convincing evidence of regular time measurement.

In the interests of standardising a working version, several small amendments have been made. Towards the end, the transcription exhibits four beats, superimposed after beat 62, where also L.E.R.P. was uncertain in transcribing. Of the four beats in question, the third and fourth are already present in the transcription at the same place, with only slight variation; and the first and second beats of the variant fall into place immediately following beat 62, where the rise to the mode-final begins. At the cadence, the mode-final quarter-note, before the repeating double bar in the transcription, has been changed to a half-note, so as to complete the binary beat. The ten-beat coda constitutes no problem.

Example 14. Conflation: *Amma*

Conflation

Nothing is certain regarding the origin and history of *Amma*. Japanese literary sources state that its admission to the suite, *Ryō-ō*, as final movement (in place of the *Sada-chō* 'Modal Prelude' *Chōshi* 調 子) was the result of an Imperial Decree, issued about the time of the consecration ceremonies of the Tōdaiji Temple in Nara in 752, or soon after.

RMS reports the addition of this movement to the set, and a performance of *Ryō-ō* on that occasion (with or without *Amma* is not known); a century later, *KKS* infers that the change was made about 85 years after the events at the Tōdaiji, and adds that *Amma* was first offered to the throne, in the Jōwa reign-period, by Ōto no Kiyogami who 'made' the piece.

KKS adds that, contrary to those who say that *Amma* was a Japanese composition, it is properly to be regarded as an Indian piece (Fascicle 5, pp.24-7). More than four centuries later, *HPGS* [in *Gakkaroku* (1690)] supplies a song text, and repeats from *KKS* that this piece was transmitted to the Japanese Court from Champa by Buttetsu (Champa having formerly been regarded as an Indian kingdom) (see Fascicle 3, p.31).

Three of the four basic source manuscripts for this series say nothing about *Amma*, but in *JCYR* the indefatigable and inexhaustible Moronaga cites Prince Sadayasu, Hakuga (Minamoto no Hiromasa) and Ōwari no Hamanushi, on its history, and gives directions for performance.

Like the Free Prelude, *Amma* consists of two parts, with an additional cadential phrase, to be used in concluding repetitions during dance performances. The number of repeats is not given; but *Amma* certainly became the piece performed for the exit of the dancers. The centuries-later manuscript *RTYF* (1688) states that *Amma* was danced by one or two men, wearing masks and holding batons; but nothing of the choreography or symbolism of the performance is known.

The conflation consists of 82 unit-beats – including the final cadential phrase. Apart from the ending, the two halves amount to 72 beats, 36 in each half, with cadences on *b* and *d* respectively. The Free Prelude also consists of two halves that cadence on *b* and *d*, but the form of *Amma* is simply A + B, unlike the Free Prelude, where the halves share the same material – to the extent that the second half is a variant of the first, and the form is ABA'B'. In *Amma* there is no significant melodic resemblance between the two halves. It might be suggested that the periphrasis of beats 53-66 in the second half is an extended reminiscence of beats 1-5 in the first half; but the suggestion scarcely convinces. The first half consists almost entirely of falling phrases, the second, mostly of rising phrases, and their structural profiles are dissimilar.

In the second half of *Amma* (bound as it is, almost entirely, within the interval of a perfect fourth) there are only two descending intervals: *c♯' - a*, and *d' - b*; and these occur over the comparatively long time-span of beats 37-52. In itself, what follows (beats 53-64) does not suggest any return to, or reminiscence of, the opening of the first half (beats 1-8), but rather introduces something quite different. Part B of *Amma* is subjected to a procrustean operation in two stages. Beats 37-40 are extended into beats 43-50, and then drawn out still further into beats 53-70. Musically speaking, Part B has little to say of itself, beyond what is heard in the first six beats. In course of time, the first six beats (37-42) become the next 24 beats (43-66), to which is added the mode-final ending that replaces the earlier cadence of Part A on the sixth (*b*) of the scale.

On the basis of modality, another way of looking at beats 53 onwards may be posited. The scale formation of the first half moves in descending phrases through *b - a - g♯ - e*, with a final lift (in the last three beats) to cadence on *b*. The first note, *c♯*, makes no real contribution to the piece, beyond acting as the initial note of the melody – a role that only achieves prominence for a moment. The sub-final is not a frequent opening note; and indeed the traditional status of auxiliary notes (in Chinese heptatonic scales) is minimal and lightweight. In this respect the Entering Broaching of *Ryō-ō* is exceptional. It too starts from the sub-final, but casts it in a particularly important role in the first four measures.

In contrast to the scale of the first half, the phrases of the second half of *Amma* cover the notes of the upper tetrachord: *a - b - c♯ - d*, with *g♯* (the other auxiliary note) sounding only as the cadence is approached. Beats 37-52 – rising and falling three times (through *a - d' - b*) – are followed by beats 52-72, during which the contour changes to *b - g♯ - b - d'*. This is where *g♯* makes its brief appearance (beats 62-5). The movement towards *g♯* stretches over fourteen beats, from *d' - g♯* (beats 49-62); and this is followed by a return to *d'* in half the time. The note *g♯* – the nadir of the second half – is thus aurally prepared, placed in its peculiar relationship with the final, and then laid aside in a prompt bid for the mode-final in cadence position, and thence in cadence formula. Before the nadir, the fourth of the scale has not been heard in *Amma* for 30 beats (out of a total of 72).

Textural evidence of this kind lends substance to the view that, at the present stage of our experience of this kind of music, *Sada-chō* melodies exemplify increased flexibility of modal and stylistic behaviour. In the movements of *Ryō-ō* – as known from quite late sources – intermediate tonal centres occur and are prolonged in sizeable segments of melody. The treatment of melodic structures provides clear and formed elements of variety and contrast; this treatment extends the technical range of 'genuine', early *Tōgaku* pieces. The heptatonic scale has become less inhibited by old pentatonic practices; and the musical style of *Ryō-ō* movements – except perhaps for the Entering Broaching – is freer and less conventional.

It remains to present a formulaic analysis of *Amma* in illustration of some of the previous descriptions.

Example 15. *Amma*: formulaic, aligned analysis

Dissimilarity between the two parts is evident; activity in each tetrachord differs, exhibiting no formulaic connections. The possibility that beats 56-62 are a reminiscence of beats 1-5 is remote, and the same may be said of beats 53-61 being a further variant of the first three notes of the second half of the melody, beats 37-9. The absence of the mode-final from the first half, and its weak status in the second, is surprising. Weighted-scale figures reveal that neither the mode-final, nor the dominant, is the heavyweight of the tune.

Table 9. Amma. *Weighted-Scale Data*

	e	f♯	g♯	a	b	c♯	d'
Beats 1 - 36	18.5	19	11	18	19.5	6	-
Beats 37-72	-	-	6	13.5	37.5	18	12
Parts A and B	18.5	19	17	31.5	57	24	12

Most weight is laid on *b*, which note holds both dominant and final down to one third of its own weight in the second half. In the line-up of totals, the mode-final sits very low at 21 percent of the score of *b*, and only 7 percent of the weight of all notes of the tune together. The dominant reaches 18 percent of the total weight of all notes. In the final count, the respective positions of the two auxiliary notes are extraordinary, as compared with that of the mode-final. Through repetitions in beats 54-9, the sub-final raises its weight from lowest in the first half to second highest in the second. Even so, both auxiliaries overshadow the final in the end. The order of notes as determined on the basis of these data, strongest to weakest, is as follows:

Table 10. Amma. *Orders of notes, strongest to weakest, as determined from weighted-scale data*

Part A: beats 1 - 36,	b,	f♯,	e,	a,	g♯,	c♯,	
Part B: beats 37- 72,	b,	c♯,	a,	d,	g♯,		
Parts A and B: beats 1 - 72,	b,	a,	c♯,	f♯,	e,	g♯,	d.

The four movements of *Ryō-ō* are distinctive in their differences. Probably unconnected in ethnic origin and style, and reshaped by foreign cultural and social influences in the course of transmission, they stand together as a monument to the true hero, transformed to legend, whose reputation and character are with difficulty separated from the accretions of romance. Of the four movements themselves, something similar may be said. Practically nothing is known of the origins or originators of many of the Tang entertainment pieces, except that some of the tunes must have sprung from the musical imagination of musicians in imperial capitals, while others, of less elitist origins, were imported from far and wide, to be absorbed into the style and repertory of the popular genre. With transfer of knowledge of many kinds eastwards across Asia, in the second half of the First Millennium, went many other aspects of culture; among them: a living embodiment of materials, experiences and brilliant achievements of the far-flung, multi-racial Tang Empire. As is abundantly clear, music from other parts of the vast Asiatic continent was also transmitted to Japan, there to be absorbed, acclimatised and preserved, in the heritage of the rising Island Nation.

Ryō-ō unquestionably became a much-favoured performance at centres of *Gagaku*-performance in Japan – not only at the Imperial Court but also at the great religious houses, and in homes of the nobility. It is likely that the suite, as we know it today, was assembled and established as a performance in that country. The legend of Changgong of Qi undoubtedly developed in China, from the date of the victory at Mangshan onwards; but in Japan the *Ryō-ō*, the *Ling-wang*, The Prince of the Grave-Mound, was utterly transformed into the dragon-masked being seen today wielding an insignificant trifling baton, last pitiful reduction of a demon-expelling whip, first acquired in China before he reached Japan. Today this quasi-suite lives on in three movements: part of the Free Prelude, the Entering Broaching and the mysteriously coupled *Amma*. The popularity of the Entering Broaching, even with foreigners, is evinced whenever nowadays the Imperial Musicians perform abroad. Recently, indeed, a group of Japanese musicians and dancers performed *Ryō-ō* in China at the grave-site of Prince Changgong of Qi (see *Nihon Gagakkai Kaihō*, p.3, 1992).

Erratum (L.E.R.P): Professor Emeritus Piet van der Loon has most kindly indicated (his letter of 15th October 1992) that the translation of the passage from the text of a commemorative inscription on the gravestone of the Senior Princess of Daiguo (see Fascicle 5, p.3) is inaccurate. He gives permission for his translation to be published here:

'The Empress Zetian paid a formal visit to the Sacred Hall. During the banquet the [present] Emperor, six years old and holding the title of Prince of Chu, danced "The Long Destiny". The Abdicated Emperor [Li Xian] who was twelve years old and [at that time] Senior Imperial Grandson, performed "The An Gongzi". The Prince of Qi [Li Fan], who was five years old and [at that time] Prince of Wei, played "The Prince of Lanling" and also made the following address as leader of the troupe:

"The Prince of Wei enters the scene,
To offer congratulations to the Divine Saint:
A myriad years to Her Majesty the Empress!
Her grandchildren form a file."

The Princess [of Daiguo], then four years old, and the Princess of Shouchang together danced "The Western Liang". The officials in the Hall all shouted "A myriad years!" '

The quatrain of the address is then:

衛 王 入 場
咒 願 神 聖
神 皇 萬 歲
孫 子 成 行

The charm of the scene is renewed, and the five-year-old's address is enhanced by becoming a quatrain with three rhymes: 場, 聖 and 行 – [respectively *d'iang*, *śiäng*, *γɒng* – as pronounced in the Tang period (see phonetic values in Karlgren, 1957: **720 x**; **835 z**; **748 a**)]. The date of this earliest testimony to a performance of 'The Prince of Lanling' (as established by Professor van der Loon) is 690.

A further change to be proposed here concerns Appendix 2 of Fascicle 4 (p.113), where it was already suggested that the piece *Sōba/Caopo* 曹 婆 might have some connection with the state of Caoguo 曹 國 – on the border between Kazaks and Üzbeks during the Tang. Rather than 'Mother-in-Law Cao' or 'Stepmother Cao' it seems much more appropriate (as suggested by Professor Wolpert) that this title (known only to the mouth-organ manuscript, *SSSTF*) should be translated as 'Girls of Caoguo'.

25. A New "Prince of Luoling" (Volume 6, pp.1-12)

Shin Raryō-ō

Conflations

The Broaching

Primary versions of the Broaching, from the mouth-organ scores and *SGYR*, show no significant differences. The mouth-organ versions agree on the *Shangdiao* (Mixo-Lydian-type) scale, and on tablatures measured off (in *KF/HSF/RK*) in sixteen measures of eight beats each, with drumbeats on the penultimate metrical beat of each measure. Apart from Moronaga's insistence on the *Gongdiao* (Lydian-type) scale, *SGYR* differs only in six notes from the mouth-organ versions: the first beats of recurring measures 2, 6 and 14; the fifth beats of recurring measures 7 and 15; and the final beat of measure 10. Discrepancies are therefore minimal. Following the practice adopted in the conflations of *Ryō-ō*, the conflations of *Shin Raryō-ō* are set here in the scale of the Chinese *Gongdiao* on *D*, and the conflation of the Broaching follows the notes of the transcriptions of the mouth-organ scores.

Example 1. *Shin Raryō-ō*, Broaching: conflation of primary version

The secondary version of the Broaching, only found in the string sources, is an eight-measure tune, quite closely related to the first half of the primary version. Comparison of the two (Example 2) shows the secondary version (the only one tabulated in *JCYR*) to be a *gakubyōshi* variant of measures 1-3 and 6-8 of the primary version. It will be seen that measures 7-8 of the primary version are repeated in measures 15-16, and measures 5-6 of the secondary version (of half the length), in measures 7-8. Measures 5-8, therefore, vary primary measures 7-8 and 15-16. Primary measures 4-5 are omitted from the secondary version. When embellishments are withdrawn from the transcriptions of the secondary versions, all principal notes are found to be the same as those of the primary version.

Example 2. *Shin Raryō-ō*, Broaching:
conflations of the primary and secondary versions compared

The Quick

Of the Quick there are four, primary versions, in sixteen measures, and two secondary versions, in twelve measures. The initial measure of the primary versions is amended for repetitions of the tune after the first time through. The

127

secondary versions (not shown here) are the first twelve measures of the amended primary versions. A small number of source differences required reconciliation in measures 3, 7, 11 and 15, the results of which are evident in the conflation (Example 3). In measures 3 and 11, the conflation has adopted an order of notes taking *a* as first beat, and *b* as third beat. Since the two measures are clearly intended to be the same, *a - d - b - c♯* is a supportable solution for both. In measures 7 and 15, so far as they apply to the six source versions, *b* is selected for the first beat in the conflated version: *b - f♯ - e - d*. As in the Broaching, the Lydian octave-species is maintained as scale formation of the Quick.

Example 3. *Shin Raryō-ō*, Quick: conflation

The Broaching, Analysis

Since the primary version of the Broaching also contains tonal and structural elements of the secondary version, analytical comments are confined here to the primary version. Structurally, the Broaching melody resembles several *Tōgaku* movements of sixteen measures, and an unmeasured one with sixteen drumbeat periods; but tunes of this length are few in the modal repertory so far presented. The binary principle produced many tunes with phrases of two and four measures, in total lengths of eight, ten, twelve and fourteen measures, but tunes of sixteen measures are less common.

A recently discussed example in the same time as the Broaching, and in the same mode, is the Entering Broaching of *Ryō-ō* (Fascicle 5, pp.21-4; conflation on p.114 of this volume). Three further examples are to be found in *Shunnō-den* 'The Singing of Spring Warblers' (transcriptions Fascicle 2, pp.52-71; conflations Fascicle 3, pp.70-3): the third movement, Stamping; the fourth movement, Entering Broaching (but in triple time – six beats to the measure); and the second movement, Prelude, unmeasured, with sixteen drumbeats (irregularly distanced in time). Attention is drawn to the analytical commentary on *Shunnō-den* in Fascicle 3, pp.86-90. There are six movements in this last suite, five of which are tabulated in the mouth-organ and string sources. The first movement, Processional, is in fact the latter part of the Prelude, and the final movement, Quick Tune, is a repeat of the Entering Broaching. As to the four ostensibly independent movements, analysis has shown them to be variants of each other (Fascicle 3, pp.86-90).

The four movements named, from *Ryō-ō* and *Shunnō-den*, exist in melodic textures not dissimilar from the patterned design of the Broaching of *Shin Raryō-ō*, and this movement shares with them a basic ABCB form in which approaches to the repeating section from A and C are negotiated by similar methods, A-B and C-B. All these pieces have their own internal factors that identify the particular composition; yet they have a commonality that regulates the medium and manner of expression. They evince a craft of musical composition, over small time-spans, which complements the skill and constructional ability previously discovered in compositions of longer time-span, the most remarkable of which has been the great suite, *Ōdai hajin-raku* 'The Emperor Destroys the Formations' (Fascicle 1; Fascicle 2, conflations, pp.76-9).

Features of the Broaching of *Shin Raryō-ō* common to the movements mentioned above can be pointed out from the conflation. The Broaching consists of two equal parts; these divide into quarters of the whole, and these in turn, into eighths. Of these divisions, measures 5-8 recur in measures 13-16, initially suggesting an ABCB plan. Measures 3-4 also recur in measures 11-12, where measure 11 is a variant of measure 3. In fact, measure 3 is itself a variant of measure 1, which yields further variants in measures 5, 11 and 13. Measure 2 recurs in measures 6 and 14, and measure 4 in measure 12. One is now describing single-measure units.

The ABCB plan requires more detail. At first, a description in two-measure phrases will be convenient; the varied recurrence of measures 1-2 in measures 5-6 and measures 13-14 can be detailed; but if a finer point were drawn, the relative significance of *each* measure would be recognized more easily. Varying recurrences of the simple formula that underlies measures 1, 3, 11 and 13, coupled with the recurrence of measures 7-8 in measures 15-16, make a tidy and compact construction. If one hears measures 9-10 as related to measure 7, the plan of eight two-measure phrases will stand as follows:

Table 1. Shin Raryō-ō, *Broaching: formal plan*

A, A^1, A^2, B ‖ B^1, A^3, A^2, B ‖

Table 2. A fuller measure-by-measure, structural description

a,   b,   a',   c,   a",   b,   c,   d,   ‖
c',   c",   a''', c,   a",   b,   c,   d,   ‖

An aligned table of analysis clarifies the descriptions.

Example 4. *Shin Raryō-ō*, Broaching: aligned analysis.

Further study of the Broaching leads to observations on modal behaviour and consequent tonal profile. There is only one mode-final cadence before *hanjō* in measure 8, and only one after *hanjō*, where measure 8 repeats in measure 16. Until the *hanjō* the ear is not informed of the fundamental role of *d*, although it sounds in passing in measures 2, 4 and 6, and again in the same positions in the second half, measures 10, 12 and 14. In itself the mode-final gives little identity to the tune, except where modal definition is prescribed for the most important cadential points of an entire composition; in the Broaching these are in the middle and at the end.

In contrast to the infrequency of the final in this melody, and the absence of specific modal identification at the beginning, is the strength of the dominant. It appears twice in almost every measure except measures 8 and 16, and thrice as cadences, in measures 4, 10 and 12 – the same number of cadences as fall on *b*, in measures 2, 6 and 14. In this movement, the fortunes of the sixth of the scale

130

fluctuate according to its contextual position. In the hierarchy of notes, it has a commanding position relative to the dominant, but pales when the mode-final is about to emerge at its two cadential points. More curious is the poverty of the superfinal, the least heard note of all, entirely dependent on the final for its five brief appearances.

With the help of the weighted-scale procedure, applied on the same basis as in earlier analyses, data concerning the hierarchy and interrelationship of notes in the tune can be sought and sighted objectively. In a first exercise, data assembled from the total durations and numbers of occurrences of each note, and from notes that act as initials and finals of each measure, are tabled to compare the modal perspectives of the four phrase-units, each of the same length.

Table 3. Shin Raryō-ō, *Broaching: weighted-scales, according to sectional structure; cadence notes underlined*

		a	*b*	*c#*	*d*	*e*	*f#*	*g#*
Measures	1 - 4	<u>18</u>	28	9	5	-	8	2
"	5 - 8	10	21	7	<u>16</u>	4	9	2
"	9 -12	<u>28</u>	12	2	11	2	9	6
"	13 -16	10	21	7	<u>16</u>	3.5	10.5	2
Measures	1-16	66	82	25	<u>48</u>	9.5	36.5	12

In three sectional entries, the sixth far outweighs other notes of the scale, while in the remaining phrase the dominant is supreme. In the first and third phrases the mode-final is heavily depressed by the dominant, while in the second and fourth phrases, containing the only mode-final cadences, it rises significantly above the dominant, but remains subdued by the sixth of the scale – the dominant's neighbour. The weak rating of the superfinal (lowest in the scaled totals) is a surprise not recognized in perception of the tune. Of the auxiliaries of the scale, the fourth is not prominent, but the seventh assumes importance in measures 1-2 and their variants – that is, measures 3, 5-6 and 13-14.

In the light of this survey, a second exercise may now be conducted from a position of projected modal divisions, rather than melodic phrases. Earlier examinations of *Tōgaku* pieces have shown that modal perspectives vary in parts of some items of the *Ichikotsu-chō* repertory, and that, on the basis of analysis of the *Ryō ō* suite, movements of the *Sada-chō* sub-category may be conspicuous in this regard. It is now proposed to apply the weighted-scale procedure once more, demarcating sections of the melody that reflect specifically dominant- and mode-final orientations respectively, bearing in mind that the mode-final assumes no identity as such in this piece, except in the context of its cadential appearances. Looking back to the aligned analysis of the primary Broaching, one sees that measures 7-10 and 15-16 adhere to the mode-final as tonal centre; and that measures 1-6 and 11-14 recognise the fifth and sixth of the scale as central to their existence. Another Table of data from the Broaching is now presented.

Table 4. Shin Raryō-ō, Broaching: weighted-scales of the primary version, according to modal inference

1. Ten measures where dominant and sub-mediant lead:

		a	b	c♯	d	e	f♯	g♯
(1) Measures	1-6	24	46	14	7	-	12	2
"	11-14	22	28	5	5	-	8	2
Subtotals		46	74	19	12	-	20	4

2. Six measures where mode-final leads:

		a	b	c♯	d	e	f♯	g♯
(2) Measures	7-10	16	6	4	22	6	10	6
"	15-16	4	3	2	14	3.5	6.5	2
Subtotals		20	9	6	36	9.5	16.5	8

Measures	1-16							
Totals		66	83	25	48	9.5	36.5	12

This latter table gives quite a different impression from the previous one. In sections where the mode-final functions as prime-tone of the mode-key (measures 7-10 and 15-16), it dominates other notes decisively. The final, dominant and median-third are the structural backing of these sections; and the lightest notes in these parts of the melody are the auxiliaries: the fourth and the seventh. One can appreciate an *Ichikotsu-chō* description of the six measures 7-10 and 15-16.

In formulaic and modal language, the aligned analysis of the Broaching gives no hint that measures 1-6 and 11-14 belong to measures 15 and 16. In measures 1-6 and 11-14, the mode-final fails to maintain itself as prime tone of the mode-key. The weight of evidence shows that *b* dominates these sections, with *a* the next note in line, but not numerically close; the two notes carry 69 percent of the total weight of the ten measures. With *c♯*, the three notes *a* - *b* - *c♯* take 79 percent of the subtotal. The one other note that attracts attention is *f♯* which, with *c♯* in this tune, belongs to the dominant rather than to the final. If one were to propose a basic scale on *A*, backing these parts of the melody, *d* and *g♯* would theoretically stand as *bian* notes – the two lightest notes, one fourth apart; but the scale would lack a true dominant. Moreover there is no convincing precedent for a *Tōgaku* movement that behaves so extravagantly as to relegate the final of the named mode to the status and role of an auxiliary note, nor for changing mid-stream from one form of modal scale to another. The Broaching remains a member of the *Sada-chō* sub-category of *Ichikotsu-chō*.

Since *Sada-chō* is assuredly a Lydian octave-species on *D*, no challenge to theory, so far as we know it from experience, is invoked. The Broaching functions with *d* as final, and with *g♯* and *c♯* as its traditional auxiliaries. The final is strongly supported by its fifth and sixth notes, the extent and degree of support varying according to the note formulae, and the structural constraints imposed thereon. The melody holds firm, while two perspectives of the one mode demonstrate the variety and texture of the music.

Shin Raryō-ō: the Quick

The Quick of *Shin Raryō-ō* consists of sixteen measures in duple time, with the bass-drum marking the second binary beat of each measure. Consequently, in a symmetrical melody such as this, with half-notes at the ends of alternate measures, the phrasing falls naturally into well-defined, two-measure lengths, as in stanzas of poetry with seven syllables (characters) to each line, the last syllable being held for two beats. Like the Broaching, the Quick divides into halves, quarters and eighths.

The form of the Quick embodies repetitions and variations of structural and formulaic elements. Measures 5-8 return in 13-16, and 3 returns in 11. More interesting is the affinity between 1-4 and 9-12. By intuitive craftsmanship on the part of those who made the tune, 9-10 are a modal transposition of 1-2, and 11-12 a transposition of 3-4. Measures 9-12 are a close variant of 1-4, in which the order of cadences is reversed: in 2 and 4, cadences fall on the mode-final and dominant, to be answered (in 10 and 12) by dominant and final.

Example 5. *Shin Raryō-ō*: Quick; comparison of measures 1-4 and 9-12

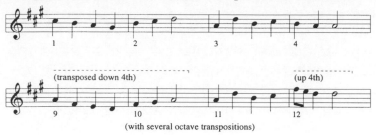

(transposed down 4th) (up 4th)

(with several octave transpositions)

In the light of comments on the adaptation of measures 1-4 in measures 9-12, the atypical commencement of the Quick – on the sub-final, in descending motion to the dominant – should not be overlooked. In this context there are two examples to note: the Entering Broaching of *Ryō-ō* has a more spacious sub-final-to-dominant opening than the Quick of *Shin Raryō-ō*; it spreads over eight beats of the first measure, and continues to an implicit mode-final cadence in the second measure. A similar example opens Section 3 of the Broaching of *Ōdai-hajin-raku*. Admittedly Section 3 is not the beginning of the movement, but the first two measures are a dominant-final mode-key affirmation, bolder than the incipits of other Sections, in so far as a full triadic structure on the dominant is stated before the mode-final is addressed. The first two measures of Section 3 are not unlike the first two measures of the Quick; both declare the dominant of the prevailing mode-key, and follow this with an explicit cadence on the mode-final. Comparison of the first four measures of the *Ryō-ō* Entering Broaching in 4/2, with the first four measures of the *Shin Raryō-ō* Quick in 2/2, uncovers similarity of musical idea and expression at centre, and the relevance of both excerpts to a *Gongdiao* context.

Example 6. Radical similarity between unconnected movements:
Entering Broaching of *Ryō-ō* & Quick of *Shin Raryō-ō*

The brevity of phrases in the Quick has ensured a precise statement, aided by the fourth of the scale. Aurally, *g♯* seems to strengthen the position and power of the final in this passage. The two subfinal-dominant incipits make their points, not as modal licences or random liberties, but as parts of opening mode-key definitions. The initial two measures of each movement belong together in structured and formal predications of mode-final identity. In the total span of these movements, the openings are convincing; but this may not necessarily apply in other circumstances, where movements begin from the sub-final.

A movement that remains puzzling to the analyst in this regard is *Amma*, 'Durga', of *Ryō-ō* (Fascicle 5; conflation in this fascicle, p.120), the concluding movement of the first suite listed in *Sada-chō*. Not only does it begin on the sub-final and descend to the dominant, it continues to descend to the super-final, several times tracing a meandering path from dominant to super-final, before reaching a halfway cadence, not on *a*, nor on *d*, but on *b*. The scale of the first part of *Amma* is *e - f♯ - g♯ - a - b - c♯*; that of the second part: *g♯ - a - b - c♯ - d*, in which, according to previously tabled data (drawn from this piece, p.123), *d* registers 14 percent of the combined weight of all notes of the second half. Of the weight of all notes of both halves, the mode-final carries just 7 percent of the total.

On this evidence, and on information from *Ryō-ō* (movements given earlier) one moves cautiously towards what determines the classification of the items before us as *Sada-chō*. Only a few general pointers are in sight: pieces that terminate on *d* as final; the scale being the Lydian-type octave-species on that

135

note; and the contemporary belief that they or some emanated from Kuchā, or were influenced in the course of transmission by the musical taste of that state in early Tang times. The question remains open until all *Sada-chō* items have been introduced, when it may be addressed in more detail.

At this point, items grouped in *Sada-chō* have yielded evidence that they are not strictly attuned to the historical and modal contentions we have learned to recognize, and in general terms to expect, in compositions in *Ichikotsu-chō*. Some technical explanations may lie in the diverse origins of Asian mainland tunes, their various means of transmission, and in the types of human contact to which they were likely to have been subjected *en route* to the Tang capital *via* Kuchā. *Sada-chō* items appear not to be moulded in quite the same language as 'standard' *Tōgaku* compositions of our earlier studies.

Turning to observations on tonal perspectives of the Quick, numerical data (elicited by weighted-scale procedures) disclose interesting facts about the melody which explain its tonal balance, apart from symmetrical balance, and internal note relationships.

Table 5. Shin Raryō-ō, *Quick: analysis of four-bar phrases by weighted-scale procedures, with cadence notes underlined*

		a	*b*	*c♯*	*d*	*e*	*f♯*	*g♯*
Measures	1 - 4	<u>11</u>	10	8	6	-	-	3
"	5 - 8	7.5	7.5	-	<u>9</u>	5	5	6
"	9 - 12	10	2	3	<u>11</u>	3.5	7.5	2
"	13 - 16	6	6	-	<u>9</u>	3	10	6
Measures	1-16	34.5	25.5	11	<u>35</u>	11.5	22.5	17

After the first, four-measure phrase-unit, the dominant gives ground to the mode-final, which note then maintains a small lead thereafter to the end. *b* frequently attends the dominant as neighbour-tone, however, in the same way as *e* precedes the final. Comparing combined entries of *a + b* and *d + e*, progress of the pairs of notes through the sectional entries can be read: 21 and 6, 15 and 14, 12 and 14.5, and 12 and 12. In totals over the sixteen measures, 60 and 46.5, the difference is not suppressed; but no melody is ever heard or experienced as a whole, in one concentrated moment, as if in a flash. The conflation represents elements of sound organized in the movement of time. One can see and hear that the mode-final of this tune establishes a relationship with the dominant which, in progress, redresses an initial imbalance. The piece thus displays its own tiny bit of growth, which renders it creative within a small form.

To conclude a first analysis of the Quick, weights of the auxiliary notes of the four sections catch the eye. Both notes complement the musicality and contour of the melody; at the same time, it is not difficult to imagine the tune with dominant and final replacing their half-tone neighbours, *g♯* and *c♯*. A melody remains, but one that reflects a conservative, conventional style. The presence of the auxiliary notes is musical, each adding its colour independently of the other. In measures 1-4, the sub-final is prominent in formulae drawn from the upper tetrachord; the adaptation of these measures in 9-12 reduces this effect in transposition. The sub-dominant, the under-dominant, *g♯*, makes its particular contributions in measures 5-6 and 13-14, gestures that are effective in their concision and repetition, promptly introduced and promptly dispatched. Neither *bian*-note is exposed in the same phrase; their separated positions in the hierarchy of notes are declared in the first six measures. The musical and technical features of this melody will be more appreciated if the contour of the *JCYR* (*gaku-sō*) version of the tune is followed.

26. Piece: **Western Liangzhou** (*Sairyōshū* [西] 梁 州)

Conflation

The case for the scale of *Sada-chō* being the Chinese *Gongdiao* scale, originally on *E*, later transferred to *D*, has been stated repeatedly in Fascicle 5 and Volume 6. Moronaga supported this view (Fascicle 5, pp.xii, xiii) and moreover upheld it in all *Ichikotsu-chō* and *Sada-chō* items in tablature, in his comprehensive collections. The *Ryō-ō* transcriptions from the later Chū Ōga flute scores (Fascicle 5) call for this scale; and there have been several *Ichikotsu-chō* items: *Shō-ō-raku*, *Kasui-raku* and *Shuseishi* (Fascicle 4), where mouth-organ tablatures of the fourth and/or seventh notes of the scale on *D* indicate raised pitches, outside the standard notes of the *Shangdiao* octave-species. *Shangdiao* is the prevailing scale on *D* of the *Tōgaku* mouth-organ tradition in *Ichikotsu-chō*, as we know it down the Toyohara line of descent. The preceding conflations of *Ryō-ō* and *Shin Raryō-ō*, however, are notated with three sharps, and this practice will continue in conflations of *Sairyōshū* and the remaining *Sada-chō* items. Readers who have been looking ahead will undoubtedly have noticed the insistent raising of fourths and sevenths in transcriptions from mouth-organ scores of three of the five *Sada-chō* items that follow *Sairyōshū*.

Sairyōshū is an interesting and important item to come forward at this juncture, because of the relations between Liangzhou and the state of Kuchā, on the Western border of China, where music was known to sound in the distinctive *Sada-chō* mode-key (*Huangzhong Gongdiao*) equating with the First Kuchean Mode, a Lydian-scale formation. The extensive and extra-musical introduction to *Sairyōshū*, 'Western Liangzhou', when introduced in this volume (pp.13-47), is a timely introduction to *Sada* and Kuchean modality on which rests authority for restoration of the *Gongdiao* modality to all items of this group.

Conflating sources of 'Western Liangzhou' raised no problems; the version of *KF/HSF/RK* is complete and clear. A difference of rhythm between the mouth-organ and string versions of measure 3 is of no real account, nor are the discrepancies in measure 4. The slightly extended cadence form in measure 4 has been adopted, and repeated in measures 12, 16 and 20. The more concise cadence in measure 8 is common to all versions.

Example 1. *Sairyōshū*: conflated version

Analysis

This item has been thoroughly examined (L.E.R.P.) earlier in this Fascicle, where attention was drawn to its musical impulse not being confined to Central and Eastern Asia, nor to the first millennium of the Common Era. The earliest known written versions of *Sairyōshū* – partial evidence of how the Japanese may have heard it close to one thousand years ago – reveal a melody formal and urbane.

Simple in design, its phrasing is regular, an opening out (measures 5-8) and closing back (measures 11-12), and a number of patterns recur. The contour of the melody is marked by triadic progressions, many thirds and sixths, and some tritonal leaps. Excluding the single occurrence of the sub-final, the scale of the melody is hexatonic in which the remaining auxiliary, the fourth of the scale, plays a major part. Aligned analysis shows that frequent repetition of formulae limits variety and spread; almost the whole tune comprises literal and slightly varied repetitions of the first four measures. Lest a disparaging note be heard in that observation, let it be added that, far from innuendo, the tone in this case is one of commendation. It endorses the opinion that *Sairyōshū*, as we have it today, might be a version of the tune to which was performed the song-text, attributed to Taizong, Emperor of Tang, on the occasion of his visit to the Blessed Goodness Palace in 632 (L.E.R.P., p.33).

The twenty measures of the melody are marked off in sections of four measures each, with firm cadences where movement momentarily ceases. Equidistant cadences define five stanzas of four lines, one line per measure of music, each measure capable of articulating five characters of rhyming text, as is shown in the reduced version of the tune with underwritten text (Volume 6, p.41). The stanzas advance in sequence, but the musical verses are simple variants of each other, the first four measures forming the basis of the composition to which all that follows relates. Measures 5-8 take measures 1-2, but continue to a dominant cadence instead of the mode-final cadence of measure 4. Measures 9-12 begin with two measures drawn from 2, then continue with 3-4. Measures 13-16 imitate 9-12 including the mode-final cadence; and 17-20 repeat 13-16. The following aligned analysis proves that the first four measures, possibly the first verse of the song, contain all the melodic formulae, except for measure 8, of the whole composition.

Example 2. *Sairyōshū*: aligned analytical table.

The table illustrates twenty measures apt for twenty lines of text. There are five four-measure phrase-units appropriate for five four-line stanzas, with repeating mode-final cadence formulae, except in measure 8. There are ten two-measure sub-phrases applicable to ten poetic couplets with final rhyming syllables; cadences in measures 2 and 6 rhyme, as do those in measures 10, 14 and 18. The entire melody complements the form, repeating structures and rhyming schemes of the quoted text.

A singularity of *Sairyōshū* is its five sections of four measures each, a distinction which further strengthens the possibility of an early association between the imperial text and this tune. Data from the verse-stanza sections are these; cadence notes are underlined.

Table 1. Sairyōshū: *weighted-scale application*

		a	b	c♯	d	e	f♯	g♯
Measures	1 - 4	17.5	8.5	-	19	5	15	6
"	5 - 8	30.5	13.5	2	5	-	6	11
"	9 - 12	8	5	-	22	15.5	12.5	8
"	13 - 16	3	6	-	20	21.5	11.5	8
"	17 - 20	3	6	-	20	21.5	11.5	8
Measures	1-20	62	39	2	86	63.5	56.5	41

Numerical analysis, and the aligned analytical table, prove the repetition of measures 9-12 in 13-16 and 17-20; heavy weight is thus piled on to *d-e-f♯* in the slightly varying repetitions from measure 9. It also shows a simultaneous withdrawal of weight from the dominant. At the outset, measures 1-4 set the *Gongdiao* mode. The notes *d, f♯* and *a*, with *d* a little in front, establish the basic tones, with *b* and *e* providing modest support adjacent to the dominant and final. The modal fourth, *g♯*, also supports the dominant, but not consistently. Measures 5-8 reciprocate measures 1-4; the dominant and its neighbours are powerfully asserted, while the final and its attendants are abandoned: 55 points (*g♯, a* and *b*) to 7 (*c♯, d* and *e*) (one might say), at the same time noting the almost doubled weight of *g♯*.

From measure 9, the second part of the binary composition, concentration centres on the tetrachord on the final. The super-final stands close to the final, backed by the third and auxiliary fourth of the scale. The fourth, *g♯*, has quite a prominent profile, growing from measures 2 and 6 into the extended patterns of measures 9-10, 13-14 and 17-18. Clear to the eye in aligned analysis, and equally to the ear, *g♯* is not primarily dependent on the dominant, but acts rather in the capacity of third in a secondary tetrachord on *e*: *e - f♯ - g♯ - b*, whereas the primary tetrachord is *d - e - f♯ - a*. Only in measures 1, 5 and 7 does *g♯* lean on the dominant. Examples of this kind of modal ambiguity are gathering as experience of the *Sada-chō* group unfolds, but in the second part of *Sairyōshū* the weight of the basic notes of the *d-a* axis outweighs any pressure from a secondary structure independent of it, or competing with it. Only in measures 7-8 might the initial perspective of the mode seem insecure, and then only briefly. After the mode-final the dominant is the next important cadence note, and *g* (or *g♯*) and *b* are common elements of dominant cadence formulae.

The presence of *c* (or *c♯*) in dominant cadence-formulae of *Ichikotsu-chō* is less usual, while cadential movement of *a - b - c♯ - a* occurs seldomly, notwithstanding examples located in: *Toraden*, Prelude Section 2, measures 4 and 8 (Fascicle 2, p.28); *Shunnō-den*, Stamping, measure 12 (Fascicle 2, p.60); *Katen*, Broaching, measures 2 and 8 (Fascicle 3, pp.23-4); and *Ka-kyokushi*, measures 4 and 8 (Fascicle 4, p.13), all of which bear authenticated titles found in Tang lists; but measure 8 of *Sairyōshū* is an individual case. Although the dominant cadences above are cited, none has the dogmatic rhythm of the *Sairyōshū* example; and the identical note pattern is absent from other dominant cadences indicated by Moronaga in the *Sada-chō* group.

From this point, suspicions of any divergence in modal identity in this item can be abandoned. There is no instance in *Sairyōshū* where a change of modal perspective is demonstrated for sufficient time to assert a counter-claim, such as happens in three of the four movements of *Ryō-ō*. The weighted-scale procedure has exposed specific data relevant to *Sairyōshū*, proving that the first four measures are a normal *Sada-chō* musical stanza, and that the third, fourth and fifth stanzas, in so far as they retain the same structure, are repeating modal statements of a kind familiar in four-measure phrase-units of this genre. The second verse is the only one to hint at possible abnormality, but nothing comes to light except a temporary concentration on the dominant and its neighbours at the expense of the final.

In an overview of the structure of this piece, it is within past experience that *Tōgaku* melodies often introduce the two most important notes of the mode in the first phrase, then move away from the final to promote a surrogate, often the dominant or the note above, returning later to restore and re-assert the final in conclusion. Such is the description of *Sairyōshū*; seen as a whole its modality is quite stable. It is because of phrase-repetition that the notes *e*, *f♯*, *g♯* and *b* claim 57 percent of the total weight of all notes of the tune, and thereby attract disproportionate attention. These notes have no stanzaic cadences, but of initials and finals of measures, they take 19 of a total of 40, *i.e.* 47.5 percent; whereas of cadences, initials and finals of measures, the mode-final and dominant claim 21 of the same total, namely, 52.5 percent.

If one were to weigh up the notes of the first three stanzas only (all that counts musically in the tune), the result would contain the central measures 5-8 in a shorter but still satisfactory context; that is, followed by just one four-measure statement of the thrice repeated verse. The totals of all notes of measures 1-12 would register as follows:

Table 2. Sairyōshū: weighted scale, measures 1-12 only

	a	*b*	*c♯*	*d*	*e*	*f♯*	*g♯*
Measures 1-12	56	27	2	46	20.5	33.5	25

d + *a* would total 102, and *e* +*f♯* +*g♯* + *b*, 106. In this narrower frame, the mode-final and dominant would share 15 of the 24 cadence, initial and final notes; while the remaining notes, *e* +*f♯* + *g♯* + *b*, would account for 9 of the same: 62.5 percent to 37.5 percent. The repeating verse form stretches the composition without adding to the musical content, and it is these repetitions that extend the length to 20 measures. This, presumably, is the form in which *Sairyōshū* was known, and played, about the time it first entered Japan.

27. Piece: **Spear-Play** (*Rosō* 弄 槍)

Conflation

Since the first conflated version of a *Tōgaku* item was made in this series, it has
been customary, when reconciling instrumental sources, to place slightly more
weight on evidence from the mouth-organ manuscript, *Ko-fu/Hōshōfu/
ritsu-kan/ryo-kan* (*KF/HSF/RK*), completed by Toyohara no Toshiaki in 1201
(Fascicle 2, p.72). This is because of the authority and lineage of members of the
Toyohara clan who played at court for many generations, and preserved the
mouth-organ repertory in tablature for many centuries (Fascicle 1, pp.33-4).
Apart from this is the nature of the instrument which, with its fixed tuning,
peculiar construction and technical limitations, imposed natural restrictions on
extravagant departures from a basically simple, melodic style of performance.
Early mouth-organ versions of *Tōgaku* items thus remained closer to their
prototypes than was the case with developing performance practices of stringed,
and of other wind instrument, traditions. Respect for the initiative and reputation
of Fujiwara no Moronaga (1137-1192) who compiled the string sources germane
to this study, is not reduced thereby. Thorough consideration is always given to
all versions when conflating from diverse sources, and it will be understood that
solutions adopted are not necessarily the only ones possible; they are judged to
be the best under the circumstances, based on knowledge, experience and
evidence at the time. The reason for this summary preamble is that the conflation
of *Rosō* waives its allegiance to the Toyohara line at several points in favour of
Moronaga's records.

    Comparing the transcriptions of *Rosō*, and remembering the *Gong* scale
inherent in *Sada-chō*, their similarity is unmistakeable; they are undoubtedly
versions of the same melody. What differences there are lie between two self-
sufficient instrumental traditions, rather than four individual lines of
transmission. Looking closer at specific discrepancies, there are only three places
calling for discretion: the last two beats of measures 3 and 5, and the first beat of
measure 10.

With regard to measures 3 and 5, the conflation takes up Moronaga's versions,
the same in both string scores, thereby capturing intrinsic Chinese tonal colour,
reduced in the mouth-organ versions.The prominent *g♯* initial note in measures 4
and 6, preparing for a dominant cadence in the first instance, and a stepwise
descent to the mode-final (for an implicit super-final cadence) in the second, is
thus thrown into strong and characteristic relief. A genuine Chinese predilection
for this quality of coloration has been noticed in two recent *Sada-chō* items: in
the Quick of *Shin Raryō-ō*, measures 5-6 and 13-14; and in *Sairyōshū*, where
quite a striking passage is heard three times, in measures 9-10, 13-14 and 17-18.

144

Turning to measure 10 of *Rosō*, the initial note of the conflation retains the mouth-organ reading. Analysis will show later that measure 10 is a variant of measures 3 and 5.

Example 1. *Rosō*: conflation

Reference has been made to mouth-organ versions of the *Tōgaku* repertory being less subject to variation and stylistic change over time, than versions for stringed instruments, the latter lending themselves more readily to advancing technical skills and practices. In string style, delineation is achieved through frequent use of mordents, appoggiaturas, passing-notes and other devices that decorate and add superficial movement to what, in the mouth-organ versions, is a plain, basic statement of the tune. A variety of embellishments and treatments brighten the texture of Moronaga's versions. Mouth-organ versions may generally be nearer the original melodies from the mainland, though in this instance 'The title [*Rosō*] does not occur in the Tang lists of entertainment music-with-dance' (Volume 6, p.48).

At this point three critical observations can be made: that the versions for zither and bass-lute transcribed here result from, or have been directly influenced by, retardation of performance tempi of Tang music in Japan; that this music endured comparatively speedy adaptation to fashionable taste there; and that it enjoyed great popularity at the Japanese court, and for a long time. In formal and informal music-making, *Tōgaku* and other imported musical styles were central attractions. Be that as it may, R.F.W. has demonstrated convincingly that *Gakubyōshi, Tadabyōshi* and other forms of rhythmic variation and prolongation, were standard treatments included by Moronaga in his various collections (Fascicle 4, pp.117-33). In the example under discussion, the zither and lute versions, although permeated with rhythmic and melodic decoration, have recognisable features absent from the simpler mouth-organ versions, features that overlay their melodies with colour and character. One striking feature may exemplify a point in the present discussion. Mouth-organ versions of *Rosō* exhibit no tritonal leaps or implications, whether reading with a signature of one or three sharps; the only hint of such tonal colour in these scores comes in measure 6, but it fades with measure 7, fulfilling a dominant objective. Both the

145

zither and lute versions, however, display four tritonal leaps, and they occur at places where accentual stress draws attention to them. Such leaps have been pointed out previously in *Sairyōshū*.

The form of *Rosō* attracts comment. While we may compliment Moronaga on preserving the musicality of the melody, his account of the piece in tablature does not clarify its structure precisely. His unwitting oversight of several cadences disguised with added notes conceals the musical punctuation, with consequent loss of shape. Moronaga's *ichi*-markings describe the first two and last two phrases; the two central phrases have, however, lost definition.

Experience of *Tōgaku* analysis has demonstrated that, in general, cadences will be apparent or implied at fairly regular intervals in a composition, even when written tablatures continue without indicating them. *Rosō* appears to be another example where specific indications of musical punctuation are deficient or disguised. All even-numbered measures have recognisable cadence formulae embedded in the texture: well-defined in measures 2, 4, 10 and 12, implicit in measures 6 and 8. Structurally the melody of twelve measures consists of six two-measure phrases, with cadences on *d*, *a*, *e*, *d*, *a* and *d*.

Example 2. Conflation: measures 6-10 reduced, showing cadence implications

The six phrases incline towards three groups of two phrases each; pairs of cadence notes support the possibilities: *d* and *a*, *e* and *d*, *a* and *d*. Cadence formulae in measures 8 and 12 on *d* are dissimilar, while measures 11-12 identify quite fully with measures 1-2, including the mode-final cadences.

Aligned analysis of *Rosō* draws further attention to the unmatched dominant cadences in measures 4 and 10, to the involvement of notes of the lower tetrachord of the mode-scale on *d* in measures 6 and 7, and to the prominence of the tritone in measures 5-7. The fourth of the scale, *g♯*, attends the dominant in measures 4, 5 and 9, while measures 5-8 are moving from a dominant context towards the mode-final. A similar movement underlies measures 9-12. Comparison of these measures with measures 9-12 of *Sairyōshū* shows the same tonal movement over the same space of time.

Example 3. *Rosō*: conflation; aligned analysis

Yet the modality of *Rosō* is stable. Not opposing several perspectives of modal behaviour, as do some *Sada-chō* movements, its cadence notes, literal and implicit, are regular, but limited to three. There is only one cadence outside dominant and mode-final, and it falls on the super-final. But the tune has interest in its choice and use of materials, its melodic formulae. Variety is achieved through two kinds of contrast. The first is the nature of formulae in measures 6 and 7, where new elements are introduced. The second is effected through formulae disposed to lie principally in one or other tetrachord of the scale. Formulaic textures tend to vary the tonal area, measure by measure, in this way assisting forward movement and uncomplicated variety. Putting the two points together, measures 5-8 may be heard as the centre-piece of an ABA form. The aligned Example 3 demonstrated that measures 5-8, though the central group of twelve, have formulaic connections with measures 1-4 and 9-12, in that measure 5 is a variant of 3, and 8 a variant of 1 and 11, and also of 7 (transposed down a fifth).

Tonal structure of the melody merits further comment. Prominence of the fourth of the scale in the centre of the tune emphasises a particular relationship of the fourth to its final; the fourth lends tonal colour that cannot be missed. The amount of conjunct movement in the texture is apparent, and contours would be smoother if one remembers that large intervals of the mouth-organ versions are passages rendered more disjunct because of the instrument's physical limitations. A weighted-scale application throws light on the relationship of notes to each other, to the final, and to the scale. The Table presents sub-totals of data, concerning each note, four measures at a time, and a grand total of sub-totals in a composite statement.

Table 1. Weighted-scale data in three equal parts, and of the whole

		a	*b*	*c♯*	*d*	*e*	*f♯*	*g♯*
Measures	1-4	<u>17</u>	9.5	8.5	22	3.5	6.5	5
"	5-8	13	11.5	6.5	<u>16</u>	11	6	9
"	9-12	11.5	6	7	<u>16</u>	17	10	3.5
Measures	1-12	41.5	27	22	<u>54</u>	31.5	22.5	17.5

Points from the summary data to be observed are:

the strength of the final in all sections, and the secondary role of the dominant – not observed as such in movements of *Shin Raryō-ō* and *Sairyōshū*;

the gathering importance of the super-final as the melody progresses, albeit in close association with the final;

changes in texture, influenced by the four weakest notes in each block of four measures, the notes listed here in declining numerical order: in measures 1-4: *c♯, f♯, g♯* and *e*; in measures 5-8: *e, g♯, c♯, f♯*; and in measures 9-12: *f♯, c♯, b* and *g♯*;

the active roles of the auxiliary (*bian*) notes, the textural significance of which can be seen in perspective, when the combined weights of auxiliaries are compared with the combined weights of dominant and final. In percentages, with dominant and final standing together at 100 percent, in measures 1-4 the *bian* notes achieve proportionally 35 percent; in measures 5-8, 53 percent; in measures 9-12, 38 percent; and over the whole melody, 42 percent;

the full involvement of the heptatonic scale. In the final count, notes of the *Gong* pentatonic structure, over measures 1-12, claim 82 percent of the total weight of all notes, the *bian* notes (in consequence) rating just 18 percent of the entire melody.

The historical study of *Rosō* (L.E.R.P., pp.48-50) shows that this item had performance associations in Japan with three other *Tōgaku* items (this volume, p.49): *Shinnō hajin-raku*, 'The Prince of Qin destroys the Formations'; *Ōjō*, 'The Yellow-and-White Spotted Roebuck'; and *Jūten-raku*, 'The Ten Heavens' or 'Ten Devas'. *DNHS* notes that *Rosō* was used as an 'answering dance' with the first two of these titles, and *KKS* records a connection (unspecified) with the third. One can expect associations of items of different titles to happen for various reasons, including social circumstances bringing them together, imperial decisions, or chance couplings retained for convenience; and a possible basis for choosing items for linkage in performance may sometimes have been made on purely musical grounds – resemblances recognized as existing between them, for example.

A detailed study of the tonal material of 'The Prince of Qin Destroys the Formations' (see R.F.W.'s transcription in *Musica Asiatica 3*, pp.123-4) reveals an item in *Taishiki-chō*, the Mixo-Lydian octave-species on *E*, with no connections, musical or technical, to suggest common ground. The same may be said of 'The Yellow-and-White Spotted Roebuck' (see the melody in *Hyō-jō*, the Dorian octave-species, also on *E*, to be extracted from the mouth-organ version in Shiba, 2, 1969, pp.126-9); no connections between it and *Rosō* are discernible (see also R.F.W. 1981, p.78). The third named item, *Jūten-raku*, 'Ten Devas', is the final title in Moronaga's *Sada-chō* modal group (see this volume, pp.78 and 167). For the present it may be affirmed that *Jūten-raku* and *Rosō* do indeed share note patterns, in consecutive measures at some points, and that Japanese musicians can be credited with musicality sufficient to recognize the common language. Under the heading of item **31**, 'Ten Devas', a comparison of the two tunes will be tabled.

28. Suite: **Bird(s) of the Qin River** (*Shingachō* 沁 河 鳥)

Conflation

Transcriptions of this title (pp.61-2) present independent traditions surviving in varied forms. The barring systems and drumbeat locations of each are differences that cannot be reconciled in a single conflated version. The distinctive mouth-organ and string traditions of 'Bird(s) of the Qin River' are sufficiently diverse in style to be irreconcilable without loss of one, or other's, individual identity. Each is a complete formation consistent in its idiosyncratic self. In the past, when determining which of several variants of a tune might be the basis of conflation, general policy has been to lean slightly towards the mouth-organ tradition. As previously explained, its tradition is thought by us to be less susceptible of variation in transmission, and in the case of *KF/HSF/RK*, the tradition is more likely to have been protected, since it remained in the possession of the Toyohara clan from the eleventh until at least the early nineteenth century (Fascicle 1, pp.3-4). However, in idiomatic style the two mouth-organ versions and the two string versions of *Shingachō* adhere quite closely to their own, equally important, instrumental traditions.

Remembering that the *raison d'être* of our conflations is primarily to facilitate analytical scrutiny and technical discussion, the conflation of this tune will, therefore, conform to the bar structure and mid-measure drumbeats of most other Broachings of the *Ichikotsu-chō* and *Sada-chō* modal groups (exceptions are Broachings of *Koinju* and *Shin Raryō-ō*). Nevertheless, while implementing this decision, a conflation of each pair of transcriptions has been provided for comparison, showing that they are not fundamentally opposed, either in ten-measure form or linear texture. Each may be respected in its own line of transmission; but for the discussion that follows, the mouth-organ conflation will be the choice, and will be referred to as 'the conflation'.

Example 1. Conflations: from mouth-organ and string transcriptions

Although one cannot explain in detail how, or why, differences occur between versions of some *Tōgaku* tunes that survive in Japan, and not others, it is surprising that the range of variation is not wider and more frequent. These tunes had been known and played in Japan for at least four hundred and fifty years by the time the *MSS* studied here were written down, and in China they have a history of a good deal more than two hundred years before that. Bear in mind that the only learning process at home and abroad was by rote; and that there is no evidence, in the copious social and historical writings of both countries, that musicians ever attempted to collate, or reconcile, remembered versions of their regional instrumental repertoires. Written *MSS* were 'secret' library treasures; they were rarely, if ever, consulted in learning or performing. That would have been entirely foreign to the Asian musical experience.

What was written down in tablature by early musicians appears to have been copied and re-copied by scribes through the centuries, occasionally with brief, added asides of a few characters noting a slight amendment or alternative, and at times attributing an imperial or other name in authentication. Preservation and copying of sources was dissociated from possible practical relevance, a paradox confusing to accepted twentieth-century attitudes and standards, but one peculiarly rewarding to historical musicologists in Asian music. It is just this segregation that disallowed direct contact with primary, source-collections of repertory-tunes in their simple forms and styles, and gave birth to what became, in the course of time, the totally artificial style and art-form to be heard in Japanese court-music performances of the Edo and post-Edo periods.

Areas of disagreement between the conflations above are seen at a glance, the first of which is striking: the *JCYR* and *SGYR* versions of 'Bird(s) of the Qin River' are two unit-beats behind the *KF/HSF/RK* and *SSSTF* versions. The technical cause of this is the first note, the mode-final of minim value, which delays the string melody from moving forward as promptly as the mouth-organ version, thus upsetting the binary-beat structure, essential to all items of the repertoire. The delay of one beat at the start of the melody is partly redressed by repeating the mode-final (double value again for the same note) at its next appearance, the third binary beat in the same measure. Two beats have thus been added in the first measure of the string version, so that this melody remains one binary beat behind the mouth-organ; and thus it stays to the end.

One could also argue that the wind version is at fault – and who is to gainsay it – save that the more usual Broaching structure is evident in the mouth-organ version, and the string instruments, though possibly deviating in the movement of time, have retained drumbeats on the same notes as the mouth-organs, but now sounding on the seventh beat, instead of the more usual fifth beat, in eight-beat measures. The mouth-organ tradition can be said to have the stronger claim to Tang authenticity, on the basis of a more conservative reputation, and support of over eight hundred years of Toyohara clan-leadership in this field.

A second and basic conflict exists in phrasing and rhythm, as determined by the drumbeats and *ichi*-signs. Moronaga's *ichi*-signs have been applied to both conflations of the comparative Example, although the primary mouth-organ tablatures, it will be remembered, have no *ichi*-signs. Applied to the mouth-organ conflation, they confirm the natural, musical structure of the tune: five, equal, two-measure phrases, with cadence formulae reinforced by drum-strokes that mark the third binary beat. Formulaic cadence rhythms are positive, the weaker, second binary beat followed by the stronger, third binary beat, carrying over termination of the phrase into the fourth binary-beat. In the string conflation, phrasing by Moronaga's *ichi*-signs is singularly inappropriate, musically false. Cadence rhythms sound unquestionably convincing in the first conflation, so clearly are they defined. In the second conflation, delay of one binary beat causes cadences to move from the second and third binary beats to the third and fourth binary-beats, dragging over to the first of the next measure. All five cadences are thus awry. Moronaga, one might conjecture, remembered where phrases end, but had not realised what an extra binary beat at the outset had done to falsify the rest of the melody.

Little remains to be added in justification of the recommended conflation. All fundamental unit-beat pitches of the four transcriptions agree. There is no doubt about the scale of *Shingachō*, as mouth-organ tablatures specify which notes are raised and which are natural. Of the two notes concerned, the fourth and seventh of the scale, all save one (before the final cadence) are raised. Here the accidentals of the transcriptions are stated in the signature of the mouth-organ conflation, and this agrees with Moronaga's applied signatures also.

Analysis (Mouth-Organ version)

Shingachō is one of a number of tunes in this mode-key with ten measures of eight beats to the measure. Fascicle 5 (pp.70-83) includes conflations and short

152

analyses of six ten-measure tunes, and a brief comparative discussion of them in relation to each other. 'Bird(s) of the Qin River' is a seventh similar example in the most popular, ten-measure form of the *Ichikotsu* and *Sada* mode-groups. It consists of five, two-measure phrases, cadencing on *a*, *a*, *a*, *b* and *d*. The first three phrases are strongly weighted in favour of the dominant as tonal centre, the mode-final being unable to maintain itself as an important note after the first half-measure. Not until the fourth phrase does the final begin to gain strength; but even here the two measures (7-8) fit comfortably into the preceding dominant context, rather than prepare for an imminent modal rally, pending conclusion. The last two measures (9-10) restore the final to belated prominence, by quickly reducing the activity of other notes to allow the final to be heard. The final now sounds three beats in the penultimate measure, which it has not done in any measure before, and occupies six beats in the ultimate measure. Weighted-scale data illustrate clearly the strong, dominant, tonal bias in measures 1-6, and restoration of prime position to the mode-final in the remainder (measures 7-10). Cadence notes are underlined in the Table.

Table 1. Weighted-scales

		a	*b*	*c♯*	*d*	*e*	*f♯*	*g♯*
Measures	1-2	<u>15</u>	5	-	5	2	9	-
"	3-4	<u>14</u>	11	1.5	3.5	-	7	-
"	5-6	<u>11.5</u>	7	2.5	3	1.5	8	5.5
"	7-8	3	<u>10</u>	4.5	7.5	5	2	2
"	9-10	2	3.5	1.5	<u>18</u>	5	4	-
"	1-10	45.5	36.5	10	<u>37</u>	13.5	30	7.5

The notes *a* and *f♯* feature prominently at first (measures 1-2), then *a*, *b* and *f♯* (measures 3-6), followed by *b* and *d* (7-8), and finally *d* alone (9-10). The auxiliaries, the fourth and seventh of the scale, contribute only 10 percent to the total weight of the piece.

Strong dominant influence in the first six measures (more than half the tune) is borne out by note patterns in which it becomes central to the linear texture, its importance reinforced by two neighbouring notes, *b* and *f♯*. From an aligned analysis, it can be seen that the majority of the melodic movement falls on the left side of the table, where phrases and part-phrases appear to reiterate, directly reaching towards the dominant: cadence formulae in measures 2, 4 and 6; interim linear finals in measures 3 and 7; dominant repetitions in measures 2 and 4; and accented dominants in measures 1 and 9.

Comparison of cadence formulae in the even-numbered measures shows a prominent change in measure 8; of the five cadences, three on the dominant have passed, and only one remains which must be final. Measure 8, cadencing on the sub-mediant, differs from patterns on 5 and 1, in so far as dominant and final-note cadence formulae are structurally the same in transposition: *b*, *a*, *f♯*, *a* and *e*, *d*, *b*, *d*, while the penultimate cadence-formula is *a*, *c♯*, *d*, *c♯*, *b*. Once again it is noticed from the weighted-scales, that the super-final is the weakest note of the pentatonic scale, that the strongest notes of the tune are the first, third, fifth and sixth of the scale, and that the *bian* auxiliaries register 10 percent of the total.

Example 2. Aligned analysis

Looking back to the previous table of ten-measure *Ichikotsu-chō* items in 4/2-time (Fascicle 5, pp.80-3): none shows three successive dominant cadences; none, such a pronounced dominant attraction; and none, a sub-mediant cadence. *Shingachō*, however, relates to another repertory item that recalls birds and bird song, namely, the fifth movement of *Shunnō-den*: 'The Singing of Spring Warblers', *Tesshō*, 'Bird Tune'(Fascicle 2, pp.67-71, conflation Fascicle 3, p.76). Calls of the Japanese Bush Warbler were carefully considered when the item *Shunnō-den* was prepared for publication (L.E.R.P.), and indeed it seems

154

feasible, from the evidence submitted, to credit an original composer, Bo Mingda or other, with making music intentionally reminiscent of the song of Bush Warblers at dawn.

The same might be said of 'Bird(s) of the Qin River', identified as Bean Geese, of which the calls and the locations of the bird have been explained in some detail in this volume (p.63). There it is suggested (L.E.R.P.) that the first two notes of the string versions of the tune, as transcribed, mimic the falling pitch of the creature's natural call. Unfortunately, the Moronaga zither version has no other fall of d-$f\sharp$, a minor sixth, to strengthen the idea. The lute version, nevertheless, has five appearances of this descending interval (one octave lower). The mouth-organ versions are unable to attempt a sixth below d; they play the inversion – a major third – since the basic pipe-set to which the tablatures apply has no $f\sharp'$ below d''.

The Bird Tune of 'The Singing of Spring Warblers' is a more remarkable piece than 'Bird(s) of the Qin River'; nothing like it has hitherto appeared in our studies, and after a lapse of nine years, something more may be said about its structure. The title of the suite is listed by Moronaga in the *Ichikotsu* modal group; and the Bird Tune is unmeasured and like a prelude, but played 'very quickly' (*KF/HSF/RK*; Fascicle 2, p.67). It consists of three sections of 14, 16 and 16 unit-beats, each repeated, making 92 beats in all, and the third section is a measured trill, e''-$f\sharp''$, concluding the movement on the latter note. The sustained notes of two beats, and the trills, were (it was suggested: Fascicle 2, pp.70-1) imitations of calls of the Bush Warbler, as recorded on tape in Japan. All four primary sources in tablature agree on the long notes and on the trills. The brevity and directness of the musical structure make an interesting case for naturalistic symbolism in this genre of Chinese traditional music.

The curious nature of the 'Bird Tune' in 'Spring Warblers' is exposed by weighted-scale data (Table 2), and relative percentages of the notes can be deduced. In the first two sections, the most important note is a, with b nearest to it, but registering just over half its value; $a + b$ occupy 76 percent of the rating of all five notes in these two sections. In the final section, where the scale is reduced, and the carolling of birds can be imagined, $e'' + f\sharp''$ are alternating notes, the higher note of the trill gaining two-and-a-quarter times the weight of the lower, the dominant being all but silent. Weighted-scale data cannot disguise the fact that, for two-thirds of the 'Bird Tune', a and b are the principal tonal materials, despite four cadences on g; for the remainder of the tune, these three notes are of no significance, all activity being compressed into reiteration of e and $f\sharp$.

Table 2. Weighted-scales, octave span (Shunnō-den, *Bird Tune*)

		$f\sharp'$	g'	a'	b'	c''	e''	$f\sharp''$
Beats	1-28	4	6	33	11	-	-	-
"	29-60	8	6	25	19	4	-	-
"	61-92	6	-	4	-	-	16	36
Beats	1-92	18	12	62	30	4	16	36

The final part of the 'Bird Tune' is strikingly different from what has gone before, and this is more noticeable from one of the source transcriptions. The pitch range of mouth-organ tablatures is limited, and similarly that of the lute; not so of the thirteen-string zither which covers two-and-a-half octaves. The first 60 unit-beats of the *gaku-sō* version are restricted to the lower two octaves of its register, the melody remaining in the middle area within the space of the fifth, $f\sharp'$-c'', with notes on the odd-numbered beats strengthened with lower octaves or mode-final resonances. But with the legendary imperial command to copy the songs of Bush Warblers at dawn (Fascicle 2, p.45), texture and pitch suddenly change. After two beats, the zither – the only instrument represented here with a range and capability of further pitch-response – leaps to the high, bright strings, plucking octave-accentuations on the first of every binary beat. Perhaps it is not too much to fancy the initial swoop of the upward seventh as the intuitive impulse that begins the song, exerting physical power in the throat, for a spontaneous vocal exercise.

There may also be support for the notion that the first two beats of the third section (beats 61-92) are part of the bird's song. The two notes before the upward leap can be played on *gaku-sō* in either middle or high register, as proved in transcriptions from *JCYR* of which the 'Bird Tune' is one; but here height is sought only after the second beat of the phrase, which suggests that the leap to the high trill may be placed intentionally at that moment. If the creature in the wild opens the throat, and lifts its voice with a quick rising swoop in a brilliant roulade, the zither is the only instrument of those presented here that can effectively imitate the complete performance.

Questions of this kind, arising from a critical examination of the music before us – and they do attract attention sometimes, apart from associated extra-musical factors – are worthy of further examination when time and space permit. Tang art, poetry and literature are filled with images and experiences associated with nature; and birds have inspired many a creative imagination to artistic imitation and achievement. The musical mind has been equally responsive to nature's own performers. Their spectacular repertoire of exuberant vocalises has enriched the timeless heritage of world music, and enlivened the intelligence and sensitivity of the human species.

156

29. Piece: **'Introit to "Perfect Virtue" '** (*Ittokuen/Yide yan* 壹 德 鹽)

Conflation

The conflation is the *KF/HSF/RK* version, with which other versions agree almost *in toto*. The scale is the heptatonic *Gong* mode on *d*, which allows the accidentals to be collected in an appropriate mode-key signature at the beginning. In transcription, the eighth-notes of measures 1 and 2 (*SSSTF* version) illustrate readings of the tablature characters for the natural and raised pitches of the seventh degree of the scale before us. Minor discrepancies between versions are due to ornamental devices, characteristic of string-playing techniques, established and formalised by Moronaga's time.

It can be said, however, that by the twelfth century it had become customary in *gaku-sō* practice in this genre, to stress the melodic note on the first beat of most binary units, with an open string, plucked simultaneously at lower pitch. Often this note was one octave below the principal note of the beat; but this was not always possible. If the main note was the second or third above *middle d*, or a *bian*-note, no open string was available. In *gaku-sō* tuning-systems of *Tōgaku* modes on *d*, the super-final and mediant are not present in the lowest octave; and *bian*-notes lack open strings at any pitch. In these instances, another note, a ninth, tenth, or even an eleventh below, was sounded in place of the octave; this note was often *d*.

Looking again at the two beats in question (in measures 1 and 2), it will be seen that the lute and mouth-organs agree on *g♯*, thus giving weight to acceptance of this note in the conflation. In measure 9, the first beat again offers the choice of *g♯* or *a*; in the winds, *g♯* is undoubtedly the main note, while the strings insist on *a*. As the raised sub-dominant was characteristic of Tang style in the *Sada* context, *g♯* has again been adopted into the conflation.

Example 1. Conflation, 'Introit to "Perfect Virtue" '

Analysis

Layered analysis of the melody, measure by measure, shows a simple form and an economical structure. There are two unequal sections, of eight measures (the first four repeating) and six measures, respectively; they are musically compatible, and share formulaic material. The opening half-measure consists of notes from a common, mode-final cadence formula, which pattern closes measures 4 and 8 of the first section, and measure 14 of the second. It is thus heard five times in the course of the total of fourteen measures. There is also an alternative mode-final cadence formula in measures 2 and 6. The third measure, repeating in the seventh, is also heard twice in the second section, as measures 12 and 13; and measure 11 repeats measure 10. Measures 1, 3 and 10, therefore, yield eleven measures of the whole.

The melody is conspicuously heptatonic, the fourth of the scale assuming some importance by the frequency of its appearances, rising (from mediant to dominant), or (conversely) falling, while the seventh operates similarly, between sub-mediant and final. More striking are the tritonal leaps, from mode-final to fourth, which mark the first measure and its repetition, and the bold thrust from the cadence of the first section onto the first notes of the second, measures 8 to 9. These measures are not striking for the tritonal intervals alone, but rather for their evidence of Chinese taste for the Lydian-type scale, before it declined in favour of the Mixo-Lydian formation, which subsequently became fashionable in the later Tang. Another feature of 'Introit to "Perfect Virtue" ' is the pairs of repeating notes within binary-beat durations. In the manner of the conflation, dictated by that of the transcriptions, there are nineteen pairs of repeating quarter-notes; and all of them occur on the final, its mediant and its submediant. A more extended example of this is the pressure on the mediant in measures 10 and 11, where repetitions occupy fourteen beats of musical time.

Example 2. Aligned analysis

Items of fourteen measures are not numerous in this series, but three have been introduced so far, with features interesting to recall at the moment: *Gyokuju gotei-ka*, 'A Jade Tree's Rear-Court Blossom' (Fascicle 3, pp.1-19; conflation, Fascicle 5, pp.34-7), *Hokutei-raku*, 'The Northern Courtyard' (Fascicle 4, pp.22-6; conflation, Fascicle 5, pp.66-9), and the item before us, *Ittokuen*. These compositions employ the full heptatonic scale, with due weight placed on notes of the pentatonic scale, but also allowing *bian*-notes to function as material assets. Data relative to tonal weights and perspectives have been assembled by the same method as in earlier analyses.

'A Jade Tree's Rear-Court Blossom' places 86 percent of total weight on notes of the pentatonic scale, with 14 percent taken by the *bian*-notes. The dominant is by far the strongest note, *d* and *f♯* being next in line; but cadences fall five times on the mode-final, and twice on the dominant. Weighted-scale figures are these:

Table 1. Gyokuju goteika, *weighted-scale*

Measures 1-14	a	b	c	d	e	f♯	g
	64	37.5	20	49.5	29.5	48.5	17

'The Northern Courtyard' places 87 percent of tonal weight on pentatonic notes, and 13 percent on *bian*-notes. The dominant is again the strongest note, with *d* and *e* coming next. Four cadences occur on the dominant, two on the mode-final, and one on the sub-mediant.

Table 2. Hokuteiraku, *weighted-scale*

	a	b	c	d	e	f♯	g
Measures 1-14	56	36	11.5	48.5	46	33	20

'Introit to "Perfect Virtue"' expresses itself rather differently. Although the pentatonic scale takes 89 percent of total weight, within that figure the individual distribution of weight has changed. The mode-final has risen sharply, and both it and the mediant outweigh the dominant quite heavily. Of the seven cadences, five fall on the final, two on the mediant. This item is the only one of the three with cadences on *f♯* and none on *a*.

Table 3. Ittokuen, *weighted-scale*

	a	b	c♯	d	e	f♯	g♯
Measures 1-14	34	24	9	82	21.5	58.5	19

Summary figures drawn from these pieces show their physical forms to be broadly similar: fourteen-measure durations, heptatonic *Gongdiao* scales, reliance on the pentatonic formation with its powerful triadic backing, regular two-measure phrases, and cadences confined (but for one) to 1, 3 and 5 of the scale. They are differentiated from each other by details in profile: individual melodic textures, respective note-relationships within the mode-key, the adopted patterns, and the order of cadence notes along the way. In an earlier study it was shown that, to some extent, the ten-measure tunes (in the mode-key on *d*) share common formulaic material and structural organization (Fascicle 5, pp.80-3). The same cannot be said of the three fourteen-measure tunes of this group (a closer comparative study of which is postponed for a later date). *Ittokuen* does not share affinity with *Gyokuju gotei-ka* and *Hokuteiraku*, but it bears a family resemblance to another melody of the *Sada-chō* group, namely *Sairyōshū*, 'Western Liangzhou' (pp.13-47; conflation pp.41,139).

Example 3. Comparison: 'Western Liangzhou' & 'Introit to "Perfect Virtue" '

Looking at the two compositions together, there is more than a casual resemblance between them. Both tunes include repeating sections which, when removed leave them simpler and reduce their lengths. 'Western Liangzhou' consists of five sections of four measures each: sections 4 and 5 repeat section 3; and half of section 1 repeats in section 2. 'Introit to "Perfect Virtue" ' repeats the first four measures in measures 5-8, and also repeats several measures within the final six. For convenience, 'Western Liangzhou' is tabled here in a twelve-measure form; all the music is present without the repeats.

Comparison of these tunes draws attention to quite prominent likenesses in their initial six measures and final sections. The pitch difference, in the area of measures 7 and 8, is an interesting diversion, where cadences are placed on the dominant in one tune, and on the mode-final in the other; formulae are similar but contrasting – a fourth apart in modal transposition. The musical mind practises adaptability in involuntary action. Outside cadential circumstances, a similar variance is noted about measures 9 and 10. The assured openings of both melodies in measure 1, repeated in measure 5, must be more than coincidental, and so possibly is the tritonal leap, in measure 10 of 'Western Liangzhou', preceded (as it is) by the same move from measure 8 to measure 9 in 'Introit to "Perfect Virtue" '.

The comparative table exposes curious extensions in the latter part of 'Introit to "Perfect Virtue" '; measures 10 and 11 stretch measure 11 of 'Western Liangzhou', and measures 12 and 13 duplicate, and so draw out, preparation for the final measure and inevitable cadence of 'Introit to "Perfect Virtue". Could the latter have originally been a twenty-measure tune like 'Western Liangzhou'? In his introductions to the two titles, L.E.R.P. has informed us that both had strong links with Japanese ceremonial: 'Western Liangzhou' was used as Entrance Music (Introit?) on private imperial occasions from 813 onwards (p.18). Was 'Perfect Virtue' part of 'Blessed Goodness Music' in times gone by?

30. Piece: **'Introit to "Peace-Music"'** (*Anrakuen/Anyue yan* 安 樂 鹽)

Conflation

For analytical and critical purposes, an acceptable conflation is provided in the *KF/HSF/RK* version. Discrepancies between music sources are few, no more than differences of one note in a version, against other versions in general agreement; *ichi*-signs also agree in both string scores.

Example 1. Conflation: *Anrakuen*

Analysis

There are six phrases, making a tune of twelve measures in all. Moronaga's penultimate *ichi*-sign is misplaced with regard to the unvaried repetition of measures 3-4 in 7-8, which occur again in measures 11-12. It is safe to describe the structure of the melody as six two-measure phrases, with cadences on *a, d, a, d, f♯* and *d*. The cadence of the fifth phrase, in measure 10, is undoubtedly on the mediant, allowing repetition of the second, fourth and sixth phrases to be precisely defined and aurally discerned. Further evidence for the mediant cadence in *Anrakuen* is provided by comparison with measures 9 -11 of *Ittokuen*, where almost the same, two-measure phrase is extended to three measures, throwing greater emphasis onto the mediant as phrase-terminal. *Ittokuen* is, in fact, a slightly longer version of *Anrakuen*. The first eight measures of *Anrakuen*, measures 1-4 repeating, identify closely with the same measures of *Ittokuen*. Measures 9-10 are recognizably similar in both melodies, as are measures 13-14 of *Ittokuen* with measures 11-12 of *Anrakuen*.

The noticeable difference occurs in measures 11-12 of *Ittokuen*. Measure 11 is an extension of measures 9-10, and measure 12 anticipates the return of measures 3-4 and 7-8 in measures 13-14 (which – it has been said – are identical with measures 11-12 of *Anrakuen*). In the earlier exposition of these titles (this volume, pp.91-120) there is no explanation of how they came to resemble each other so closely, nor why; but there have been other melodies in which extensions of phrases may have come about, where melodic impulse, in purely musical terms, hesitates or wavers – perhaps for some extra-musical purpose not explained ('no dance' is recorded in comments above both pieces in three of the four current sources), or where historical memory may have foundered or faltered during centuries of oral transmission and rote-learning.

162

An earlier instance of momentary loss of direction occurs in measures 3-6 of the Broaching of *Katen*, 'The Palace of Congratulations' (Fascicle 3, pp.20-9; conflation, Fascicle 5, p.35), but this kind of periphrasis is more frequently encountered in unmeasured movements, of which a prime example is the Prelude of *Ōdai hajinraku*, 'The Emperor destroys the Formations' (Fascicle 1; conflation, Fascicle 2, pp.76-7). There is an abundance of prolixity in three movements of *Ryō-ō*, 'The King of Lanling': the *Ranjo*, the Wild Prelude and *Amma* (Fascicle 5, pp.14-26; conflations, this volume, pp.91,108,120); but these are not pieces of Tang origin.

At this point it is interesting to observe Moronaga's placing of *Ittokuen* and *Anrakuen* in sequence, without historical or other comment on their likeness to each other. Of *Ittokuen* he records only basic facts, that it is a 'small' piece of 'old' music, of fourteen beats (or ten in another version), without a dance. In the case of *Anrakuen* of twelve beats, or measures, he gives similar information, and adds two relevant comments from Nangū's (Prince Sadayasu's) 'Transverse-Flute Score' (completed in 921): that *Anrakuen* is to be played before *Amma* ('when commoners emerge for *Amma*, first do this tune'); and that when this is done, it expresses the highest moral virtues, beyond anything known before. *Amma* will be remembered (from its first appearance in this series) as the fourth movement of *Ryō-ō*, 'The King of Lanling' (Fascicle 5, pp.24-5). To the Nangū instruction, *ZKKS* (late thirteenth century) adds that the dancer, coming forward to dance *Amma*, advances with special, particular steps. Perhaps his entrance was made to *Anrakuen*, but we are not told so. Later musical sources following *ZKKS* – manuscripts of the Ōga family, starting from c.1330, *CORYF* and *RTYF* – address *Amma*, but with no reference to *Anrakuen*.

In English translation, Nangū's use of the word 'commoners' is unusually specific. It has been suggested it may refer to untitled persons, and its meaning may possibly include those external to the political and social structure of imperial government, those (for example) in temples and shrines, where *Tōgaku* was also accommodated and performed. As to the second statement about moral virtues beyond estimation, it is translated literally by L.E.R.P. with sensitive choice of words: 'the sincerity (purity, genuineness, integrity) of this is incomparable' or 'has never been seen' (this volume, pp.78,89). In any form it evokes metaphysical concepts of fanciful and supernatural conceits and images.

Although *Ittokuen* and *Anrakuen* are versions of the same melody, Japanese records credit *Anrakuen* with a certain prestige. *ZKKS* and *HPGS* name a musician of the Tang as its 'maker' (of an early version supposedly, not likely to have been the first), and *Anrakuen* seems to have been held in some regard by Prince Sadayasu, by Moronaga who often quotes from the Nangū score, and by *ZKKS*, which coverage spreads over a number of centuries. Review of the note-perspectives of *Ittokuen* and *Anrakuen* uncovers some of the technical differences between them.

Table 1. Weighted-scale data of Ittokuen *and* Anrakuen

	a	*b*	*c♯*	*d*	*e*	*f♯*	*g♯*
Ittokuen	34	24	9	82	21.5	58.5	19
Anrakuen	53	15	5	74	19	45	6

Variation between two similar versions of the same tune is due to differences of length, and relative perspectives between notes within the scale. The two extra measures of *Ittokuen*, measures 11-12, increase weight on the mediant and, to a lesser degree, on the dominant. The mode-final is unaffected in this item, as the note is not heard in those measures. In *Ittokuen* the mediant registers its weight equally between the final and its dominant; but in *Anrakuen* the dominant is 21 points behind the final, and the mediant eight points further back. The second and sixth of the scale are comparatively weak in both hierarchies of notes; each melody relies most heavily on one, three and five. The primary notes of the pentatonic structure prove the mode to be very strong in both pieces. Auxiliary notes in *Anrakuen* are of little value; but in *Ittokuen* the fourth is prominent owing to three tritonal leaps, absent from *Anrakuen*. Conversion of figures to percentages enables a more rational and equitable summary-comparison to be made.

Table 2. Comparative data from Ittokuen *and* Anrakuen *in terms of percentages*

		Ittokuen		*Anrakuen*	
Notes of the primary pentatonic scale:	*d, e, f♯, a, b*	89 percent		95 percent	
Three triadic notes:	*d, f♯, a*	70	"	79	"
Final and dominant:	*d, a*	47	"	59	"
Mediant:	*f♯*	24	"	21	"
Second and sixth:	*e, b*	18	"	16	"
Auxiliary notes:	*g♯, c♯*	11	"	5	"

Comparison of percentages confirms that the primary pentatonic scale furnishes almost the entire tonal material of both pieces, particularly of *Anrakuen*, and that *bian*-notes are consequently very light in this tune. Of pentatonic notes, the final and dominant are strong in *Anrakuen*, and with the mediant are principal providers of its modal and melodic strength. *Ittokuen*, however, gains a certain colour and character through the presence and higher profile of the fourth of the scale, and its three tritonal leaps from the mode final. Differences of this kind sometimes occur between conflations of like tunes, owing to conflation guidelines observed since this series began.

164

Two such differences concern a point under discussion: first, to give slightly more attention to the significance of the Toyohara mouth-organ tradition, because the Toyohara clan history constitutes the oldest recorded line of court musicians and court repertory; and second, when discrepancies arise, to compile a version guided by the larger body of received opinion contained in these sources. In the present comparative analysis, each title exists in four primary versions, and in the main each conflation is determined by this policy. It so happens that sources of *Ittokuen* allow three tritonal leaps to be included in conflation, and that sources of *Anrakuen* are divided, two each way in measures 1 and 5, while in measure 9 three sources display *a* as first beat, and only one (*SSSTF*) displays *g♯*. In measures 1 and 5, therefore, the Toyohara tradition was the deciding factor; in measure 9, the majority made the decision, of which *KF/HSF/RK* was one.

In *Ichikotsu* and *Sada* modes, melodies of twelve measures of eight beats are few. Both the Entering Broaching and Stamping of *Toraden* (Fascicle 2, pp.36-42; conflations, Fascicle 3, pp.72-3) have sixteen drumbeats, of which the first four repeat, as in *Anrakuen*. Ignoring repeats, 4+8 suggest reduced alternative versions. Some items were shortened, on occasion by omitting repetition of the first four measures, but no *Toraden* source recognizes the existence of abbreviated versions. Moreover, the Entering Broaching is partly unmeasured, and the Stamping, wholly so.

Gyokuju goteika, 'A Jade-Tree's Rear Court Blossom' (Fascicle 3, pp.12-17; conflation, Fascicle 5, p.35) has fourteen measures, of which the first two and the last two are the same. The piece is played eight times, each being a *Section* in the entire performance. As directed in the scores, the first Section is to consist of all fourteen measures, after which repeats begin from the third measure; consequently repeats will consist of twelve measures. Again, however, comparison with *Anrakuen* is not helpful, as the whole tune, with or without the initial two measures, is through-composed and closely knit, without definite four- or eight-measure divisions. A sequence of two-measure phrases is the order throughout.

Finally, attention can be drawn to two other *Sada*-melodies cast primarily in twelve-measure forms: *Sairyōshū* and *Rosō* (this Volume, pp.13-47 and pp.48-54). *Sairyōshū* has twelve measures of through-composed melody, followed by two repetitions of measures 9-12, making 20 measures in all. *Rosō* is complete in twelve measures. Conflations and sufficient comments on these pieces have been offered earlier in this Appendix, so nothing further is needed here. Like *Gyokuju goteika*, all the tunes named in this context are individual in their modal groups. They have a variety of structures and dispositions, to which those of the *Sada*-class add a hint of exotic colour inherent in the *Gongdiao* scale, and – a not unreasonable inference – in foregone Kuchean connections.

31. Piece: **Ten Devas** (*Jūtenraku* 十 天 樂)

Conflation

Once again, well supported by other sources, *KF/HSF/RK* provides a suitable conflation. A minor variance occurs in the second half of measure 2, where the Toyohara tradition records *f♯e - f♯ - a - ba*, while Moronaga has *f♯ - a - c♯b - a*. At this point in both scores, an alternative version, noted by Moronaga (which happens to agree with the mouth-organ version, *KF/HSF/RK*), has been retained in conflation. In keeping with the ethnic origin and structure of the *Sada-chō* scale (Fascicle 5, pp.xii-xiii), conflations of all items listed in Moronaga's *Sada-chō* 沙 陀 調 are written with a signature of three sharps, appropriate to a Lydian-type octave-set in the mode-key on D.

Example 1. Conflation: 'Ten Devas'

Analysis

Four two-measure phrases form the structure of *Jūtenraku*, a short melody of which dominant and final are the mainstays, with the mediant leading towards each of these notes in turn: *f♯ - a* in measures 2, 3 and 6, and *f♯ - d* in measures 4 and 8. From the weighted-scale exercise, these three notes take 72 percent of total weight; the auxiliaries, 10 percent – mostly earned by the sub-final.

Table 1. Jūtenraku, *weighted-scale data*

	a	*b*	*c♯*	*d*	*e*	*f♯*	*g♯*
Measures 1-8	41.5	11.5	11	39	15	26	3

The tonal structure of this tune is primarily dependent on its first two measures; they expose material for all that follows. These measures are familiar from other repertory items, each (in various forms) being capable of cadential and non-cadential functions. The presence of variant forms of measure 1, in measures 4, 5 and 8, provides related beginnings and endings for each half of the tune, and thus declares the mode at important parts of the binary divisions.

166

Analysis demonstrates: that the melody, a simple tune in itself, is generated from measures 1 and 2; that the number of formulae is thereby small; and that they are used economically.

First and last notes of the two-measure phrases are limited to three primary notes: first-phrase opening and closing on *a*; second-phrase opening on *f♯* and closing on *d*; third-phrase, on *a* in both places; and fourth-phrase, on *d* in both places. Measures 3-8 are traceable to the same initial source. Measure 3 interchanges the halves of measure 2; measures 4, 5 and 8 relate to measure 1, and to each other; while measures 6 and 7 share elements of measures 1 and 2. The compact nature of *Jūtenraku* is evident from the following comparative table.

Example 2. Aligned analysis

Jūtenraku is the last item in Moronaga's listings of the *Tōgaku* repertory in the *Ichikotsu* and *Sada* modes; and these brief comments close a series of initial analyses of the music of 33 titles (including the two appendices of Fascicle 4), that amount to 52 movements in all. While moving through a first investigation of this music, and the remarkable historical, cultural and explanatory material that accompanies it, one is reminded from time to time of the nature of the musical language in which it was made. A scale of seven notes, up to this point operating in the one mode-key, and without a developed, written theory of practical composition or technical procedures, is bound to have produced many pieces modelled on experience, memory-recall and imitation, some of which sound similar, at least in part, if not in whole.

This was first discovered while examining the Processionals of 'The Emperor destroys the Formations' and 'The Singing of Spring Warblers' (Fascicles 1 and 2; conflations, Fascicles 2 and 3), the two initial movements of these suites. When it was found that they are simply the latter drumbeat periods of the Preludes of the same suites, excised, perhaps in Japan, to serve in another capacity, the possibility of their being independent compositions was by chance removed; they are too like their models to be independent structures, and remain so to their final cadences.

If the Processional movements were made in Japan, Tang musicians would not have known of them. There is no reference to Processionals in the introductory information from China on these suites, but as shown in Fascicle 5 (pp.26-8) the term itself *is* known in China. Be that as it may, it is hardly credible that Tang folk did not know that some pieces resemble others. Surely musicians, including the players themselves, recognized that the three preludial Sections of *Toraden*, 'The Whirl-Around' (Fascicle 2, pp.18-35; conflations, Fascicle 3, pp.70-2), are variants of themselves. There are examples: of movements within a suite being variations *on*, rather than variants *of*, each other, as in *Koinju*, 'Sogdians Drinking Wine' (Fascicle 4, pp.1-9; conflations, Fascicle 5, pp.57-62); of borrowing a movement of one suite for use under a changed name in another suite: the Quick of *Tori*, 'The Bird', is the Way-Walking of *Katen*, 'The Palace of Congratulations' (conflations, Fascicle 5, pp.50 and 38); and of unrelated pieces, of different lengths, being similar melodies devised independently – presumably at different times and under different circumstances. Musical invention, experienced and conditioned in familiar and socially accepted styles, fashions random assemblies of tonal clichés into phrases of one sort and another, to make new pieces.

Jūtenraku is made up of familiar-sounding phrases that together make a satisfactory and balanced tune. Taken in isolation, however, each measure is a reminder of patterns heard many times during exploration of items in the same mode-key, whether in *Ichikotsu-chō* or *Sada-chō*, or in pieces of two or four binary-beats to the measure, in Lydian or Mixo-Lydian scale-types. Rather than prolong discussion when so many examples lie ready to hand, an illustration centred on *Jūtenraku* will be useful. Two passages from diverse items, distinctly individual in musical styles, are lined up with the first four measures of *Jūtenraku*. Each excerpt is contained in its own sub-structure as part of a greater whole; and note patterns, shared in various forms, are contributory details.

The patterns themselves are unobtrusive, fragmentary elements, and what is important is that they serve the musical impulse and skill of the 'composer', making melody subject to natural human direction. As patterns they have no musical value of their own; they only assume value when applied at some level of purposeful, creative exercise. Such points are better seen in the following comparative table of excerpts from the conflations of three items: the first four measures of *Jūtenraku*, the last two-and-a-half measures of *Gyokuju gotei-ka* (Fascicle 5. p.35), and the final four measures of *Shō-ō-raku* (Fascicle 5, p.70).

Example 3. Comparative table: excerpts from three repertory items

In conclusion, evidence asserts that modal language, mosaic texture, and structural organization are the materials of the *Tōgaku* repertory. On the great continent to the West of Japan, where the repertory originally developed, accumulated and flourished, *Yanyue* – the Banquet Music – proves the capacity of the Sui and Tang Dynasties to assemble and establish a versatile and flexible genre of music, both tuneful and functional; this is an achievement indicative of the cultural energy, and social response, of people of that time, during the second half of the First Millennium of the Common Era.

169

Appendix 2

Is the Free Prelude of 'The Prince of [Luo]-ling' (*Ryō-ō /Ling Wang* 陵 王) a Japanese Composition? (N.J.N.)

Music from the Tang Court 5 includes an intensive study of the etymology and history of the terms *Ranjo* and *Ranjō* – titles of several movements in large instrumental suites (*Taikyoku*) of the Japanese *Tōgaku* repertory. One *Ranjo* of particular interest in the context of that Fascicle is the first movement of *Ryō-ō*, 'The Prince of Luoling' (in its Chinese context more properly 'Lanling' – see Preface, p.xi), the music-and-dance Suite featured in Fascicle 5 (p.14). Of questions exposed in the substantial investigation of the Suite, this Appendix reviews the formation of the *Ranjo*, and its analysis, in the commentary on *Sada-chō* items in this fascicle (p.92), and proceeds to address the origin of the music of the *Ranjo*: whether it is a 'Chinese' composition or acquisition, or (feasibly) a Japanese composition. In several parts of the text (L.E.R.P.), the author's opinion points in the latter direction (Fascicle 5, pp.15 and 31).

Discussing the early history of the *Ranjo*, one is mindful that all the extant primary music sources are Japanese, written down in tablature much later than general references to the existence of an item of this or similar name, in the *Ryō-ō* suite. *Ranjo* was not unknown as the title of a composition in Heian times; written accounts that affect the interpretation and possible significance of the name have varied forms of the title, in *Kanji* and in *Kana* syllables. Laying aside that area of criticism, this essay explores the question of *origin* in relation to the musical language and style of the *Ranjo* of *Ryō-ō*, in terms of formulaic and structural analysis of its materials.

Before looking into the work more closely, let it be said that there are few factual answers to questions about the origin of any single piece of music of this repertory. Formal analysis, of the materials and modal practices of a composition taken in isolation, will only disclose information about that one composition. How the music of one selected item was composed, and how it reached the condition from which the Cambridge scholars eventually transcribed it, did not interest authors and scribes in Japan in the first millennium; nor has it done so in the second millennium. By whom any one piece was written, where, when, on what occasion: these are questions that will tease historians and musicologists for the rest of time.

Several written descriptions of the *Ranjo* are to be found in the reconstruction and examination of the history of *Ryō-ō* (L.E.R.P.) in Fascicle 5 (pp.1-33). In the preface to the suite, *KF/HSF/RK* (p.12) records 'Old Music' as the general and only description. *Ranjō* and *Ranjo* (Free Tune and Free Prelude, both forms of title are used in this source, probably implying the same movement) are named there without further information. *SSSTF* omits all subtitles from its introductory sentence, except *Netori*. In *JCYR* Moronaga records the names of four movements, including *Ranjo* (Free Prelude), the text of a chant, and some qualifying instructions on performance; in addition he quotes from two tenth-century flute scores. Using 'Free Tune' (*Ranjō*) and 'Angry Prelude' (*Shinjo*), in addition to 'Free Prelude' (*Ranjo*), Moronaga omits comments on history or ancestry. In *SGYR* there is no entry on the subject of the *Ranjo*. *RSCY* classes the Free Tune as 'New Music'. None of these sources supplies music tablatures of the movement; and the transcription in Fascicle 5 (p.14) was made from four, late, Japanese manuscripts, written down, and recopied, over a time-span of three-and-a-half centuries – *c.*1330-1688 (p.15) – by members of the Ōga family of flute-players. It is thought that the absence of string versions from the primary sources may have been due to the fact that, at least by Moronaga's time, *Ranjo* were played by winds and percussion alone (L.E.R.P.). As from this point, the form of title: *Ranjo*, 'Free Prelude', will be adopted on grounds of typological convenience.

Attribution of the *Ranjo* to both 'Old' Music and 'New' Music indicates the unreliability of these classifications (see Volume 7, Chapter 3 – in preparation). Adopted by the Japanese, the terms were repeated, unquestioned, by copyists, for centuries after social, political and cultural changes rendered this kind of music anachronistic, even obsolete, so far as the public was concerned. However, Fascicle 5 states (L.E.R.P., p.15): 'That this piece [*Ranjo*] is a Japanese composition of pre-tenth century date would seem probable.' Thorough examination of all the historical evidence has hitherto come no nearer than that, to an opinion on the origin of this unusual piece, only to be found in Japanese sources.

What can be discovered about the *Ranjo* from the music itself? Certainly nothing about when, how or why it was made; but on purely musical grounds, a particular item can sometimes demonstrate its affinity with, or independence from, the main stream of *Tōgaku* items to which it traditionally belongs. All items of Fascicles 1-5 have now been examined, analysed and discussed, and broad guidelines relative to the structure and style of *Tōgaku* compositions in the mode-key on *D* have emerged. In some ways, however, the *Ranjo* falls outside the bounds of recognized precedents.

The Conflation
Justification of the conflation of the *Ranjo* is fully supported where conflations and analyses of the complete suite, 'The Prince of Luoling', are given (pp.88-120). Repetition of this material is not necessary here, but the conflation bears repetition for the investigation that follows.

Example 1. Conflation of the *Ranjo*

The Mode

An interesting and unexpected feature of the *Ranjo* is that it exists and functions
on what appear to be two modal levels, but there is no written evidence, in
Chinese or Japanese historical sources, to suggest that a single composition was
capable of operating in two different keys of the same mode. The Song poet and
composer, Jiang Kui 姜 夔, otherwise known as 'Daoist White Stone' (*Baishi
Daoren* 白 石 道 人),writing at the end of the twelfth century AD, had
described 'clashing tunes' (Picken 1966, p.161), using the term as a description
of a particular type of modal irregularity. Jiang Kui, however, was concerned –
and most explicitly so – with tunes in which there was a clash between two
different modes; and he expressly excluded the possibility of clash between
different *Gong* modes on different finals.

172

Notwithstanding historical silence in Chinese or Japanese sources on this matter, the *Ranjo* is a melody to which this description of functioning on two modal levels may properly be applied. In a coherent manner, providing variety and contrast, various parts of the melody exhibit independent profiles, according to their individual structural patterns and internal scale formations. It is convenient to recognize that the basic scale of the *Ranjo* is a Lydian octave-series on *D* (the scale of the modal group and sub-group to which the *Ranjo*-piece belongs), and that this scale contains all the notes of the entire melody. Two 'aspects' or 'perspectives' of the mode are evident (these terms were first used in connection with analysis of *Tōgaku* items in Fascicle 2, pp.89-91), according to the area of the scale on which the separate parts of the melody concentrate, and according to how the notes of these parts relate to their cadences or central notes.

The Form

The form of the *Ranjo* includes the following structural divisions:

Table 1. Ranjo, *sectional outline*

‖: A - B | b - A' - B' - a :‖ a'.

A and B are the principal contrasting sections within each half of the composition; the second half is a variant of the first. There is a short transition passage, b, derived from B, and a short codetta, a, derived from A, and attached to B'. The final eight beats that act as coda, a', are played only at the end on the last time through; it is a variant of the codetta, a. With reference to the conflation and numbering of beats (quarter-notes), the binary plan becomes more clear when accompanying details are added.

Table 2. the Ranjo, *broad formal plan*

1.

A	beats 1-31,	duration	31 beats	
B	" 32-56,	"	25 "	
				56 beats

2.

b, transition,	beats 57-64,	duration	8 beats	
A'	" 65-87,	"	23 "	
B'	" 88-106,	"	19 "	
a, codetta	" 107-112,	"	6 "	
				56 beats
				112 beats
a', coda	" 113-120,	duration	8 beats	
				8 beats
			Total	120 beats

To illustrate independence of the two principal sections and their adjuncts, and to bring forward technical details differing between sections A and B, relative analytical data from weighted-scale applications (this volume, pp.95,96) are summarized in sectional tables.

Table 3. the Ranjo, *summary of weighted-scale data*

	d	e	f♯	g♯	a	b	c♯
(i) Sections A (beats 1-31), A' (65-87), and a (107-12)	36.5	17.5	13	-	41.5	20	3.5
(ii) Sections B (beats 32-56), B' (88-106), and b (57-64)	2	3	14	45.5	1.5	32.5	10.5

Analysis of the *Ranjo*: Mode and Form

The A sections as a whole demonstrate the usual formalities relative to heptatonic *Gong*-mode scale practices; in this instance the scale is a Lydian-type, hexatonic scale on *d* as mode-final. The only cadences of these sections occur on *d*; one concludes each repeat of the *Ranjo*, and one is added on to complete the entire performance, after the last repeat.

Intermediate cadences on the dominant are implicit at beats 31 and 87 of the conflation (see Example 1, p.172). Dominant and final are well established and well defined throughout. Theoretically, *Gong* expectancies are recognized and upheld. The only *bian*-note, *c♯*, has no status; it makes two slight appearances at beats 64 and 108. Percentages (drawn from Table 3) support the conventional nature of A-related sections.

Table 4. Elements of A-related sections expressed as percentages of the whole

---

Mode-final, *d* = 28; dominant, *a*, 31 percent; *d* + *a*, 59 percent;
Pentatonic scale, *d* + *e* + *f♯* + *a* + *b*, 97 percent;
Bian-note, *c♯*, 3 percent.

B sections support a reduced scale, consisting mainly of four notes that underlie several distinctive melodic patterns. Notes *d*, *e* and *a* are of no consequence in these sections, while the remaining underlying scale, *f♯* - *g♯* - *b* - *c♯* and its patterns prominently expose the interval *g♯-b*. The only cadence occurs on *b*, which is well defined in rhythm, structural position and time-duration. The question is: what is the modal relationship of the second scale to the first? Data that may bear on an answer are these: *b* is the most important note by position and function; *g♯* is the most weighted note of weighted-scale ratings; and *g♯-b* is the most frequent disjunct interval of the B sections, with *c♯-f♯* occurring, but rarely. From weighted-scale data for B sections can be drawn the following percentages of pairs of notes, single notes and scale sequences, with reference to modal and tonal implications, and to the modality of the B sections in relation to the A sections.

Table 5. Elements of B-related sections expressed as percentages of the whole

---

Fourth of the scale, $g\sharp$ = 42; sixth, b = 30; $g\sharp$+b, 72 percent;
Third + seventh scale-notes, $f\sharp$ and $c\sharp$, 22 percent;
Pentatonic scale, $d + e + f\sharp + a + b$, 49 percent;
Bian-notes, $g\sharp + c\sharp$, 51 percent;
Third, fourth, sixth and seventh notes of the scale, 94 percent.

The high ratings of $g\sharp$ and b in B sections of the *Ranjo* suggest that these notes
will have bearing on the modal enquiry; they are the two most heavily weighted
notes in the B sections. Although $g\sharp$ is the most weighted, it cannot be mode-final
according to traditional, Tang, modal theory (see Picken 1969, iii, p.98, for Duan
Anjie's list of modes, translated and amended), as all heptatonic modal scales,
derived from pentatonic forms, require the distance of two half-tones between
mode-final and super-final, whereas in the scale of the B sections, if $g\sharp$ were final,
the interval would be one half-tone. Moreover, the interval between $g\sharp$ as final
and d as its dominant would be six half-tones, not seven (as imposed by the cycle
of fifths). Similarly, $g\sharp$ could not be dominant to $c\sharp$, since the note next above $c\sharp$ in
this scale is also only one half-tone from it. Could b, then, be dominant or final in
the scale of the B sections, since intervals between e (as final) and b (as
dominant), and between final and super-final, e-$f\sharp$, would then be satisfactory?

   If b is dominant, the scale formation on e would be an octave-series formed
from the primary *Gong*-scale on d. The scale on e would begin from the second
note, *Shang*, of the primary scale, which note would function as mode-final,
creating in this case the *Shang*-mode scale, a Mixo-Lydian-type structure, in the
mode-key on e. The most important notes of the B sections are (as shown) $g\sharp$ and
b, with b providing the cadence-definition at the end of the first half of the
composition. The two notes, $g\sharp$ and b, carry weight in B sections owing to
repetitions of the broken third, and repetition of the B section in the second part
of the movement. However, *bian*-notes of the primary *Gong*-scale of the A
sections (in the parent mode-key on d) are $g\sharp$ and $c\sharp$; and (theoretically) modal
inversions would retain the light weight of original *bian*-notes on the same
pitches in the inverted scale. The *Ranjo* does not accept this practice, however,
since percentages show that $g\sharp$ and $c\sharp$ together collect more than 50 percent of the
total weight of all other notes of the B sections. Additional evidence against b
being the dominant of a *Shang*-mode scale on e in this context is the inescapable
fact that, in these sections, e is so undernourished as to accrue only 3 percent of
the total. No mode-final could sustain itself at such an ignominious level so as to
function and survive as final of a modal inversion, or as key-note of a mode,
whether temporary or permanent.

176

A more favourable approach to the modality of the B sections is that from the note *b* itself as final, key-note of the only cadence, and strongly asserted by virtue of its structural position, its binary rhythm and time-duration. The scale on *b* is an inversion on the sixth note of the heptatonic, primary *Gong*-mode scale on *d*, a Dorian-type octave-species; its notes, therefore, are: *b - c♯ - d - e - f♯ - g♯ - a*, in which *f♯, g♯, b* and *c♯*, are essential to the formulaic structure of the melody, to the extent that their total contribution amounts to 94 percent of the whole. Furthermore, intervals between mode-final and super-final, and dominant and sub-mediant are (in both instances) two half-tones. The dominant is seven half-tones above its final, and none of its four strongest notes are *bian*-notes in the inverted scale on *b*. Observing that *g♯* and *c♯* (primary *bian*-notes of the parent *Gong*-scale on *d*) are important to the melodic fabric of B sections, providing as they do 51 percent of the whole, analytical experience in this genre suggests that this may be condoned with reference to other analyses of *Tōgaku* items under the present title. The *bian*-notes of a primary mode have sometimes been known to follow a temporary transposition of the final – when a change in modal perspective has assumed an inverted position of the same mode-scale within the same mode-key – and this would explain what happens in the *Ranjo*. The final of the inverted scale of the B sections has fallen three half-tones from the final of the primary *Gong*-scale on *d*, and the *bian*-notes of the inverted scale, *e* and *a*, now *bian*-notes of a Mixo-Lydian-type octave-series, have of necessity fallen four half-tones. Together the *bian*-notes claim only 4 percent of tonal weight in the melodies of the B sections of the *Ranjo*.

Analysis of *Tōgaku* tunes from Fascicles 1-5 and this volume corroborates that a shift had taken place in China, by the middle of the first millennium, affecting the fundamental pitch of the ground-tone of the modal system, for convenience named here as *C*. Around this time the ground-tone appears to have re-established itself one degree higher on *D*, which move, observed in tablature in some repertory collections after 838-9, appears to have introduced a complementary shift whereby *bian*-notes of the *Gong*-scale on *C*, notes that normally remained auxiliaries in inversions of that mode, tended also to move a whole tone upwards *with* the transposed ground-tone. Practical evidence of the result of this significant movement is found in consequent modal ambivalence among source materials, confirmed in tablatures, as to whether the adopted pitch-level on *D* as final predicated the higher scale to be a direct transposition of the basic *Gong*-scale structure from *C* to *D*, together with traditional Han modal theory and practice; *or*, whether the new pitch level on *D* instigated replacement of the *Gong*-scale with that of the first inversion of the *Gong*-scale, namely the *Shang*-scale, *Shang* being the second degree of the *Gong* pentatonic order. In simpler terms, the difference is that the one scale is a Lydian-type octave-series of tones and semitones: T·T T S T T S, while the other is a Mixo-Lydian-type octave-series: T T S T T S T.

Now, let us particularise the difference. If the *Gong*-sequence of intervals was to be upheld on transfer of the basic mode-key to *D*, one might expect *bian*-notes in the former mode-key (*f♯* and *b*), to be replaced by *bian*-notes in the new mode-key (*g♯* and *c♯*); but if the *Gong*-order gives way to *Shang*-order on the super-final of the old mode-key, then the new mode-key will have, not *f♯* and *b* as *bian*, nor yet *g♯* and *c♯*, but *g* and *c*, the fourth and seventh notes of the new *Shang*-scale on *D*. The first inversion of the *Gong*-scale, in which *Shang* becomes mode-final, and in which the *Shang* octave-species is defined by the natural order of *Gong* notes, read from super-final to super-final, thus yields a Mixo-Lydian-type scale, in which the circumstances of consecutive notes alter, in relation to their mode-final, and in relation to each other. As *bian*-notes of *Shang* thus lost the strong semitonal slant towards dominant and final, characteristic of the *Gong* mode, so they became somewhat ineffectual in the new manner, assuming a degree of independence in melodic formulae, and sometimes even cadence functions and responsibilities.

To return to the *Ranjo*, Duan Anjie's enumeration of scale formations, with names of the twenty-eight mode-keys of Tang modal practice (Picken, 1969, iii, p.98), provides names for the two modal scales engaged in the *Ranjo*. Applying to the lists a simple transposition from the mode-key on *C* to that on *D*, the scales of the *Ranjo* become identifiable, and their relationship is clarified in their being primary and secondary formations of the fundamental *Gong*-mode scale in the mode-key on *D*. The clarification of their identity accounts for their mutual tolerance in close proximity under conditions, such as the *Ranjo* imposes on its form, by its modality.

The figures shown in Table 3 (summarising weighted-scale data), together with the modal analysis that follows, establish that A sections and B sections do not share the same modal perspective and physical structure, nor are they of the same melodic profile. It can also be seen (from the conflation: Example 1, p.172), that where A changes to B and A' to B', the same distinct and immediate step is taken from one section to the other; it happens before the ear realises an incident of change has occurred. In both places, the change is made promptly within the duration of one binary beat (two quarter notes); *g♯* is substituted for *a*. The latter note is not sounded again until the transitional passage (the first eight beats of the second half of the composition), when the return of A is imminent. Following A', the dominant, in B', is again silent, until the final cadence, marked codetta, a', is introduced.

The transitional passage (beats 57-64) is ingeniously designed. Simple as it was to move from A to B, and from A' to B', through conjunct notes *a* and *g♯* (the strongest notes in each section, as the weighted-scale proves), the return from B

178

to A' required more time. This was necessary since the *Gong* pentatonic scale of section A had been completely supplanted by the new tonal structure of section B, and had later to be reinstated as the primary mode-key, to which all elements of the composition are expected to relate. It is worth indicating that the return, from b to A' and from B' to a, is made through the same notes in reverse order, *g♯* and *a*, that made the initial step from A to B.

The same problem of restoring the primary mode-key arises again at the end of the *Ranjo*, but here the solution is less convincing. In support of this contention, let it be defended in non-musical terms. The *Ranjo* acts out a power-struggle between neighbouring territories, represented by sections A and B. Following the outset, where A is overrun by B, B assumes power and sets up its own centre of reference, formally declared by the half-way cadence. In the second half, A rallies and drives B out, having taken time to prepare for the return (by way of the transition) before claiming rightful possession. B attacks a second time, however, and A is once more expelled. If A is to gain and retain victory once and for all, it will need more time to prepare a stronger comeback, not only to subdue the aggressor, but to annihilate him totally and restore dominion beyond further dispute. This last stage is the most important.

In the conflation of the *Ranjo*, final reinstatement of the primary mode is left to a brief codetta, consisting of the last six beats, 107-12. In full performance, however, the *Ranjo* is repeated a number of times, so that the cycle of conflict keeps recurring, as does the temporary truce (for just six beats) at the end of each repeat. Only the very last time – when immediate repetition of a modal cadence provides an additional eight beats, thus lengthening the codetta into a coda to mark final reinstatement of the primary mode-key – is an extended conclusion of fourteen beats (a + a' = 6+8 beats) made. The illustration of warring neighbours is fanciful, but there is a point to be made. Aesthetically and structurally, the ending of the *Ranjo* is lightweight compared with the comparatively heavy, and more imposing, dimensions of other parts of the composition. A and A' account for 31+23 = 54 beats; B and B', for 25+19 = 44 beats.

The cadential six beats of a, and even the ultimate 14 beats of a + a', are barely adequate to establish, and confirm, unequivocal modal supremacy in favour of the prime mode-key, at the conclusion of a modally ambivalent composition. Comments such as these – on the necessity of deploying adequate time, if an effective final return to the primary mode-key is to be made – are not carping criticisms. Were they so, an appraisal of this kind would be unwarranted. The *Ranjo* is otherwise skilfully crafted in detail. Its deficiency, if admitted, is one of proportional balance of time-blocks of the parts of the composition in relation to the time-span of the whole. The problem is one of craftsmanship and aesthetic judgement. The *Ranjo* is not a composition by a named composer; but folk and traditional musics are rich in anonymous melodies that prove that qualities of developed technique and refined musicality are a common property of mankind. Inspiration is commonly activated and elevated in communal creation that needs no composer's studio.

It has been said that the *Ranjo* operates on two modal levels. The reason for this view rests, broadly, on the form of the piece, and more particularly on its melodic ingredients: the formulae, or note patterns, and the scales contrived by the note patterns. A peculiarity of the *Ranjo* is that the A and B sections are identified in disparate groups of patterns; and yet the notes of both groups are contained in the *Gong*-scale, a Lydian-type octave-series on *d*. Each section is identified, therefore, through its own group of note patterns and the scale formation that underlies them. For this reason, the A and B sections cannot be subjected to comparative and continuing analysis since they have no material in common.

Example 2. Analysis of the *Ranjo,* sections A and B

Although prefatory notes to *Ryō-ō,* translated from the sources (Fascicle 5, pp.12-13), contain no direct statements naming the modal category of the *Ranjo* (or indeed of the Suite itself), Moronaga lists *Ryō-ō* first among *Sada-chō* items. This mode-key is a sub-group of the *Ichikotsu* mode, the sole mode of all music from the Tang court thus far studied, under the general title of this series.

Moronaga quotes, however, a statement by Owari no Hamanushi – who lived four centuries earlier, and is said to have visited China in 835 – that before *Amma* was adopted as retiring-music, the tradition had been to play the *Sada-chō* Modal Prelude (Fascicle 5, p.12) after *Ryō-ō* had been danced. Apart from this reference, the terms, *Sada-chō* and *Ichikotsu-chō*, are barely mentioned in the comments and notes that precede movements of the suite in tablature.

Analysis of Melodic Elements

In the light of the closely protected and precious traditions of *Tōgaku* in Japan, and Moronaga's painstaking efforts (in the twelfth century) to revise and restore Tang modal practices as he understood them – practices from which he must have believed the musicianly practice of the Chinese court to have strayed – it is proposed now to compare melodic passages of the *Ranjo* with similar passages from other items of the repertory, in the same mode-key. The purpose of the exercise is to determine whether the musical language of the *Ranjo* is at one with that of other compositions in the same mode-key group (*Ichikotsu-chō* and *Sada-chō*), reported to have reached Japan from Tang China. All written historical information about the musical nature of *Sada-chō* vis-à-vis *Ichikotsu-chō* is available in L.E.R.P.'s preliminary explanation of *Sada-chō* (Fascicle 4, p.8) and the translation of Moronaga's preface to such items in *SGYR* (Fascicle 5, p.xii).

To set up a viable comparative exercise, it has been assumed that versions of melodies classed in the same mode – or in a mode and a sub-category of that mode, though nominally in the same mode-key, but reflecting two scales, Lydian and Mixo-Lydian – have indeed a sentential correspondence harking back to homogeneous sources. In asserting his belief that items from the Tang court, classed by the Japanese in *Ichikotsu-chō* and *Sada-chō*, properly belonged to the Chinese *Gongdiao* scale, Moronaga was consistent throughout his two great compendia. If melodies composed of note patterns drawn from a Lydian note-set at a certain pitch are read as though from a Mixo-Lydian octave-set at the same pitch, they will then be effectively identifiable as the same basic materials, and belonging to the same modal genus. In the present context, this argument prevails, even though Moronaga was mistaken in imposing his theories on the contents of Japanese, historical, musical records.

The *Ranjo* cadence formulae

Except for the middle and end of the *Ranjo*, cadences are only implicit. In the absence of drum-beat markings in sources for this item (*COGRTYF*, Fascicle 5, p.12), all that tradition has to say about the structure of the *Ranjo* is: that it is in one Section (*JCYR*), that it was played several times consecutively (*JCYR*), and gained an additional eight beats the last time through (*COGRTYF*); transcription proves that the tablatures and binary-beat markings are similar in the four manuscripts (*CORYF* and *COGRTYF*). As the oldest extant version of the *Ranjo* (*COGRTYF*, *c*.1330) is centuries later than the first literary references to a *Ranjo* among movements of the *Ryō-ō* suite, or to a *Ranjo* in any other connection, Ōga-family musicians and copyists through the generations may have lost personal contact with an item no longer performed in the repertoire, and thus have recorded and copied it (with tablatures and accompanying information) as a part of family history due to be passed on with respect. The tablatures and transcription tend to support this view; the necessity for slight amendments when forming the conflation has earlier been explained (this volume, p.89). In the light of previous analysis (see p.91), the conflation adopted 56 beats in each half – that is, 112 beats repeating – and (finally) 120 beats in conclusion. Without loss of detail, each half is capable of sub-division into seven measures of eight beats each, with an extra measure added on the last time round.

Example 3. The *Ranjo* edited in eight-beat measures

From this slightly edited conflation, it can now be seen that the fourteen eight-beat measures function as fourteen sub-phrases, yielding a string of transitory cadences, in keeping with the preceding structural analysis of the *Ranjo* into A and B sections, with a transition, b, and two mode-final cadences a and a'. Since the conflation (Example 1) repeats the same notes on both sides of nearly half of the binary beat markers, it has been feasible and convenient – where the eighth beat of a sub-phrase or quasi-measure is the same as the first beat of the next – to regard that (eighth) beat as anticipating the next sub-phrase and to take the seventh beat of the eight as the probable cadence note. This does not compromise the guidelines by which to distinguish essential from non-essential notes, as explained in introductory comments to the conflated version (this volume, p.89). On this basis, cadence notes of the fifteen eight-beat sub-phrases of the *Ranjo* are tabled (in terms of the above) as follows:

Table 6. Ranjo: *cadence notes of edited version in eight-beat measures*

First half,   measures 1-7,
         section A: cadences on   *a, a, e, a*
         section B: "   *b, g♯, b*

Second half, measures 8-15,
         transition, b: cadence on   *f♯*
         section A':   cadences on   *a, d, a*
         section B':   "   *b, g♯*
         codetta, a: "   *d*   :‖

         coda, a':   cadence on   *d*   ‖

The two principal cadences at the ends of the major sections define themselves physically in time, rhythm and structural position, and hence are unmistakable. The mode-final cadence is a four-note pattern over six beats, first time, and a six-note pattern over eight beats, second time. Of the seven short passages (Example 4) culled from conflations of other items – all (except one) from Fascicle 5 – none is exactly the same as the *Ranjo* cadence formula on *d*. All have strong cadence rhythms, and occur where such cadence formations and rhythms emphasize their functions. The two measures from *Tori*, 'The Bird' (p.50), are note structures close to the *Ranjo* cadence (dominant to mode-final); the cadence from the Broaching comes halfway through its eight measures, while that from the Quick is the conclusion of the movement, and of the suite. The four examples, one from *Katen* 'The Palace of Congratulations' (p.38), two from *Ka-kyokushi*, 'Ka's Piece' (p.65) and one from *Ikinraku*, 'All Gold' (p.75) vary the *Ranjo* pattern, while retaining cadential rhythms and formulae at the ends of their phrases. The example from *Ōdai hajin-raku*, 'The Emperor destroys the Formations' (Fascicle 2, p.78), where the same notes occur without the same meaning, is an interesting instance of a pattern that appears to be something that it is not. It is merely the first measure of Section 3 of the Broaching, with no cadential effect in place, time or rhythm; and the principal note of all three binary beats is the sub-final, *c*.

Example 4. The first final cadence of the *Ranjo*, and seven like passages

Two further extracts are now offered for comparison (Example 5), both undoubtedly of Chinese origin; their resemblance to the *Ranjo* formulae is possibly more than coincidental. The two final cadences of the *Ranjo* are comparable, in that their last six beats are marked by the prominence of the same three notes, *a*, *e* and *d*; repetition of the cadences reinforces not the formula alone, but also finality, pattern and function. There are other pieces in the repertory which end with a double statement of cadence: the Entering Broaching, Stamping and Quick Tune (periods 15 and 16) of *Toraden*, 'The Whirl-Around' (Fascicle 3, pp.72-3); the Prelude of *Tori*, 'The Bird' (Fascicle 5, p.50); *Hokuteiraku*, 'The Northern Courtyard' (Fascicle 5, p.67); and yet another example, not to be overlooked: the conclusion of *Ōdai hajin-raku* (Fascicle 2, p.79). The four final drumbeat periods of Section 6 of the Broaching of this piece (periods 17-20) are very short, with a direction to be played 'very quickly'

184

(Fascicle 1, p.80). Rising over a long span to the mode-final in period 19, and through the same three notes as the *Ranjo* exemplifies, the cadence is then reformed (in period 20) in the classic *Gongdiao* cadence formula. Example 5 shows the two mode-final cadence formulae (of six and eight beats respectively) from the conflation of the *Ranjo*, superimposed on the last eighteen beats of the Broaching of *Ōdai hajin-raku*. Common elements will be noticed, as will the effect of the cadences in succession. In performance, the second *Ranjo*-cadence follows directly on the first, just as drumbeat period 20 of *Ōdai hajin-raku* follows, and emphasizes, the cadences of period 19.

The ending of the Prelude of *Shunnō-den*, 'The Singing of Spring Warblers' (Fascicle 3, pp.74-5) – a variant of the ending of *Ōdai hajin-raku* – provides a second comparative example. It follows the melodic line of the Broaching, but in a less dramatic style; in fact, the same two drumbeat periods close both halves of the *Shunnō-den* Prelude, in periods 7-8 and 15-16. The presence of the sub-final (in the last period of the Prelude) is a feature of the movement. Not only does the whole period move through *c* to cadence on *d*, but the passage comes round four times in the course of the piece (periods 6, 8, 14 and 16), thus emphasizing its importance in this suite, both structurally and aurally. Furthermore, the sub-final takes three cadences to itself, in a kind of interrupted version of the same formula, in periods 7, 11 and 15.

The last notes of the Broaching of *Ōdai hajin-raku* make a decisive conclusion of a different kind. As though calling up the greatness of the past, the imperial suite concludes with a precise classical gesture, the prototypical cadence formula of the primary pentatonic *Gongdiao* mode, a stronger form of statement than that adopted in *Shunnō-den*. The *Ranjo* cadence variants eschew tradition – assuming its authors knew, and esteemed, the great age of tradition – in favour of a less conventional expression of cadential and modal finality.

Example 5. Two further cadence passages compared with the *Ranjo*

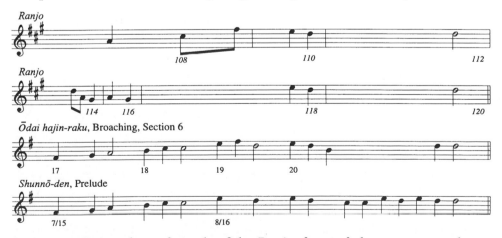

The intermediate cadence formula of the *Ranjo*, *f♯* - *g♯* - *b*, has not occurred elsewhere in the repertory, as a cadence on the sub-mediant, in the mode-key

185

on *d*. Furthermore, only one other movement in this mode-key calls on the sub-mediant for a median-cadence in a binary composition, namely: *Amma*, the final movement of *Ryō-ō*, which deserves examination independently from the one before us. [An introductory analysis of *Amma* is set out in the critical commentary on the suite (this Fascicle, p.122).] In some ways, the *Ranjo* is an oddity as compared with other repertory-items, and it warrants full attention *sui generis* at this stage.

It has been argued that the A sections of the *Ranjo* exist in normal terms of the *Gongdiao* (Lydian-type) scale in the mode-key on *d*, with principal notes relating to that mode-final; while the B sections function independently, in terms of a modal inversion on the sixth note (*Yu*) of the primary *Gongdiao* scale in the mode-key on *d*, the scale of the inversion being the *Banshediao/Banshiki-chō* (Dorian-type) scale in the mode-key on *b*, sub-mediant of the primary *Gongdiao* scale on *d*. In Tang theory the *Banshe* mode was an inversion of the *Gongdiao* scale, rising from the sub-mediant, which note became its final. The two modes function independently. Both are members of the Tang modal system centred on *Huangzhong*, in this case on *D*. On *Huangzhong* was raised a *Gong* pentatonic structure, which itself then generated modal inversions. *Banshe*, a modal inversion of the *Gong* scale, is thus directly related to the primary *Gong* mode, in so far as the notes of its scale are of the same order; but because they begin from a note other than *Gong*, the tonal perspective is individual. The order of notes in the *Gong* scale defines, and decrees, the parent scale from which other modes proceed; and in Tang practice they proceeded from *Shang*, *Jiao* and *Yu*, the second, third and sixth notes of the parent scale (Picken, 1969, iii, p.98).

Following the notion of a modal change a stage further, reference back to the numerical data of Table 3 – in which comparative figures from the *Ranjo* are tabled, in respect of the tonal contexts of the two sectional groups – will allow percentages to be deduced. These show that, in sections A, dominant and final provide 59 percent of the total, and *bian*-notes 3 percent of the total weight, as might be expected; whereas in B sections, *a* and *d* merit only 3 percent of the total weight, while *g♯* and *c♯* merit 51 percent – a complete reversal of the primary situation, due to the change in modal perspective effected by modal inversion. The A sections operate normally, while the B sections operate unilaterally, the strongest notes being *g♯* and *b*, sixth and final of the secondary scale. In the B sections of the *Ranjo* these merit 72 percent of the whole.

No other melody of the repertory in this mode has provided such a clear opportunity (as does the *Ranjo*) for introducing the possibility of extended modal practices in *Tōgaku* items. A single example proves nothing, however, save its own existence. What can be said with reference to the *Ranjo* intermediate cadence on *b* is: that interim sub-mediant cadence-forms, in other items in this mode, approach the cadence-note from the mode-final or mediant; and when from the mediant, the likely approach will be through the dominant: $f\sharp$ - a - b. The *Ranjo* cadence-form, however, is $f\sharp$ - $g\sharp$ - b. In all cadence-formulae, passing-notes may grace the melodic line; but their presence will not alter the basic approaches as here described. This case is different, however, in that, technically speaking, $g\sharp$ is not a passing-note. If the premiss of a secondary mode, or modal inversion, influencing the B sections of the *Ranjo* be sustained, and if the pattern of notes which forms a mode-final cadence in the secondary mode-key ($f\sharp$ - $g\sharp$ - b) be transposed to the primary mode-key on d, then the resulting succession of notes, leading to the primary mode-final (a - b - d) will be found in a number of pieces; for example: (1), in drumbeat period 13 of the Entering Broaching of *Toraden* (Fascicle 3, p.72); (2), in measure 9 of the Stamping of *Shunnō-den* (Fascicle 3, p.75); and (3), in measure 8 of the Way-Walking of *Katen*, and the Quick of *Tori* (the same piece) (Fascicle 5, pp.38 and 50). In addition, examples in various items in the same mode-key can be found, where the three notes: $f\sharp$ - $g\sharp$ (or g) - b, are sounded consecutively, but not in formal cadence-positions. If a cadence *is* imminent, b will often be a note leading to a cadence on d by way of c and/or e.

The two principal sections of the *Ranjo* contain different types of formulae. In Fascicles 2 and 3, where much was made of the tessellated or mosaic texture of *Tōgaku* melodies, the aim of analytical effort accompanying the conflations (Fascicle 2, pp.80-99; Fascicle 3, pp.77-90) was to examine evidence of the creative process, and to assess the skill and invention displayed in centonate methods of composition, in the latter half of the first millennium.

A useful means of illustrating the craft of Tang composers, and their imitators, has been to align tables of variant formulae. While retaining the continuity of each composition in horizontal staves, recurring patterns of note-groups are assembled vertically, like under like, showing their similar identities and degrees of variation, in continuous columns down the page. Applied to the *Ranjo* as a single composition, this method has shown itself to be suitably unambiguous in proving both the continuity of melody within each section, and the discontinuity of melody between sections (Example 2, p.180).

It is proposed now to adopt an aligned method to illustrate how non-cadential material of the *Ranjo* relates to that in other compositions, previously analysed. The intention is to see if the *Ranjo* is cast in the same language as they; and, if not, whether its differences can be put down to external influences during the time and process of transmission, or perhaps to an attempt to emulate Tang style by musicians inexperienced in the creation of Tang composition at first hand. It matters not whether the *Ranjo* is a movement by named or unnamed musicians, or a compacted creation of folk-culture. Our purpose is not to dismiss those who made the *Ranjo,* but to enquire after its origin and derivation.

187

The material of the A sections of the *Ranjo* is almost entirely drawn from the basic pentatonic scale on *d*; there is only one additional note (*c♯*) in the total of 60 beats (= A + A' + a), and it occurs twice: at the beginning of A', and again in the final cadence. It should, therefore, be easy to find other pentatonic passages that share formulae in terms of the basic scale. Two fragments from the Broaching of *Ōdai hajin-raku* – the most respected suite in Japanese, historical estimation – are shown compared with non-cadential passages from the *Ranjo* (Examples 6 and 7). For closer comparison, the two extracts superimpose the fuller texture of the *Ranjo* transcription (Fascicle 5, p.14) and the simpler conflated version (Example 1, p.172), above the Broaching excerpts transferred to the Lydian scale. The rhythms of the *Ranjo*-conflation are plain beside the decoration of the flute-playing, Ōga versions; but it can be seen that the conflation loses nothing in its simplicity, nor does the Broaching gain materially from appearing in the complementary scale. In addition, it will be remembered that the increased elaboration of *Tōgaku* melodies, as recorded in tablatures of the fourteenth century, imposed a much reduced tempo on the music, and that this imposition already sustained the solemnity and imperial dignity that became part of the ritual and aesthetic of music and dance in the Japanese court-tradition, as we know it today.

The first comparison, Example 6, aligns two versions of a *Ranjo* passage (from fourteenth century and later sources, Fascicle 5, p.14) with the first two measures of the conflation of Section 1 of the Broaching of *Ōdai hajin-raku* from late-twelfth and early-thirteenth century sources (Fascicle 1, p.65; conflation, Fascicle 2, p.77). The material of all versions shares a common pentatonic modality; but one version has retained spontaneous musicality, the others have not. Primarily it is the skeletal formula that is under discussion; at core this has not altered. What have altered are the style and tempi of the *Ranjo* versions; the nature of change over time is no part of the present exercise.

Example 6. From the *Ranjo*, Transcription and Conflation,
and from *Ōdai hajin-raku*: Broaching, Section 1

The second comparison, Example 7, drawing on Section 2 of the Broaching of *Ōdai hajin-raku*, is of different quality. The odd-numbered notes of the Broaching grace a phrase of melody that disguises the importance of the auxiliary notes supporting it: *c - c - a - d - g - a.*

Example 7. From the *Ranjo*, Transcription and Conflation,
and from *Ōdai hajin-raku*: Broaching, Section 1

A more surprising correlation is with the Entering Broaching of *Shunnō-den* (Example 8). Both A sections of the *Ranjo* can be laid out, in continuity, against almost all of the conflation of the Entering Broaching, measures 1-16 (Fascicle 3, p.76). The melodic formulae of both tunes are shared, the *Ranjo* drawing out the length of the composition in repetitions, while the Entering Broaching is purposeful, with regular phrasing and stronger rhythms. Although the A and A' sections of the *Ranjo* are variants of each other, they bear upon separate parts of the Entering Broaching. Section A shadows measures 3-4, 6-7 and 14-15 of *Shunnō-den*, while Section A' shadows measures 10-12. The comparative Example also shows both A and A' to be compatible with measures 3-8; that is, with most of the first half of the *Shunnō-den* movement.

Of the two movements, what there is of interest in the *Ranjo* lies in the second half's being a variant of the first half; sections A and B are varied as A' and B'. The Entering Broaching is also repetitive, but in detachable measures or phrases. Measures 11 and 12 are not-so-distant relatives of measures 3-4; and measures 13-16 are, indeed, measures 5-8. As a composition, the *Shunnō-den* movement gains over the *Ranjo* from its AB|CB form (the form of the *Ranjo* is AB|A'B'), and from the apt, yet modest appearance of auxiliary notes as passing-notes: the sub-dominant sounds only in the first quarter, in measures 2 and 4; and the sub-final sounds only in two measures of the third quarter, measures 9-10. Furthermore, the vigour of the disjunct B phrases of the Entering Broaching complements the less active lines of the A and C phrases.

Shunnō-den is a title recorded in lists of items known at the Tang court since the seventh century (Fascicle 2, pp.45-7). That it is a Chinese composition is

189

beyond doubt. The same cannot be said of the *Ranjo* as an introductory movement; nor is evidence of the Japanese method of performing a *Ranjo* to be found in any of the historical sources of Chinese music (Fascicle 5, pp.13 and 27).

Example 8. The A sections of the *Ranjo*, and the Entering Broaching of *Shunnō-den*

measures 13-16, as m. 5-8 above

The B sections and A sections of the *Ranjo* have no visible connections. Modality, scale and formulae all differ; and their independence is maintained in both halves of the composition. Whereas the primary A-related sections are founded on the standard five-note scale on *d*, the secondary B-related sections are

190

contained in a four-note scale: *f♯* - *g♯* - *b* - *c♯*, with concentration on the central interval, the minor third. In fact, reference to the weighted-scale data provided earlier (Table 5), shows that the notes *g♯* and *b* contribute 72 percent of the total weight of the B sections. The only relief from reiteration of these two notes comes in the form of a momentary textural ellipse, when each note, *b* and *g♯*, moves stepwise, and in contrary motion, to form a fifth: *c♯* and *f♯*, which immediately returns to its former position (Example 1, beats 40-44). It has been indicated that the secondary scale – if it be admitted as a self-determinant entity – resembles part of a *Yu*-mode structure on *b*. A description (put forward previously) was that, while remaining related to the basic mode-key on *d*, the B sections alter the modal perspective of the primary scale away from concentration on *d*, *f♯* and *a*, to focus attention on an opposing pitch-area, marked by strong use of *f♯*, *g♯* and *b*, 'opposing' (it is suggested), because of the unpredictability of the alteration, its non-triadic structure, and the extraordinary prominence accorded to *g♯* (one of the *bian*-notes of the primary mode-key). As if to confirm a tension of opposition within the total structure, the cadence on *b* makes a positive statement on its own behalf at the second most important place in the music, by closing the B section and the first half of the movement. After the return of B in B', opposition is temporarily abandoned when B' fails to reach a cadence, and is finally resolved by the surprise-announcement of not only *one*, but *two* consecutive cadences on the mode-final *ad ultimum*.

Finding passages from other items to compare with non-cadential formulae of the B sections was difficult. The patterns of the B-related sections are two, and they are alike. The close imitation of one pattern: *g♯* - *b* - *c♯*, chased by the other: *f♯* - *g♯* - *b*, gives the B section its peculiarity. Other *Tōgaku* items have not overtly displayed the proximity of two pentatonic scales consecutively active within each half of the one form. The *Ranjo* achieves this notoriety through its foundation on a Lydian-type *Gong*-scale, and on that scale's potential for generating further modes modelled from inversions of its pentatonic structure.

To make this comparison, eight fragments from six familiar repertory-items in their original mode-key, have been aligned, under a passage common to B sections of the *Ranjo* (Example 9). The Example quotes from *Tōgaku* movements in the *Shang* mode-key on *d*, which may be read (for the moment) with a signature of three sharps, as for a *Gongdiao*-scale in the same mode-key. Alternatively, the signature of the *Ranjo* can be reduced to one sharp for reading in the *Shangdiao* scale, also in the same mode-key. Whichever choice is made, reducing all examples to a common scale affects: (1) internal note-relationships; (2) modal perspectives; and (in particular) (3) the position of the tritone and its relevance to phrase-structure. Be that as it may, with the exception of the sample from the *Shunnō-den* Prelude – where all essential notes of the *Ranjo* B sections appear in the same order – the selected examples are not close to the singularity of the *Ranjo*. The musical ear may listen for connections; but resemblances are superficial, tenuous, elusive.

Example 9. From B sections of the *Ranjo*, and from six other movements

What appears to affect the modal complexion of these selections (Example 9) is not so much the appearance of similar, melodic profiles, but rather the relationship of their respective cadence-points to the operation of the scale in their immediate vicinity. The choice of a *Gong* or *Shang* scale has bearing on the matter; but this may be of less importance for musicians trying to hear the music as it was heard more than a thousand years ago. As transcriptions repeatedly show, Heian and early Kamakura musicians were hearing and playing these tunes in both scales, collectively and individually, according to their separate, isolated traditions, a practice still evident in *Tōgaku* performance today. The special point, germane to the *Ranjo* in the context of Example 9, is that the first B section is the only one that cadences on *b*. That note is the objective of the section, and the section is designed to achieve it. When the same passage returns for the second time, it is denied its cadence, and thereby is rendered less proficient. All other examples cadence elsewhere; consequently their pitch-elements move in relationships different from those of the *Ranjo*. They are fulfilling different functions in their individual expressions. The nine excerpts display visual likenesses; but physical attributes are not necessarily a basis on which to claim an association of creative and musical ideas.

Some determinant issues

The present study set out to investigate the nationality of the *Ranjo*, but the piece guards its secrets closely. Fascicle 5 includes a Table (p.11) that collates the historical sources of the movements of *Ryō-ō*; it includes references to the titles: Free Tune (*Ranjo*) and Free Prelude (*Ranjo*). All are Japanese writings from 1133 (*RMS*) to *c*.1330 (*CORYF*), and none records the piece as having either Tang connections or Japanese origins. It is known that a composition named *Ryō-ō* was danced at the first Eye-Opening Ceremony of the Great Temple, Tōdaiji, in Nara in 752, and that this item was a favourite of the Empress Kōken (Takano-Tennō), 749-758 [later Shōtoku Tennō, 764-70, daughter of the builder of great temples, the Emperor Shōmu, who reigned from 724-49]. What that performance in fact included, is not recorded. At the court of Japan, the eighth century was a period of immense admiration for China, when all things borrowed from there, tangible and intangible, were copied and cultivated; but that a *Ranjo*, or this *Ranjo*, was played at Nara in 752, in association with 'The Prince of the Grave-Mound', is not stated.

The earliest Japanese reference to a *Ranjo* / Free Prelude, in relation to this piece comes in *Nangu's Transverse Flute Score*, from which Moronaga quotes, in prefatory notes to *Ryō-ō* in *JCYR* (Fascicle 5, p.12). Although movements of *Ryō-ō*, including the Free Prelude, are named in the Flute Score, only tablatures of the Entering Broaching are provided in *JCYR*. Nangu is identified as Prince Sadayasu, whose now extinct manuscript was dated 921 (Fascicle 3, p.11). Absence of earlier reference to the movement in Japanese official records, strengthens the view that the *Ranjo* in question may have been composed, or introduced, some years later than the 752 Consecration Ceremony at the Great Tang Temple in Nara. A *Ranjo* was played, early on a day when *Ryō-ō* was performed in the evening, on the occasion of the reconsecration in 862, but, even then, there is no evidence that the piece was the present item under discussion or that it was linked with *Ryō-ō*. Nevertheless, the record of the *Tōdaiji-yōroku* confirms the existence of such a musical form in the ninth century.

The present technical analysis has revealed that, in some respects, the *Ranjo* fails to adhere to guidelines previously drawn from analysis of other *Tōgaku*

193

items in the same modal category (Fascicles 2-5 and this volume). Attention to the modal ambivalence of the *Ranjo* does not, necessarily, preclude the possibility of an item straying beyond the traditional confines of its modal class; but none, so far as clinical tests have discovered, displays the sectional plan of AB|A'B' as its basic form, with sections A and B systematically adhering to differently structured groups of notes from the same heptatonic scale. Several notes overlap both sections of the *Ranjo*; but they are subject to different relationships and structural functions in each sectional context. How, and to what extent, the two sections differ, has been pointed out. The separate sets of note-patterns share no melodic formulae; and the individual sections are formally incomplete when detached from each other. Neither A nor A' section closes with a conventional cadence; and, until the end, only the first B section displays a formal end-of-section cadence, albeit on the sub-mediant – an eccentric choice for a halfway point in an *Ichikotsu* or *Sada* composition. To restore the mode-final in conclusion, a cadence from the primary scale has been tacked on to the incomplete B' section – as though in the nick of time – just as the sub-mediant cadence was coming round for the second time.

In the absence of a written theory of mode and modal composition, either in China or in Japan, in the first millennium, it is not possible to define directly what is convention, and what invention, when it comes to musical style and structure in the creative cultural context. Music at the Tang court was undoubtedly flexible and functional. Acquired from various sources, at home and abroad, it was a class of music accepted and approved by an educated, ruling society that governed the cities and towns of the most brilliant monarchy of the medieval world. It was a popular music, of diverse ethnic origins, a music that included song tunes and dance tunes from many parts of the Asian continent and its southern peninsula. Of pieces borrowed from China and collected by the Japanese up to about 839, there are no definitive or correct versions, nor do the words 'correct version' or 'original version' have meaning in the study of Tang music *per se*. Without contemporary tablatures, and reliable information relevant to composed or 'made' music of the period under discussion, no absolute standard of critical opinion, drawn from history, enables us to determine with confidence whether any one piece is *typically* representative of a particular style, region, or tradition.

The number and variety of tunes recorded in Japan, and accounts of music-making in Heian literature, indicate that the music of the Heian capital was popular, social and versatile, and that the repertory borrowed from the Western mainland was a highly regarded portion of it. Presumably a performance was 'correct' according to how well musicians played, sang or danced it, according to traditions protected and taught by specialists. No *Urtext* of a court composition in the hand of a named Tang musician exists. The complete accuracy and exact representation required of performers, were learned by rote; judgement was not exercised in objective terms. But, fortunately, all is not in vain. Compositions transcribed in this series form a corpus of music from the earliest extant manuscripts in tablature; it is from these that much information has been drawn. In the case of the *Ranjo*, evidence gained from comparative methods has established that, alongside other items investigated and analysed in this series, the *Ranjo* differs in its modal practice, and in structures determined by that practice.

Cadence patterns aside, comparison of *Tōgaku* melodies with the *Ranjo* has yielded interesting results. Excerpts from the Broaching of *Ōdai hajin-raku* and sections of the *Ranjo* are evidence for the existence of a musical language, received and imitated by music-makers, when the *Tōgaku* repertory was established in Japan. (It must be remembered at all times that extant manuscripts of the pieces before us are Japanese.) The likeness between some of the fragments chosen is easy to see. Their similarity might even suggest that the *Ranjo* was consciously devised from instrumental versions of passages from the Broaching – and perhaps it was! Let it be said, however: the *Tōgaku* repertory contains countless passages based on notes of the fundamental pentatonic scale on *d*; tunes of this category are, in essence, founded on the same seven-note scale, all grounded on one and the same note. The argument might then be advanced that the corpus of *Tōgaku* music is a collection of variations on variations: variations (as it were) without a theme, since a scale is not in itself a theme.

Perhaps the real theme is intangible, no more than the fertile imaginings of Tang musicians and their imitators, drawing on the same contemporary styles and experiences to make music to their own satisfaction, for their own needs and in their own ways. Common sense precludes further pursuit of that argument. Compositions brought to life by the Cambridge scholars include numerous examples of the creative manipulation of simple materials in terms of the Tang modal system and its social culture; yet a good number of pieces in the repertory evince both individuality and character. Of these melodies, one (of which the origin is not in doubt) is *Gyokuju goteika* 'A Jade Tree's Rear-Court Blossom' (Fascicle 3, pp.1-19). Example 10 places the first (and last) two measures of this piece (conflation, Fascicle 5, p.35) over six binary beats from the A section of the *Ranjo* transcription.

Example 10. Measures 1-2 and 13-14 of *Gyokuju goteika*,
and beats 19-29 of the *Ranjo*

On the basis of ordered pentatonicism alone, one resists claiming a common
origin for the two pieces, or that the two passages could have come from
different parts of one composition. What assumes striking proportions, however,
is the likeness of the A sections of the *Ranjo* to the Entering Broaching of
Shunnō-den (Example 8). In fact, the formulaic vocabulary of the A sections of
the *Ranjo* appears to have been formed, in the main, from memories of *Ōdai
hajin-raku*, *Shunnō-den* and *Gyokuju goteika* (Examples 4, 5, 6, 7, 8 and 10).

If the A sections of the *Ranjo* might be regarded as Tang compositions, the
B sections are less readily so regarded. Admittedly, Example 9 is a random
collection of samples, arbitrarily clipped from a miscellaneous selection of tunes;
but whereas comparison of the A sections with a collection of samples needed no
defence, the underlying fragments in Example 9 require calculated argument to
make a case for regarding them as variants both of each other, and of the B
sections of the *Ranjo*. Nevertheless it would be hasty, at this stage, to deny
acceptance of the formulae of the B sections in the musical language of *Tōgaku*.
Whether the change of modal perspective indispensable to the B sections exists
in other *Sada-chō* items has yet to be determined. The *Sada-chō* class awaits
careful attention; as yet, not enough is known of its modality and musical
language. It is certain, however, that tunes from Kuchā introduced local ethnic
styles and practices to the Tang and hence to the Japanese capitals.

With reference to items recorded in Tang repertory lists, are there other
characteristics of the *Ranjo* that deserve comment? In this study, one constantly
hopes for, and at times gains, insights into technical and stylistic mannerisms that
may one day lead to confident differentiation of *Tōgaku* items composed in Tang
from those coming from foreign regions, items listed and known to have been
performed in the entertainment repertoire; the latter would include such as were
imported from tributary states and beyond by itinerant traders, or returning
armies. The music of Tang was exotic, multi-racial, and valued for its variety,
colour and exuberance. A proportion of what was accepted and performed at the
Tang court was not created in Tang, however, even though adapted there to
Tang-Chinese current taste. With a time-gap of nearly four hundred years from
the early Sui to the end of Tang – whence the earliest, surviving Japanese

tablatures descend to us – it is not possible now to define indigenous modes and styles, the roots of which lie deep in the past. About these matters, historical texts are virtually silent.

What reassures is the fact that surviving accounts of the first three, great *Tōgaku* suites (*Taikyoku*), and the circumstances of their origin, leave no room for doubt that these are original creations by Tang musicians, one suite of which was amended by imperial command, and at least one movement of another was composed by command of the Emperor himself. These works, *Ōdai hajin-raku*, *Toraden* and *Shunnō-den* (Fascicles 1 and 2), are valuable compositions in that they may be regarded as authentic specimens of Tang musical styles, and therefore capable of comparison with the (most probably) later *Ranjo*, with its unconventional modality and historically obscure background, confined to Japan.

The melodic texture of the *Ranjo* now merits brief comment, beyond technical observations made earlier. Outside the field of structural analysis is the intrinsic style of the melody, spread over 112 beats. It is constructed from very little in the way of material; the formulae are few and much repeated. A condensed version of the melody can be devised that retains its structural features and tunefulness, while restraining formulae from sprawling beyond their own little idiosyncratic note-cells. Prolongation of melody by repetitions and added notes is evident in the conflations of most *Tōgaku* tunes.

The filling-out of mosaic patterns into melodies that consist of many more beats than the fundamental patterns from which they stem, is a trait of *Tōgaku* style which has been evident since the first analytical studies of *Ōdai hajin-raku* were made (Fascicle 2, pp.80-99). By way of illustration, a typical example, showing how a musical sentence of eighteen beats' duration may be generated from minimal material, is period 7 of the Prelude of that suite (Example 11). Only four notes of the scale occur in the entire drumbeat period from the first note (the mode-final) to the cadence, two degrees lower. Such treatment of insignificant note-sets is so common in this repertory as to be essential – to greater or lesser extent – to the very existence of Tang melody and musical composition, while the whole is contained within the heptatonic scale of a closed modal system.

Example 11. Drumbeat Period 7 of the Prelude of *Ōdai hajin-raku*, with reduction in three stages

The *Ranjo* exhibits similar periphrases which, if removed without destroying the essential line and direction of the melody, reduce it to less than half its present length. The first half of the conflation of the *Ranjo* consists of 56 beats; limited to its primary elements it consists of 24 beats only (Example 12). The remainder of the *Ranjo* can be similarly condensed, and yet retain continuity and tunefulness.

Example 12. The first half of the *Ranjo* reduced from 56 beats to 24 beats

(beats 1-16)   (17-31)   (32-56)

The intention of this reduction is not to signal that the *Ranjo* is inflated, tautological or vainly repetitious, but to make two points. The first is this: that many versions of *Tōgaku* items as we have them are confined within a comparatively small pitch area, even though the melody is protracted in time. In context, this trait is a constant element of *Tōgaku* style as we know it, even though such passages may at times appear prolix. In practice, however, the measurement of beats in binary groups, in regularly barred systems, invariably imposes systematic, rhythmic organization – a certain discipline – on a drawn-out musical line, that would otherwise tend to ramble. Even in unmeasured movements, the binary principle is paramount in melody as music. Not only is binary grouping essential, but its rhythmic swing (of alternate strong and weak beats) underpins the pulse and constitution of music as an intelligible experience.

The second point is, then: to recognize how few are the formulae comprised within the *Ranjo*. Is this due to poverty of musical invention on the part of 'composers' of the *Ranjo*? Or is it due to a deliberate economy of material, and a conscious organization in the generation of a movement with contrasting sections, with binary form acting to hold them together?

The comparative analyses of sections A and B (Example 2, p.180) have demonstrated simplicity and paucity of material, a high degree of reliance on repetition, and clear sectional independence. Example 12 illustrated further that section A consists, in effect, of only two or three patterns, and section B of only two, the second being a modal transposition of the first. Contrary to earlier statements about the incompatibility of formulae in sections A and B, it can now be shown that the material of section B is embedded, transposed, in section A. Example 13 places the transposed version of the B section of the reduced conflation (from Example 12) beneath the reduced conflation of section A. We see the six notes germane to both sections.

Example 13. *Ranjō* in modal transposition; when reduced, B is agreeable to A

A reduced

B reduced, and transposed down 2 semitones

Does this coincidence prove poverty of invention, then; or does it demonstrate skilful organization and economical use of materials? It would be temerarious to venture an opinion. What it proves is the capacity of a people to make music in terms of a musical language adopted and cultivated in their own environment; the capacity of a people who were competent to imitate, and to make their own tuneful pieces for the purposes of ritual, amusement and any other function. The description recognizes an achievement admissible to Japanese court ceremonial, and acceptable by contemporary standards of the elite. The inclusion of the *Ranjo* in the suite, 'The Prince of Luoling', shows that the Japanese regarded it as worthy of an important place in the court-music repertoire, even though there is no trace of it in Tang or subsequent Chinese historical records.

Summary Review

This essay has limited itself to a technical examination of the *Ranjo*, the purpose of which was to discover whether evidence of its nationality, or origin, would thereby be disclosed; or, failing that, whether evidence from the musical language of the *Ranjo* might declare it as *not* of, or from, Tang, but of a calibre that might include it in that Japanese division of the traditional court music known as *Tōgaku*: Tang music, that is, Chinese music, or at least foreign music with (in Japanese eyes) some Chinese connection. The enquiry has concentrated almost entirely on the physical form and structure of the music; style has been considered only where circumstantial evidence overlapped technicalities of style and structure, or where the one may have influenced the other.

Detailed dissection of a *Tōgaku* suite had never been undertaken at such length before *Music from the Tang Court* published an analysis of *Ōdai hajin-raku* in 1985 (Fascicle 2, pp.80-99); nor has any enquiry hitherto concentrated so closely on a single movement from a suite, solely on the basis of modal behaviour and physical construction, as has this examination of the *Ranjo*.

Since there is no contemporary theoretical, didactic, or even descriptive, account of musical composition in Tang China, the only path open to us has been to relate the piece to other pieces of its court music category, in the hope that familial (or other) group traits would emerge, on comparison with representative members of its class.

The history of this *Ranjo*, and its listing in the *Tōgaku* repertory, is purely Japanese. The division of court items into 'new' and 'old' is also a Japanese classification (see Volume 7, Chapter 3 – in preparation). Since the *Ranjo* is listed in one source as 'New Music' (*RSCY*, *c*.1261), and in another as 'Old Music' (*KF/HSF/RK*, 1201), that area of enquiry need not be pursued here; the more so, since neither of these sources includes scores of the *Ranjo* in tablature. The silence of Chinese sources does not absolutely preclude the possibility of a Chinese origin, or at least connection; but Japanese records, too, omit mention of the *Ranjo* in relation to Tang China.

Not until the twelfth century is this piece mentioned in a musical source, as part of 'The Prince of Luoling'. Towards the end of the Heian period, some 40 years after the completion of *RMS*, Moronaga (in *JCYR*) cited the respected *Transverse-Flute Score* (921) of Nangū – Prince Sadayasu – as source for a tradition that, in earlier times, the Free Prelude (rather than *Amma*) had been played as retiring music. Both Sadayasu and Moronaga direct, however, that the Free Prelude be played as the initial movement of the suite. From Prince Sadayasu's statement it is certain that the *Ranjo* was not only known, but was part of the repertory, by the beginning of the tenth century (see also p.199).

The musical language of the *Ranjo* reflects matters of style and structure. Comparison of *Ranjo* sections with passages from a number of *Tōgaku* items has shown melodic resemblances, in some cases quite remarkably close. Of selections aligned in the comparative examples, one is continually impressed by the presence of excerpts from the fully authenticated Tang suites: *Ōdai hajin-raku* and *Shunnō-den*, works known to have been favoured by emperors of China and Japan. Supreme in their time and genre, they were music-and-dance entertainments of wide cultural interest and of high social regard, and their reputations are attested by descriptions in Tang records, repeated and extended in Japan for centuries after the decline of the Tang. Compositions of imperial approbation and public acclaim capture the imaginations of nations and creative musicians as long as fame and reputation last. Such spectacles as these must have lent themselves to re-creation and imitation as long as their prestige, and their popular tonal system, prevailed. In Japan, they lingered throughout the Heian period and beyond.

Only on circumstantial evidence (such as this) can the origin of the *Ranjo* be investigated. Whether truly 'Chinese' or not, the *Ranjo* displays stylistic similarities with elements of a musical language, to be identified (in various degrees) with that of authenticated creations from the Tang repertory. It also includes elements that have not been recognized previously in *Tōgaku* items. Admitting that not enough is known of the individuality of *Sada-chō*, evidence has been produced that formulae in both A and B sections may be traced to the general *Ichikotsu-chō* vocabulary (Examples 5-9). A curious anomaly, however, is the not unimportant transition from section B to section A'; and the first of the two mode-final cadences (beats 106-12) is yet stranger in this context, with its complete dominant triad immediately preceding the mode-final. It has also been shown that formulaic repetitions and periphrases are stylistically and structurally important to the *Ranjo*, as they are to the longest movement in one Section in the Tang repertory so far examined – the Prelude in *Ōdai hajin-raku* – and indeed to sundry shorter pieces.

Concluding Comments

Of the similarities and dissimilarities between the *Ranjo* and items with which it has been compared, the dissimilarities carry more weight, when it comes to making an objective rationalization of the evidence here submitted. In the A sections, similarities concern formulae and texture: elements of a creative language and style which are common property in a well-established musical medium. Composed from an unwritten vocabulary of modal bits and pieces – a mental thesaurus of note patterns susceptible of spontaneous repetition, variation and adaptation – Tang and neo-Tang court music in Japan, like other traditional arts, both serious and popular, was fashioned on models and memory experiences generated and multiplied in various forms and guises. The particularity of an isolated example, such as the *Ranjo*, is better sought through its disparities in the light of commonalities of its kind. From that position, the conspicuous modal instability of the *Ranjo* can be described as 'inelegant and eccentric', in terms of our current knowledge of *Yanyue* – the Banquet-Music tradition. Such criticism is justifiable in terms of the Tang tradition, but would have been lost on contemporary Japanese musicians of the Heian, of limited skill in the nature amd aesthetics of Tang musical art.

The anatomy of the *Ranjo* composition suggests that its composer(s) were by no means unskilled. The handling of the moment of change of modal perspective, when the B sections are introduced or withdrawn, is economical and systematic; the change is declared, without hesitation, precisely where the A section gives way to the B section (or *vice versa*) in each half of the melody; moreover, the manner of change is consistent. The nexus of the two phrases is *a* -

g♯ (beats 31-2 and 87-8) advancing, and *g♯* - *a* (beats 59-61 and 106-7) returning, the latter return being taken promptly, so as to arrest further progress, and to finish the piece on time. Craftsmanship of this order may be the result of consciously trained skill, or of musicality unwittingly exercising a natural impulse; but among other tunes of this genre currently analysed, this kind of method is unlikely to have been wilfully contrived. It is more advanced, indeed abnormally so, than anything hitherto disclosed by other items of the repertory.

In contrast to the 'advanced', tectonic features of the *Ranjo*, reservation can be expressed over the prosaic formalism of the sections; formulae are few and conventionally repetitive. The calibre of invention reflects limited experience in the centonate construction of Tang language, and immaturity in marshalling formulae into individualized melodic strains.

The Question Answered

Being dismembered, the irregular structural organization of the *Ranjo* predicates it as possibly a very late or post-Tang composition; but taken in conjunction with its modal inconsistency, and narrow selection and treatment of musical language patterns, it is more likely to be a composition assembled by, and for, non-Chinese musicians, in imitation of the admired continental style, so far as they understood it. If the latter view is accepted, the non-Chinese musicians can reasonably be presumed to be Japanese. They, it was, who alone *listed this composition, otherwise of unknown or unacknowledged ancestry,* in the esteemed category of *Tōgaku*; they, it was, who alone *preserved the notation for posterity* in their honoured and precious national archives; who placed it *first of all movements* in the heroic suite: *Ryō-ō*, which includes one genuine Tang composition and several pretenders (apart from the *Ranjo*); they, it was, and the Japanese were not alone in this, who *aspired to Tang imperial dignity, reputation and culture*, including court music and entertainment; and they it was who, in all human aspiration and achievement, aimed to rival the glorious Tang.

The *Ranjo* is cast in a language that resembles the musical language of Tang. Its use of that language departs radically from that of Tang models, both in formal design and in consequent structural implications. This may be due to inexperience and insufficient appreciation of the traditional style and craft of the borrowed repertory. Furthermore, it is clear that the prominence of the *Ranjo* (in 'The Prince of Luoling') as the first of four, disparate movements – only the Entering Broaching being authentically Tang – confirms the character of the suite as a pastiche of materials from various sources, and in several styles. The only historical records and tablatures of the suite as a whole are those of Japan, and we may now accept that it was there assembled, and performed, in the form disclosed in Fascicle 5. On grounds of technical and stylistic analysis, as well as that of its very late appearance in Japanese sources, one may, with reasonable confidence, regard the *Ranjo* as a Japanese composition.

202

Appendix 3

A Weighted-Scale Procedure in Analysis of *Tōgaku* Compositions (N.J.N.)

Technical commentaries in *Music from the Tang Court* have frequently employed a weighted-scale method of analysis as a means of obtaining information about the physical condition of *Tōgaku* tunes. It has proved useful for surfacing technical data from which to observe structural details, modal characteristics and tonal perspectives in the language of Tang musicians and their imitators. Heretofore little has been known of the practical modality and structural design of court-music items of 'Chinese' origin located in Japan. With the aid of a simple arithmetical exercise, information capable of rational interpretation and assessment can be extracted from the music for systematic study.

An approach to understanding the workings of non-Western music, through an examination of numerical information, is not new. Early in this century Otto Abraham and Erich von Hornbostel (1903-4) warned about the transference of European musical concepts, with all their psychological significance, to the study of non-European traditions. The passage is worth citing, not only because it was an early attempt to recognize problems of concept and terminology, when European musicology was first confronted with the discovery of music outside its accepted, circumstantial condition, but also because field-workers have sometimes overstressed the phenomenon of each non-European culture being a unique expression of its own creation. Such opinions are valid indeed, so long as they are not blind to the fact that the irrepressible imagination of musical man is disposed to discover for itself, and intuitively adopt, practices similar to those of the European experience, regardless of time, place and circumstance, and notwithstanding their separate and unconnected tonal systems.

On the transference of conceptual terms from familiar European contexts to note-systems of foreign cultures, Abraham and Hornbostel (1903-4, pp.383-4) had this to say: 'In their psychological significance, the concepts of major and minor, tonic and dominant, familiar to European musicians, are still such controversial problems that their transfer to the music of foreign peoples should only be attempted with the greatest care. Accordingly we intend, in general, to recognize as "tonic" the melodic centre of gravity, that is to say: that note of a melody which is characterised by frequency of occurrence, duration, accent and position. Correspondingly, we designate as "dominants" those notes to which falls a special melodic emphasis next to that of the tonic.' (*trans.* L.E.R.P.)

*(Die den europäischen Musikern geläufigen Begriffe 'Dur und Moll',
'Tonika', 'Dominante' sind in ihrer psychologischen Bedeutung noch so
umstrittene Probleme, dass ihre Übertragung auf die Musik fremder Völker nur
mit grösster Vorsicht versucht werden darf. Wir wollen deshalb als Tonika ganz*

allgemein den melodischen Schwerpunkt, d.h. denjenigen Ton einer Melodie verstehen, der durch Frequenz, Dauer, Akzent und Stellung ausgezeichnet ist. Mit 'Dominanten' bezeichnen wir entsprechend diejenigen Töne, denen neben der Tonika ein besonderes melodisches Übergewicht zukommt.)

Several years later Hornbostel (1905-6, p.93) made a further statement: 'Yet considerations of a general kind lead to the assumption that every monophonic melody, or melodic phrase, also has its centre of gravity, that is to say, a note distinguished from others by frequency, duration, position, dynamic accent, or in some other way, and with which all notes of the melody are then connected.' (*trans.* L.E.R.P.)

(Doch legen Erwägungen allgemeiner Art die Annahme nahe, dass auch jede einstimmige Melodie oder melodische Phrase ihren Schwerpunkt hat, d.h. einen Ton, der sich vor den übrigen durch Frequenz, Dauer, Stellung, dynamischen Akzent oder sonstwie auszeichnet und auf den dann alle Melodietöne bezogen werden.)

In both essays the authors are speaking in general terms, without particular examples or applied demonstrations in the immediate text.

Later scholars have occasionally presented data along similar lines, thereby establishing the 'weight' of a particular note of a composition, and hence the 'weights' of the several notes of a tune in relation to each other. Investigating the traits of tonality in the oral traditions of Pueblo Indian groups of America, George Herzog (1928, p.192) found that the range of most Yuman songs fell between the interval of the fifth and the tenth. 'As a rule one of the tones can be established as "tonic" on the ground that it carries the most melodic weight… Tones next in importance…in general…appear above the tonic, seldom below …[and] a fourth or a fifth of the tonic usually gains melodic weight.'

Still later, among methods of describing musical style in analytical studies of non-Western music, Bruno Nettl (1964, p.146) advises students: 'Scale and mode are usually presented on a staff, with the frequencies of the tones indicated by note values – a practice started by Hornbostel. The tonic is usually given by a whole note, other important tones are indicated by half notes, tones of average importance by quarters, rarely used or ornamental tones by eighths and sixteenths.'

In the analysis of *Tōgaku* items it has been possible to apply weighted-scale practices more precisely and consistently, and they have been valuable in the process of enquiry and investigation. Although the melodies of the repertory often differ in form, structure and temperament, it has been found that they have much in common in musical language and modal behaviour. Comparative examination of the same kind of statistical data, according to the weighted-scale practices of the current series, has tended to highlight both similarities and dissimilarities between pieces. In addition, it has enabled objective assessment of groups of tunes, and tunes in isolation, to be made regarding matters of modal practice and musical language.

Though capable of flexibility according to the chosen musical specimen and the particular direction of an enquiry, the applied method of data-search has been consistent throughout analytical studies of this series. Collected and assembled data, in tabular form, summarize statistical information that represents the three most prominent physical attributes of all pieces of music of this genre: time-durations of each note of the scale sounding in a chosen passage or movement, the common unit being the quarter-note in the current context; occurrences of each note of a piece, regardless of time-durations; and in extended passages, numbers of times each note acts as the initial and final of a drum-beat period or phrase, or of measures in a regularly barred melody. The columns of entries under each note of the scale are then added up to provide totals that represent the specific contributions of individual notes to the musicality and organization of the selected specimen.

The method of collecting data from items for investigation is thus summarized:
1. The pitch names of the notes of the scale of a composition are placed in order across the page.
2. Under the name of each note is set the total duration of musical time it occupies in the selected material. The complete horizontal line of figures amounts to the total number of beats in the selection.
3. Beneath (2) is set out the total number of times each note is sounded in the passage, regardless of time-durations. The complete line of figures amounts to the total number of written notes in the selection.
4. Beneath (3) is set the number of times each note sounds as the first and last of a standard phrase, drum-beat period, or measure of time. This complete line of figures amounts to the total number of initial and final notes in the principal sub-divisions of the selection.
5. Each vertical column of figures is then added up. The individual sums represent each note's aural and physical contribution to the musicality and condition of the section, or piece, in question. This final line of totals accrued by each note will equal the sum of the three sub-totals of stages 2, 3 and 4. The checking and matching of horizontal and vertical totals is a necessary test of accuracy throughout the operation. From this point onwards, analysis and assessment of the facts gained from the weighted-scale application may proceed.

To illustrate a practical application as addressed here, reference is made to 'The Eddying Bowl', *Kaibairaku/Huibeiyue*, of which the one extant movement, the Broaching, is transcribed in Fascicle 3 (pp.49-50), from which a conflated version was made for analysis in Fascicle 5 (p.55). The conflated version is provided here in the scale of the mouth-organ transcription.

Example 1. Conflation: 'The Eddying Bowl'

Sets of figures tabled below represent the five entries collected from the conflation, totals showing the individual weights of each note of the scale of the melody, and of the notes in their linear entries.

Table 1. Numerical data drawn from Example 1, assembled and aligned

	a	*b*	*d*	*e*	*f♯*	*g*		
1. Notes of the scale								
2. Total durations of each note in unit beats	11	5	19	8	12.5	8.5	=	64
3. Total occurrences independent of note values	11	5	13	8	13	9	=	59
4. Initial and final notes of each measure	2	–	4	3	2	5	=	16
5. Totals	24	10	36	19	27.5	22.5	=	139

It is now possible to direct attention to note-relationships and tonal perspectives in the composition, and to consider its organisation and structure with respect to mode and musical language. Analysis can be carried further by dividing the melody into halves and quarters to examine modal trends and tonal pressures, phrase by phrase.

The exercise involved in acquiring the numerical data is not difficult, and the information can be useful to those interested in what makes the music sound as it does: what the relationships of the notes to each other are, which are the stronger and weaker notes in so far as they bear on the language and syntax of the medium and its aural impression, how the scale is manipulated in the voluntary creative process, how the nature of the end-result is influenced by musical and modal procedures, and what the procedures happen to be within the prescribed, musical time-span. There is also wide scope for further comparative exercise, comparing the results of weighted-scale procedures applied to several whole compositions, parts of different compositions, and parts of the one composition. Assessment can be refined by reducing data to percentages. From these, perspectives relative to degrees of difference can be appreciated in terms of modality and structural organization – degrees of difference, for instance, between elements of sections within a single piece, and between sections of several pieces. [In this volume, readers will note that percentages do not sum to a hundred at times, because of rounding-off.]

Besides being a practical utility for exposing individualities and idiosyncrasies of particular melodies, it is within the scope of weighted-scale usage – at best only a first step in the direction of analytical exercise – to uncover aspects of *similarity* between tunes in the language of Tang entertainment music.

Analytical tasks looming ahead, while searching for keys to the musical secrets of Tang, include a systematic classification of melody types in this genre; and beyond that lies a more formidable charge to differentiate traits of an authentic Chinese musical personality from unidentified foreign elements which, over centuries of transmission and assimilation from the West, impressed themselves on the Tang / *Tōgaku* style and repertory we know today.

Now let us return to 'The Eddying Bowl', *Kaibairaku*, and the numerical data tabled above, and approach it through the weighted-scales in which its general tonal elements are stated in non-tonal terms. Information surfaces immediately from the table of figures. The commanding position of the mode-final is evident. The final, third and fifth of the scale are shown to be the framework of the melody, although triadic formation, as such, impresses it only slightly. The third above the final is particularly strong, while the third below is weak. The super-final, 'the minister closest to the sovereign' in the theoretical hierarchy of notes of the historical *Gong* pentatonic scale, is only fifth (of the six notes) in numerical order of precedence; and the fourth of the scale (the traditional auxiliary of the dominant) scores very heavily, nearly matching its principal. Relative properties of the individual notes of the piece have been exposed by applying a structured weighting-system on a scale basis, thus disclosing that the basic scale of 'The Eddying Bowl' is closer to a diatonic pentachord than to the standard anhemitonic pentatonic-species.

In the context of a *Tōgaku* item in the *Ichikotsu* mode, transcribed from various sources, and conflated from them with deference to the mouth-organ tradition, the seventh note would undoubtedly be $c\natural$, if used, and the scale, a Mixo-Lydian octave-species in the mode-key on *d*. Observations on the manipulation of the scale of *Kaibairaku* address two descriptions, but neither is entirely satisfactory or technically complete. Elements of two modal precedents are evident, both of which relate to the basic *Gong* pentatonic scale: 123.56 of the Western major scale, while escaping from its rigid confines.

The first account is a palpable one, that the piece is, or was originally, in the primary *Gong* mode in the mode-key on *d*. Fujiwara no Moronaga was convinced that the heptatonic *Gong* scale, the Lydian octave-species, was the authentic scale of the *Ichikotsu* mode; and all tablatures of his string versions of *Tōgaku* items in this mode adopt the Lydian octave-species on *d*, with its auxiliaries, *g♯* and *c♯*. Mouth-organ sources differ, however; they are the unofficial, but long established, preserve of the influential Toyohara clan. The scale of the conflation is that of the mouth-organ tablatures, with *g♮*, and without calling for a seventh note, *c*. The scale of the *Gong* pentatonic mode-key on *d* is the theoretical frame of *Kaibairaku*; but, as the weighted-scale figures point out, the weak sixth and the very strong natural fourth are not quite apt for an exemplar of standard *Gong* modality. Nonetheless, the Japanese accept 'The Eddying Bowl', and other pieces like it, in the category of *Ichikotsu-chō* without question; and this has been so since the music entered the country.

A second description of the modality of this item may seem more plausible. With the distribution of weight to the notes, *d* - *e* - *g* - *a*, being as strong as it is, and those notes taking 73 percent of the total weight of all notes, a case might be argued in favour of the scale in question being an inversion of the primary *Gong* scale on *c*, the Lydian octave-species on that note. If applied in this case, the hexatonic inversion operates from the second note of the primary scale, forming what becomes a Mixo-Lydian octave-set on *d*. The suggestion is feasible; *d* rightly becomes the final of the modal inversion and of the mode-key, while the original *Gong* pentatonic structure remains by inversion, *d* - *e* - *g* - *a* - *c*, and the original *bian*-notes, *f♯* and *b*, remain auxiliary to the primary dominant and mode-final, although *g* and *c* are no longer dominant and final of the inverted scale. The move of the mode-final, from *c* to *d*, is thus one of modal inversion, not transposition. As it happens, the primary mode-final, *c*, is absent from the melody, and the first *bian*-note of the primary scale, *f♯*, is excessively weighty for an acceptable role of an auxiliary note, so weighty, in fact, as to reverse the expected dependence of *f♯* on *g*, rendering, in this context, *g* dependent on *f♯* – its consequent at all times except one (in the first measure).

Analytical exercises such as these go part of the way towards an appreciation and understanding of the real music. At the heart of the matter, theoretically, is the fact that the true *Gong* scale, by virtue of the sharpened fourth, contains two, standard, pentatonic structures, on both its *gong* and *shang* notes; and when making and arranging the music for court use, the Tang musical imagination – if this tune is indeed of Tang – appears unwittingly to have taken advantage of the flexibility and freedom this afforded.

Application of a weighted-scale procedure has revealed information about *Kaibairaku* which previously may have been felt, but not precisely known. It has also encouraged penetration below the surface of the music. Having used the exercise for an introductory investigation, one is inclined to ask how, and why, the melody and scale function as they do. The enquiry can be pursued further.

The two equal parts of 'The Eddying Bowl' invite an independent check of the data for each half of the melody. By the same process as before, the notes of measures 1-4 and measures 5-8 produce the following separate weighted-scale tables:

Table 2. Weighted-scales of the separate halves of the melody

		a	*b*	*d*	*e*	*f♯*	*g*		
Measures	1-4	18	4	12	10	14.5	11.5	=	70
"	5-8	6	6	24	9	13	11	=	69

From these figures it is clear that the melody reveals a conflict. Put simply, there is a power struggle between the dominant and the mode-final, other notes remaining fairly evenly balanced in both phrases. Putting it more specifically, the dominant holds 26 percent of the total power of all notes of the first phrase – power derived from the durations of the notes, their occurrences, and roles in important positions – while the mode-final, even with the advantage of the cadence, holds only 17 percent of the same. Compare their relative weights and percentages in the first phrase with their positions in the second phrase.

In measures 5-8, the dominant has heavily reduced its weight to 9 percent of the total, whereas the final, with the same cadence formula as measure 4, has doubled its weight to 35 percent. Since more than half of each phrase (beats 13-32 in the first, and beats 45-64 in the second) is the same, the most interesting parts of the melody for closest scrutiny will be the remaining ones, in which the individual roles of the two principal notes can be examined. What is being described here is the result of the organizational and musical skills of 'composers' at work, albeit at an intuitive level (though one cannot be entirely sure of that), and thus of musicians activated, nonetheless, in creative exercise. Turning to figures once more, the numerical data for beats 1-12 and 33-44 are these:

Table 3. Weighted-scale of the first twelve beats of each half of the melody

	a	*b*	*d*	*e*	*f♯*	*g*	
Beats 1 - 12	14	2	3	3	3.5	3.5	= 29
" 33 - 44	2	4	15	2	2	3	= 28

Although four notes of the scale are of similar weight in both halves of the melody, the dominant and mode-final contrast widely. In beats 1-12 (Table 3), the dominant almost equals the sum of all other notes; in beats 33-44, however, the final exceeds the sum of all other notes, and it is during these beats that a transfer of power from dominant to final is made. In beats 1-12, percentages of dominant and final are 43 to 10 in favour of the dominant, but percentages change radically in beats 33-44: 7 to 54 in favour of the mode-final. These findings, therefore, focus attention on measures 1 and 5, beats 1-8 and 33-41, and then on the discovery that each measure is a modal transposition of the other; in the hexatonic scale, measure 1 reads: *a - a - f♯ - g - a - a - gf♯ - e*, while measure 5 reads: *d - d - a - b - d - d - b - d*.

The weighted-scale process has the capability of affording a fuller understanding and appreciation of the melody as music in terms of its own cultural period, and of gauging its natural craftsmanship and skill as known and practised by musicians in Tang times.

Select Bibliography

Abraham, O. and Hornbostel, E.M. (1903-4) 'Phonographierte indische Melodien', *Sammelbände der Internationalen Musikgesellschaft* 5, pp.348-401, Leipzig

Herzog, George (1928) 'The Yuman Musical Style', *Journal of American Folklore* 41, pp.183-231

Hornbostel, E.M. (1905-6) 'Die Probleme der vergleichenden Musikwissenschaft', *Zeitschrift der Internationalen Musikgesellschaft,* 7(3), pp.85-97, Leipzig

Nettl, Bruno (1964) *Theory and Method of Ethnomusicology*, London

Appendix 4

Ōdai hajin-raku: Flute Scores Compared (*RTHKF* 1287 & *KCF* 1095? – Fascicle 3, p.53, L.E.R.P.; Justified Conflation, Fascicle 2, pp.76-9, N.J.N.)

The flute version of 'The Emperor Destroys the Formations' from the *Ryūteki hikyoku-fu (RTHKF)* 龍 笛 必 曲 譜 of 1287

The interest of this score arises both from its history and from what the tablature reveals. As to the first, this is the only dated manuscript in flute tablature from the thirteenth century so far encountered. The colophon (see p.231) makes plain that it is the 'secret version' of the Ōga clan. Nevertheless, it was written by a high-ranking member of the Fujiwara clan: Fujiwara no Nagamasa, and the colophon to the tablature is a holograph, since it concludes with his *kaō* (written seal). Even more remarkable, perhaps, is the fact that the entire manuscript is authenticated by Uzumasa no Hironuki in a final colophon (p.232). In the course of time, therefore, pieces in the flute tradition of the Kyōto *kata* (to which the Ōga clan belonged) have reached the Tennōji *kata*, to which the great families of the Uzumasa: Sono, Hayashi, Tōgi, Ōka, belonged and in some instances still belong.

Who Fujiwara no Nagamasa was remains uncertain. In the entire compilation of genealogical tables of the *Keizu sanyō* 系 圖 纂 要, only two Fujiwara of this name occur. The more likely of the two candidates, judging by dates of close relatives (the entry in the table is undated) is a member of the Hamuro 葉 室 family, second son of Fujiwara no Akitomo (顯 朝). His rank, however, is given as First Grade, Lower Fifth, rather than First Grade, Second Rank (as in the colophon); but his Governorships of Mikawa (Tenth Province) and Kai (Thirteenth Province) (Tōkaidō), and of Tamba (Thirty-sixth Province) (Sanindō), are recorded. His mother was a daughter of the *Chūnagon* Sadataka. The date of his birth or death is not given. His father, Akitomo, died in *Bunei* 3 (1266); and his elder brother, in *Kōan* 5 (1282), so he himself might well have been active in that decade. [The other Nagamasa was the third son (no date) of Fujiwara no Shigenaga (重 長) (First Grade, Lower Fourth Rank), whose eldest brother, Kiyonaga (清 長), died in *Kempō* 2 (1214). The dates of the latter would seem to make it improbable that it was this Nagamasa who added his *kaō* to a manuscript in 1287.]

As to what the tablature of *RTHKF* reveals as a musical document: first, it is gratifying to observe that, like the *Kaichūfu* (*KCF*) version (Fascicle 3, p.56), the correspondence in essential musical line between this and the conflation by N.J.N. (Fascicle 2, p.76) is close. The conflation is evidently an adequate approximation to the tradition, as it existed in the late-twelfth century, and as transmitted to the end of the thirteenth century. Secondly, the version of *RTHKF* is somewhat more decorated than that in *KCF*; it includes more mordents (由),

more frequent appoggiaturas, and repeated semiquavers following an appoggiatura (here interpreted as overblowing to the octave). A sequence of alternating 'delayed' and 'immediate' mordents [as described by Marett (1977, pp.10-12)] occurs in *Section* 1 of the Broaching (measure 10), and what may be a new sign appears on the first note of certain binary units: *sui/tui* 推, in Chinese 'to push', 'to expel', perhaps a *sforzato*. (In Japanese also, *suiryoku* 推 力 means 'thrust', 'driving power'.) This instruction: 推, occurs only in Sections 1 - 4 of the Broaching – a point of interest in relation to doubts regarding the homogeneity of this movement (Fascicle 1, p.77).

In accordance with the stated late-thirteenth century date, the version of the Broaching of *Ōdai hajin-raku* in this score is marked for performance in the syncopated, binary, rhythmic mode: *Gakubyōshi* (see R.F.W., Fascicle 4, Appendix 4, pp.117-33). Pursuant to our practice of transcribing so as to reflect, as closely as possible, the simplest *Tang* condition – bearing in mind that R.F.W. has argued that these rhythmic-modal variants were part of *Tang* practice, since the Chinese scribe, writing *SSSTF*, evidently had no difficulty in 'pointing' the mouth-organ score for *Gakubyōshi* or *Tadabyōshi* reading) – the Broaching is here transcribed in the simple, binary mode. In transcribing, (omitted) intra-columnary dots were accepted as evidence of binary units, whether single or multiple (3 x 2 and 4 x 2). In the manuscript both Prelude and the two final Sections of the Broaching are in places pointed (by the insertion of *hiku/yin* 引) so as to facilitate reading in the *Tadabyōshi*, ternary, rhythmic mode (see R.F.W., *ibid*.). The sharp rhythmic distinction between Sections 5 and 6, and Sections 1-4, is again of interest in view of the suggestion that the Broaching may have come into existence by combining Sections that did not, originally, belong together. These notational features are not shown in the transcription, where the three versions are set out in approximate vertical alignment; indeed, restrictions imposed by computer origination have led to the omission of all annotations in Sino-Japanese.

New notational features in this manuscript are these:

1. The appearance of three types of mordent: 由 り 由; 由 り ; 由 りり as well as single 由. The significance of these is not known.
2. Where *KCF* shows an appoggiatura *c* to the conflation's *b*, *RTHKF* adds a reduplication sign to the *b*. Following a suggestion made by A.J.M., this has been transcribed as a broken octave in semiquavers/sixteenth-notes.
3. A striking feature is the existence of two sizes of tablature signs for flute pitches. (This phenomenon had already been noted in the *KCF* manuscript.) Comparison between the 1287-stave and that of the Conflation shows the reader, already in the first system, that appoggiaturas to (or échappées, or passing-notes from) notes in the conflation, are frequently being written with

smaller note heads. These match small-written flute pitch-signs in the original. Differentiation in note-head size is shown throughout the Processional, and in the Prelude to the end of the Half-Section (*hanjō*) mark, but in the Broaching is discontinued after Section 1 because of manual difficulties in writing, and uncertainty in distinguishing 'large' and 'small' sizes of pitch signs.

4. Many written-out examples of the ornament *ren/lian* are to be seen, as in the two upper staves of the first system of the *Processional*. These remove uncertainty regarding the meaning of Hakuga's explanation of the sign: 'move the finger(s)'. In the original of 1287, mention may be made of occasional ligatures (in red in the original) that pass through intracolumnary dots, in all Sections of the Broaching. These ligatures relate to *gakubyōshi* performance.

5. In view of the somewhat greater degree of decoration of the *RTHKF* version, as compared with that of *KCF*, caution is clearly necessary in deciding whether or not the latter is (as has been suggested) a fourteenth- rather than an eleventh-century product. It will clearly be of interest to see, at some stage, what the *COGRTF* version (Fascicle 3, p.9) has to offer.

Prefaces to the movements of the suite (*RTHKF*)
'Processional: one Section'
游 聲 一 帖

'Prelude: Of the Section, beats 30.'
序　帖 拍 子 三 十

'Broaching: Of the six Sections, beats of each, 20. New music.'
破 六 帖 拍 子 各 二 十　新 樂

Processional

Prelude

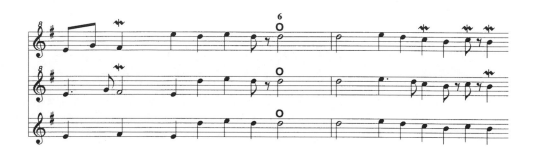

Chūhanjō

219

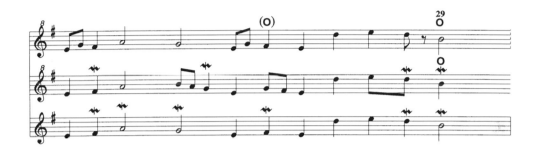

Broaching

Section 1

Section 2 (Drumbeat signs, differentiation of note-heads and mordent-signs omitted from here onwards)

223

Section 3

225

Section 4

Section 5

229

Section 6

[It will surely be conceded that the primary musical substance of this suite, as displayed in the conflation prepared by N.J.N. in 1985, based on the earliest surviving Sino-Japanese scores in tablature for mouth-organ, zither and lute (*Music from the Tang Court*, Fascicle 1, 1981), survives unchanged in the scores in flute tablature of 1095 (?) and 1297.]

Colophon to *Ōdai hajin-raku* in RTHKF

'The piece to the right [that is, preceding], the secret version of the Ōga [clan], no portion of the Sections being withheld, was imparted, and is presented.'
右 曲 以 大 神 之 秘 説 帖 之 無 所 殘 授 進 上

RECORDS of the EASTERN PALACE
Tenth year of Kōan [1287], Eighth Month, Thirtieth Day, First Grade, Second Rank, Fujiwara, Diligent Diviner [*Shintō*], Nagamasa (*kaō*)

東 宮 記

弘 安 十 年 八 月 三 十 日 正
二 位 藤 原 孜 卜 長 雅 (花 押)

Colophon to *RTHKF*

'The Dragon-Flute Score item to the right is an item copied by command by the State-Ministerial authentic brush of Fujiwara Ason Nagamasa, First Grade, Second Rank.'

右 龍 笛 譜 者 正 二 位 藤 原 朝 臣 長 雅。卿 筆 令 書 寫 者 也

From the period of the Second Year (*otsuchū*) of Jōkyō [1685], Ninth Month, Eighteenth Day, Uzumasa Hironuki (*kaō*)

于 時 貞 享 二 乙 丑 年 九 月 十 八 日 大 秦 廣 貫 (花 押)

[In preparing this transcription much information present in the original has of necessity been omitted because of difficulties in combining origination of the musical text with Sino-Japanese lexigraphs of various kinds. Features hitherto marked in transcription – such as beat-dots, binary-unit markers, signs for ornaments, marking of pace changes in the first four sections of the Broaching, etc. – have all been omitted.]

Appendix 5
Interrelationships between Tang Chinese Compositions; Three Items with Titles
in the Names of Imperial Military Leaders (N.J.N.)

From time to time, analysis of *Tōgaku* compositions has revealed degrees of
shared identity between movements of a suite, and between single tunes of
different title, as though such items are variants of each other. Bearing in mind
that analysis of the music published in this series has never been attempted
before, the first discovery of recognizable similarity, between movements of a
Large Suite, was made during analysis of the very first *Tōgaku* composition
submitted to detailed scrutiny: *Ōdai hajin-raku / Huang-di pozhen-yue*, 'The
Emperor Destroys the Formations' (transcriptions, Fascicle 1; conflation and
analysis, Fascicle 2, pp.80-99).

To begin with, the Prelude showed itself to be structurally repetitive in that
many phrases recur frequently, most notably in the first part of the movement –
the first twenty drumbeat periods in its original Chinese form (see a comparative
Table, Fascicle 2, pp.88-9). Next, the Processional proved to be a sizeable
component of the Prelude; and then, in the Broaching (a movement in six
consecutive Sections), a comparative line-up of Sections (pp.92-3) showed
repetitions of many note patterns and their variants, and repetitions of strings of
note patterns, in some instances repeating in the same place in successive
Sections.

Aware (as we were) that frequent repetition of fragments of melodic
material was likely to prove a technical and musical characteristic of *Tōgaku*
style, it soon became evident: that apart from specific repetitions that impressed
the ear as well as the eye, each movement is made up of small groups of notes of
no fixed number; that these groups appear at random in varied rhythms, both
extended and reduced in length; and that such snippets are also to be found, in
various shapes and guises, in the Prelude and Broaching. An early discovery was
that cadence formations are formal and repetitive, and that the same (and variant)
formulae are present, non-cadentially, in the continuous flow of melody.

Further penetration and study disclosed that the texture of the entire suite is
a patchwork of bits and pieces, formulae strung together, the whole composition
subject to time-honoured modal theory, and to the binary principle with its
consequent rhythmical and melodic disposition. By this means, fragmentary note
patterns from the simple heptatonic vocabulary merge quite naturally in the
musical mind to establish their own compatibility and continuity, the while
(perhaps unwittingly) stimulated by memories and impressions of familiar tunes
and styles, and thus led instinctively to form patterns into phrases, into sentences
and sections that, put together, become movements and whole compositions. In
just such a manner, *Ōdai hajin-raku* may have been created by Tang musicians

steeped in their own cultural heritage, and, at the same time, excited by the novelty of all the contemporary exotic cultures streaming into the capital, particularly from the West.

Tōgaku qualifies as a prime example of a traditional music made by performers after existing models to accompany ceremonies, rituals, festivals, feasts, games, pageants, dancing, singing and the many forms of social entertainment. In historical records of this repertory, names of performers are often mentioned: players and dancers of long-standing repute; but of composers in the Western sense of the term, only rarely is a musician mentioned in that capacity (Fascicle 2, p.45).

Experience gained from working on *Ōdai hajin-raku* proved a salutary preparation for what was to follow. Fascicle 2 brought forward two more Large Suites: *Toraden/Tuanluanxuan*, 'The Whirl-Around', and *Shunnō-den/Chunying-zhuan*, 'The Singing of Spring Warblers' (both are analysed in Fascicle 3, pp.77-90). *Toraden* includes a Prelude in three Sections, and three other movements; while *Shunnō-den* consists of six movements, each of a single Section. Analysis of these suites brought surprises beyond expectation.

Like *Ōdai hajin-raku*, both of these suites include measured and unmeasured stretches of melody in strict time; and conspicuous note patterns prove to be primary materials of melodic construction. Formulae shared between the movements of *Toraden* are unmistakable at the beginnings and endings of movements, and of Sections of movements. Sequences of internal cadence notes, and their determinant cadence forms, are similar through large portions of the movements.

With this much information to hand, it was not difficult to see that, in fact, the three Sections of the *Toraden* Prelude reflect each other with only minor discrepancies (Fascicle 3, pp.78-9). Laying aside the fact that the fourth and sixth movements of *Toraden* are the same, it was not anticipated that the Stamping would mirror them closely – as it does (pp.80-1). The greatest surprise, however, was that *all* movements of *Toraden*, notwithstanding their contrasting styles, resemble each other to a degree beyond coincidence (pp.82-6). Sections of the Prelude are variants of each other, while the following, more concise and compact movements are also related; yet disparity between the movements is marked and sustained.

In the full comparative Table of *Toraden* (pp.82-6), the part-measured and part-unmeasured Prelude (in three Sections) spreads its time leisurely; and from the same Table it can be seen that the third drumbeat periods of two Sections of the Prelude are just finishing at the point where the Entering Broaching, Stamping and Quick Tune (repetition of the Entering Broaching) are completing their first halves at their eighth measures. In fact, their ninth measures finish at the point where the First Section of the Prelude completes its fourth drumbeat period. Ramifications of major differences in length and timing have not been pursued further, but they suggest that the creation of one movement from another was not just a matter of facile imitation, but depended, in some instances, on a process of careful calculation.

Shunnō-den is in six movements, though prefatory notes in the music scores are not unanimous on the matter (Fascicle 2, pp.49-51). What the Prefaces make clear is: the order of movements in performance; that several movements are repeated later in the sequence; and that the whole suite concludes with the Modal Prelude as accompaniment for the dancers retiring from the dance terrace. The movements transcribed in Fascicle 2 are Processional, Prelude, Stamping, Entering Broaching, Bird Tune and Quick Tune. Since the Processional is the latter part of the Prelude (cf. Ōdai hajin-raku), and the Quick Tune is the same as the Entering Broaching (cf. Toraden), four movements remain as integral parts of the suite. Analysis has shown that three of these are variant forms of each other, and that the Bird Tune is to be identified with formulae employed in the first halves of preceding movements (Fascicle 3, pp.87-90).

Possibly the Bird Tune was inspired by the Bush Warbler, the characteristic song of which is marked by reiterations of notes and trills such as are present in the transcribed Bird Tune of Shunnō-den (Fascicle 2, pp.67-71). Tradition tells that when Gaozong, third Emperor of Tang, heard the songs of Bush Warblers at dawn, he commanded a musician to copy them into a piece of music. Imitation of this kind was not beyond the capacity of Tang musicians to capture in musical terms. [L.E.R.P. has pointed out several other tunes in which bird-song may be represented in melody, namely: the Quick of Tori/Niao, 'The Bird' (Fascicle 3, p.30), and 'Bird(s) of the Qin River' Shingachō/Qinhe niao (this Volume, p.55).]

Similarity between movements of a suite is well illustrated in Toraden and Shunnō-den, and comparison of formulaic passages has also been made between many single items, following through this series. The suite of two correlated movements, Koinju/Hu yin jiu, 'Sogdians Drinking Wine' (Fascicle 4, pp.1-9; analysis, Fascicle 5, pp.57-64), belongs in this context, since the two movements of Koinju are analogous – or expressed more accurately, the unmeasured Prelude apes the Broaching from which it must have been made, the Broaching certainly being the older tune, in the popular style of the Quick of Katen/Hedian, 'The Palace of Congratulations', and Sukoshi/Jiu Huzi, 'The Wine Puppet' (conflations, Fascicle 5, p.38 and p.90).

Two further examples of complementary pairs of tunes should be named in this context, because one of each pair is known to the Tōgaku repertory, the other (of the same pair) to the Saibara repertory of Court song (perhaps deriving originally from pack-horse drivers' songs). Each pair consists of versions of a single tune (see conflations in Fascicle 5, pp.61-4, and pp.103-6). The melodies themselves may have been borrowed from the court repertory for a class of popular songs in the style of the court tradition; or it may have been the other way round: because of established popularity, the court may have acquired them for its own entertainment. These two *Tōgaku* tunes were certainly foreign pieces enjoyed in the Tang capital, perhaps introduced by troops returning from distant campaigns, or by dance troupes from foreign climes, travellers along the Silk Road, or itinerant merchants and traders from the West.

Of the two *Tōgaku* items, one is the Broaching of *Koinju*, 'Sogdians Drinking Wine'; the other is *Suseishi/Jiu qing zi*, 'The Wine is Clear' (conflations, Fascicle 4, p.58 and p.93). On circumstantial evidence, the Broaching of *Koinju* is likely to have been embraced by the Tang, probably introduced there from the West, and thus classed by the Japanese as *Tōgaku*. The other item, *Suseishi*, 'The Wine is Clear', is not mentioned in Chinese records, but in three of the Japanese primary sources-in-tablature (two of which are Moronaga's compilations, *JCYR* and *SGYR*), it too is classed as *Tōgaku*.

Both tunes are also to be found in Moronaga's *Saibara* collections (*JCYR* and *SGYR*), where they appear in the *Ryo* mode-key on *G* (Markham, 1983). Their *Tōgaku* titles are *Koinju-no-Ha* and *Suseishi*, while their respective *Saibara* titles are *Tanaka no Ido*, 'At the Well in the Field', and *Mayutojime* 'Mayutojime' (Markham, vol.1, pp.208,207). Possible connections of *Mayutojime* with another item (in Japanese court-music collections) were increased by Hirade's disclosure (Fascicle 4, p.115) that the *Komagaku* item, *Kansuiraku*, 'Merrily Drunk' (Fascicle 5, pp.103-6), was associated with the *Mayutojime* song text; but this connection lies beyond the field of the present study.

The matter of appropriation and adaptation of *Tōgaku* items bears on all that follows in this essay. The nature of the musical language of the Tang lends itself to constant, kaleidoscopic change – indeed, this tractability is its subliminal method of survival; but whatever the notes and rhythms of the note-patterns and their sundry textures and impressions, the elements remain the same, constructed as they are within traditional melodic shapes and forms. All Tang court music so far examined is constructed in two primary scale-formations (pentatonic and heptatonic) and their modal inversions; and Han modal theory was still taught and generally attested (so far as we can tell) in Tang times.

Nevertheless, from about the middle of the first millennium, national imperialism and prosperity – political, economic and cultural – initiated and expanded many liberal changes in Tang society; such changes were irresistible in the onrush of exciting, exotic cultures and fashions overtly displayed in novel and daring styles of music and dance, and in other spectacular entertainments. With imperial approval and popular acclaim, extravagant, extrovert policies and practices swept the nation in the wake of great military prowess and imperial prestige. By the time Japan began to receive items from the *Tōgaku* repertory –

not later than the sixth or seventh century – cultural achievement and sophistication in China were reaching extraordinary heights of exuberance, imagination and skill – qualities that matched in good measure the styles and tastes of the exotic, multi-racial population of the capital, Chang'an.

The range of variety within the closed, Chinese modal system is declared by numberless surviving compositions: some contained in the pentatonic scale, others calling on auxiliary *bian*-notes, almost as equals to The Five. Some items show distinctive musicality; others link patterns into conventional compositions in simple binary forms. In cultural and social environments, where music is one of several arts in combination, musicality and craftsmanship complement each other. The ingenuity of the musical mind is inexhaustible, creating and re-creating music from familiar materials for every purpose and occasion. Is it then surprising that tunes, or parts of tunes, associated with extra-musical events, persons and circumstances – such as public acclamation of heroic military leaders, imperial magnificence, restoration of peace, the beauty of nature, and euphoria induced by wine, for instance – sometimes sound stylistically and musically alike? When one recalls the fixed scale formations and limited tonal resource of musicians of those days, one marvels that more tunes are not reminiscent of others.

In essence, tone-material available to the Tang was indeed limited: phrases were often short, beginnings and endings had modal obligations, forms were simple, and cadences were identified in distinctive rhythms and formulae. Originality in traditional music was neither cultivated nor expected. The concept of the recognized composer, as distinct from the scholar professed in the philosophy and theory of music, was not formed in the first millennium. So far as is known, there was no organized creation and dissemination of music; learning was by rote, and appointments for musicians were limited to those providing for imperial and temple rituals and ceremonies, royal and public entertainments, and teaching within established systems of education. The music itself was a common property of those who made and played it, albeit formal composition and ownership was often loyally attributed to the emperor. It was the court, the government, that directed the political and social roles of music throughout the realm. The variety and quality of Tang court music, as we know that music today, is its own testament to the musicality and ingenuity of musicians and composers of that time.

Having reached this point, it is now proposed to turn to 'Four *Tōgaku* Compositions', the titles of which convoke reputations and achievements of national leaders, including those heroic and victorious in war. The primary purpose of this enquiry is not concerned with persons, but with determining whether ideas and images addressed in a small set of related music titles – in this case, titles of compositions in honour of kings and emperors and the like, compositions that evoke qualities attributed to, or assumed, by such persons – are composed from similar musical materials, or even perhaps owe their origins to a single piece, of which others are descendants or kindred versions. Whether the compositions express ideas and images of strong leadership, fearless heroism and extraordinary courage, is not the question. What is attempted is, once more, an excursion into the nature of the musical language of the Tang, as evidenced in items of the *Tōgaku* repertory, in order to determine whether like titles imply like music, whether such pieces have relative musical identities, or (possibly) are of the same musical parentage.

Ōdai hajin-raku/Huang-di pozhen-yue, 'The Emperor Destroys the Formations'

Ōdai hajin-raku (Fascicle 1; conflation Fascicle 2, pp.76-9), the musical origin of which is not specifically recorded, is a prime, monumental composition of the category outlined above. It is now believed to honour the elevation to the Imperium of the Third Tang emperor, Gaozong, in 649, before whom a performance of a 'Destroying Formations' piece was given in that year. Current critical opinion tends to date Chinese references to earliest performances of compositions named 'Destroying-Formations-Music' not later than the seventh century. The title: *Pozhen-yue*, appears a number of times during the Tang, although the histories usually fail to clarify to which of several *Pozhen-yue* their various accounts refer. It has not been possible to settle, beyond doubt, which of those historical compositions, if any, is the Large Suite in Fascicle 1 which, one has always to remember, is transcribed there from Japanese sources of the late-twelfth and thirteenth centuries – all Chinese scores having disappeared in the wake of the Tang decline. On balance, the piece made for Gaozong appears the most probable claimant. To the Japanese this suite was undoubtedly the most esteemed, and hence the most important item in the court repertory of Heian times. It was placed first in Japanese listings of the *Tōgaku* repertory, both in the mouth-organ tradition of the Toyohara family, and in the comprehensive compendia of music for plucked stringed instruments by Fujiwara no Moronaga.

So far as extant Chinese and Japanese records provide, examination of the music and history of this item justifies its position and prestige in the supreme honorifics of the two Chinese characters of the title: *Huang-di / Ō-dai* (皇 帝), these characters being alone appropriate to the highest imperial dignity, but absent from all Chinese references to the title: *Pozhen-yue*. In addition, the dimensions and formal design of the two principal movements of the suite far exceed those of other *Tōgaku* pieces in the mode-key on *D*. Nevertheless, it is certain that the Japanese knew at least two *Pozhen-yue/Hajin-raku* compositions, and performed at least parts of them at the Eye-Opening Ceremony of the Great Buddha Temple, Tōdaiji, at Nara in 752. The Shōsō-in treasury in Nara, where Tang treasures from the eighth century are stored, includes items of dance costume worn at this ceremony, with identifying inscriptions: *Hajin-raku* and *Ōdai hajin-raku* on their respective items.

Being the greatly admired composition that it was – a spectacular dance-entertainment, appropriate to the splendour and opulence of the Tang court – one might suppose that *Huang-di pozhen-yue / Ōdai hajin-raku* would be the kind of composition likely to be a prototype of adaptations and parodies, with similar titles and features, and with elements of common phraseology, or variants thereof. So far, however, analytical scrutiny of the Suite (Fascicle 2, pp.80-99), and later comparison of its constituent materials, structures and forms with other items in the repertory, has not shown this line of thought (as applied to *Ōdai hajin-raku*) to be particularly productive.

Formulaic elements of tonal language are never absent from music of this genre; but communication through music and speech requires more than a common vocabulary of minimal sonic elements. With words, it is the choice and assembly of phonemes, and their logical assimilation in grammatical syntax, that make a word-complex intelligible in communication. Similarly, in this musical tradition, it is the ordered sequence of compatible formulae moving through time that makes phrases and sections of music capable of perception, recognition and useful comparison. Comparison of *Ōdai hajin-raku* with other *Tōgaku* compositions has not as yet produced convincing evidence that it is a prototype, or musical relative, of other *Tōgaku* items associated in name with princes and emperors.

Continuing the enquiry to determine whether equivalent titles imply similar tuneful expression, in part or in whole, there are three compositions (four movements in all) to be considered as a selected group of items within range of this study. Putting *Ōdai hajin-raku* aside for more thorough, future investigation, these are: (1) *Shinnō hajin-raku/Qinwang pozhenyue*, 'The Prince of Qin Destroys the Formations', in the *Taishiki*-mode (a *Shang*-mode scale – a Mixo-Lydian-type octave-series – on *E*), historical exposition of which item will come with complete transcriptions in a later volume; (2) the Entering Broaching of *Ryō-ō / Luoling wang*, 'The Prince of Luoling' (Fascicle 5, pp.1-33; conflation, this Volume, p.114), in the *Sada*-mode, a Lydian-type octave series, the *Gong*-mode scale on *D*; and (3) *Shin Raryō-ō/Xin Lanling wang*, 'A New "Prince of Lanling (= Luoling)" ' (this Volume, exposition and analysis, pp.126-37) in two movements, Broaching and Quick, also in the *Sada*-mode and in the same key.

Shinnō hajin-raku / Qinwang pozhenyue is one of the *Pozhen-yue / Hajin-raku* compositions ('Destroying-Formations' pieces) mentioned above. It honours the Prince of Qin, by which title the illustrious Second Emperor of Tang, Taizong (reigned 627-49), was known before ascending the throne. Identification of the monarch in this piece (of which only one movement is known) is now assured from historical and textual research; and the date of first performance is likely to have been 627, the year of enthronement. The Prince of Luoling of the *Ryō-ō* title (in origin the Chinese Prince of Lanling, see Fascicle 5), is known to have been a pre-Tang princeling in the Northern Qi dynasty (550-577).

'A New "Prince of Lanling" ' might be a later version of 'The Prince of Lanling/Luoling', or a later composition to honour the same or another monarch. This study will help to clarify these points.

Shinnō hajin-raku / *Qinwang pozhenyue,* 'The Prince of Qin Destroys the Formations'

Primary versions of *Shinnō hajin-raku* are four in number: three from the standard sources for this series (the piece is absent from *SSSTF*), and an earlier version from *Gogen-kinfu* (*GGKF*)/*Wuxian pu* (*WXP),* now judged to be of the eleventh century. This latter *MS* for five-stringed, bass lute is a collection of Modal Preludes and repertory items (Wolpert 1981, pp.107-35). Since materials in *GGKF* may precede *SGYR* (c.1171) by a couple of centuries or more (being themselves older than the *GGKF* manuscript), a slightly reduced version of the *SGYR* transcription (L.E.R.P.) has been made, without embellishments, for comparison with *GGKF*; both versions belong to *Taishiki-chō* on E.

Comparison with the five-stringed lute version of *GGKF* (in its tenth- or eleventh-century manuscript condition – R.F.W.) provides an illuminating illustration of the vagary of change sometimes undergone by a melody in the course of transmission through time; but there are no grounds for regarding the earlier manuscript version as an intermediate step towards the later one. The earlier written version might be expected to be nearer to an undiscovered original of some sort; but it cannot be so described in this instance. The two versions surely adumbrate separate lines of independent, unilateral transmissions (Example 1, p.242).

Distance in time between the two sources may have some bearing on their disparity; but the degree of difference is more likely to result from different time-scales affecting the transmission of written material: one version (*GGKF*) privately protected from wide exposure; the other (*SGYR*) orally transmitted through generations of performers. The first method is in the nature of a historical record made in tablatures owned, and retained, as someone's personal possession, whereas the second method may be perpetuated over hundreds of years by rote teaching methods and practical performance, arguably – but unverifiably – the same performance time after time.

The first method of preservation is a distinctly private matter, whereas the second is more open; tradition is upheld and protected by initiates, and passed on only to those initiated. Learning by rote has no use for written records of years long gone. An explanation of what appears to be considerable incompatibility between the two principal versions before us, is that each has survived independently from the other, having descended through unconnected lines of transmission. Moreover, in China, the five-stringed lute was falling into decline towards the end of the millennium, while in Japan, traditional four-stringed lutes have maintained themselves to the present day, in solo and group performance, as part of ritual, ceremonial and ancient narrative music.

As we have them now, both versions of *Shinnō hajin-raku* reveal certain recognizable similarities on the surface (Example 1); they share the same title, mode and mode-key, and the melodic outline of one (*GGKF*) is a somewhat rugged and wandering relative of the more tempered version of the second (*SGYR*). Beyond that, dissimilarity is striking. Their styles, lengths and states of preservation are not irreconcilable; but whereas one appears less concerned with revealing its musicality, the more refined state of the other expresses musicality on first acquaintance. Of the two versions for bass lute, the instrumental style of the *GGKF/WXP* version with a range from *E-d'*, is advantaged by the solo potential of the five-string *accordatura*, the wider range allowing a span of almost two octaves, and a certain amount of chord-playing.

The later version (*SGYR*) requires notes from *F♯ - d'*, but has no use for notes between *F♯* and *B*. A standard, five-note tuning in *Taishiki-chō* provides the low *E*, called for seventeen times in *GGKF*, but not required at all in Moronaga's version – albeit the latter calls for the broken octave, *F♯ - f♯*, seven times. Low *E* has the firm resonance of the lowest unstopped string of the five-stringed instrument, and (in addition) it is the final of the *Taishiki* mode-key.

One might question whether in practice Moronaga adopted a *Banshiki*-mode tuning in this piece, with its lowest string tuned to *F♯*, since the three upper strings of the four-note *Taishiki-* and *Banshiki*-mode tunings are the same: *B, e, a*. A simpler idea – more in accord with Moronaga's reputation as a practical musician – is that, being an experienced and admired lute player himself, he simply retuned the lowest string from *E* to *F♯*, in order to play the version of *Shinnō hajin-raku* familiar to him, the one chosen for inclusion, in tablature, in his collectaneum for lute.

Comparing the two, the five-stringed version appears as a peripatetic progression of (mostly equal) notes rising and falling in contour, lacking both precise rhythmic shape and melodic phrasing for want of frequent cadences. By contrast, Moronaga's version proffers its musicality with regular time-measurement, phrasing and positive cadences. Of the two versions, the later one (*SGYR*) – stylistically closer to a majority of items that have come down to us – may have changed less drastically, in the course of some 500 years of transmission from early Tang to late Heian; but it must always be remembered that the original state of every one of these conveniently called 'Tang' items, is not known.

Example 1. Two versions of *Shinnō hajin-raku*, 'The Prince of Qin Destroys the Formations', from *GGKF* and *SGYR*

The total of twenty-three measures in the *SGYR* version (the *GGKF* version is not measured) is unusual, as is the line-up of cadences in odd-numbered measures. If instead of numbering measures of this version 1-23 the count were to begin from measure 4 as measure 1, the body of the work would be of twenty measures duration, and measures 4-23 could be re-numbered 1-20. Respecting the score (Example 1), this has been done in parenthesis; and in doing so, nothing of the music is lost, since measures 1-3 and 21-3 are identical. This was known to Moronaga, since he prescribed a full performance of the item being the

243

movement played seven times, with repetitions beginning from measure 4 (as it is in Western notation).

Interpreting this structurally, measures 1-3 introduce the item proper, which then flows from measure 4 to measure 23 through all repetitions. Since measures 21-3 conclude the item, immediate repetition of measures 1-3 on return would have been redundant; one is therefore justified in describing the item as consisting of twenty measures, with an introduction of three measures. The first three measures act, therefore, in the dual capacity of introducing the item the first time through, and closing it in all repetitions.

Following the suggestion that the body of the movement really begins from measure 4, a structure of ten, two-measure phrases becomes feasible. By comparison, the *GGKF* version recognizes an introduction of fifteen beats, and a point to which to return to commence repetitions. The movement appears to end at beat 144, after which comes a slightly modified incipit of thirteen beats, a variant of the introduction; from this point the player is directed to repeat from the sign at beat 16.

[Another example (in this repertory) of opening and closing measures of a movement being the same – the initial measures being omitted from repetitions after the first time through – is *Gyokuju goteika/Yushu houting-hua*, 'A Jade Tree's Rear-Court Blossom' (Fascicle 3, pp.1-19; conflation Fascicle 5, p.35).]

The comparative table (Example 1) confirms that these melodies are indeed versions of common origin. Enough has been said earlier to explain how such incongruity has probably come about; and it is intriguing to observe the results of isolation and protection of a specialist tradition from external exploitation.

Ryō-ō / Ling-wang, 'The Prince of the Grave-Mound'

The background and sources of this title were explored in Fascicle 5. Its history is there translated from Chinese and Japanese primary sources, to which has been added consideration of four late flute manuscripts in the tradition of the Ōga family. (Regarding this family see Marett, 1988, pp.210-15.) The bulk of material available attests the reputation and importance of this item in the cultural history of both nations. The piece as performed in Japan consisted of four movements: *Ranjo / Ranjō*, Free Prelude / Free Tune; *Kōjo / Huangxu*, Wild Prelude; *Juha / Rupo*, Entering Broaching; and *Amma / Durga* as Retiring Music. The Entering Broaching and part of the Free Prelude remain in the modern repertoire of the Palace and of the Kasuga Shrine in particular, and the Entering Broaching is still performed publicly with dance. The only movement important to the present study is the Entering Broaching which, because of the style and regal title of the suite, calls for consideration alongside the melody of *Shinnō hajin-raku*. The Entering Broaching is perhaps the only movement of the four that originated in Tang China.

The Prince of the Grave-Mound – properly Prince of Lanling ('Luoling' in Japanese *MSS*), that is, literally: 'Prince of the Grave-mound (or Tumulus) on which *Epidendron* grows' – was Changgong of the Northern Qi (Fascicle 5, pp.1-11). His legend grew, and he acquired all manner of fantastic attributes of character, bearing and physical beauty.

To continue with *Shinnō hajin-raku* in relation to other items of which the titles refer to emperors and noble leaders, the conflation of this composition has been transposed to the mode-key on *D* – that is, transposed (for comparison) from *Taishiki-chō* on *E* to the same scale on *D*, thus adopting the mode-key of other items in Fascicles 1-5 and in this Volume. Apart from *Shinnō hajin-raku*, other items: *Ryō-ō* and *Shin Raryō-ō*, are classed in *Sada-chō*, a modal sub-category of *Ichikotsu*, and are transcribed on historical and technical grounds (following Moronaga's example) in the *Gong* mode, the Lydian-type octave-series on *D*: $d - e - f\sharp - g\sharp - a - b - c\sharp - d'$ (Fascicle 5, pp.xii-xiii). Throughout the collection of items on *D*, the primary, authenticated sources have shown that both Lydian and Mixo-Lydian-type scale patterns prevailed according to the major instrumental traditions: players of blown instruments favoured the Mixo-Lydian-type *Shang*-scale (with *g* and *c♮*), while players of plucked, stringed instruments favoured the Lydian-type *Gong*-scale.

In technical studies of this repertory, the general practice has been to adopt the Mixo-Lydian-type scale for conflations of compositions classed in *Ichikotsu-chō* (that is, items 1-23 and Appendices 2 and 3 of Fascicle 4), and the Lydian-type scale for conflations of compositions classed in *Sada-chō* (items 24-31). In comparative studies of transcriptions aligned in score, simultaneous differences of scale formations in the same mode-key have been ignored as irrelevant to the current enquiry.

One cannot dismiss out of hand the tradition of the Toyohara clan, who preserved the authentic *Tōgaku* mouth-organ repertory from Toyohara no Tokimoto, born 1058, and named as 'founder of the mouth-organ tradition of this [the Japanese] court', through to Toyohara no Fumiaki who, as late as 1813, signed a colophon to a portion of a copy of the mouth-organ *MS* referred to here as *KF/HSF/RK* (Fascicle 1, pp.33ff). Nor may one disregard the reputation of Fujiwara no Moronaga (1137-93), high-ranking nobleman and politician, lutenist, vocalist and musicologist, who compiled the two great collections of music for plucked stringed instruments, *JCYR* and *SGYR*, invaluable to Tang music research.

Only one movement of 'The Prince of Lanling/Luoling' calls for attention in this context: the Entering Broaching, third movement of the four, transcribed from tablatures present in all the primary sources. It consists of sixteen measures, in four-measure phrases that divide into sub-phrases. To assess degrees of comparability and individuality, the conflation of the Entering Broaching (this Volume, p.114) is here compared with *Shinnō hajin-raku*.

Example 2. Conflations of *Shinnō hajin-raku* and the Entering Broaching of *Ryō-ō*, in comparative alignment

At first glance the two melodies look very different: twenty-three measures do not compress into sixteen. If Example 2 is acceptable as a reliable comparison, measures 17-21 of *Shinnō hajin-raku* are not accommodated in the *Ryō-ō* movement, whereas the sixteen measures of the latter tune are all accommodated in *Shinnō hajin-raku*. Indeed, the latter is the longer tune, partly due to the repetition of the three-measure incipit as coda. *Shinnō hajin-raku* is thus quite differently formed; but the twenty-three measures are only to be played the first time through. Three-measure phrases, or sections, are not usual in melodies in this style; and the three-measure incipit is in fact a two-measure phrase (cadencing on *d*) plus a one-measure echo (also cadencing on *d*).

One could, however, put forward another view. The Entering Broaching includes two measures, 1 and 2, that are repeated in varied form with change of direction in measure 4. *Shinnō hajin-raku* also begins with a two-measure phrase, but this is followed by a varied repeat of measure 2 in measure 3. In effect there are two cadences in the three-measure incipit, the first being subsidiary to the second. The first two cadences of both movements (Example 2) are conventional formulae: *Shinnō hajin-raku* cadencing on *d* and *d*, and the Entering Broaching on *d* and *a*, so that measures 1-3 of one tune are paired, albeit unevenly, in measures 1-4 of the other. In so far as the normal usually precedes the abnormal, and the two compositions may be shown to be related, is it possible that the Entering Broaching was composed before *Shinnō hajin-raku*?

Lacking information, the question cannot be answered; but from measures 4 and 5 of *Shinnō hajin-raku* onward, structural formulae (of the two items in question) broadly correspond in sequence as far as measure 16 of the larger melody. In all comparative exercises of this kind, one has always to allow for the fact that length (in these compositions) is governed by:

1. the plasticity of note patterns,
2. repetitions and durations of notes, and
3. the boundless flexibility in adjustment and extension of note patterns, in one or both melodies.

It is not until measure 17 of *Shinnō hajin-raku* that the melodies separate, over a diversion to cadence on the superfinal, *e*. This is a modal direction that the Entering Broaching does not follow; nor does the Entering Broaching exhibit formulae that relate again to its partner until measures 15 and 16 meet measures 22 and 23 of *Shinnō hajin-raku*. A Table of aligned cadence notes shows that, from the incipit onwards, some cadence notes agree and some disagree; variance, in fact, applies less to cadence notes than to cadence measures.

Table 1. Order and Positions of Cadence Notes compared: Shinnō hajin-raku (SŌHR) *and the Entering Broaching of* Ryō-ō (JH / RŌ)

Measures:	1	2	3	4	5	6	7	8	9	10	11	12	13	14	15	16
SŌHR:		*d*	*d*	‖: *d*		*d*		*d*		*a*		*a*		*d*		*a*
JH / RŌ:	‖: *d*		*a*		*f♯*		*d*		*a*		*a*		*f♯*		*d* :‖

Measures:	17	18	19	20	21	22	23
SŌHR:	*e*	*d*			*d*	*d* :‖	

What caused the cadence rhythm of *Shinnō hajin-raku* to change after measure 19, so as not to cadence in measure 21, but to delay the cadence until measure 22? The answer is that, in measure 21, the incipit returns as coda: measures 21, 22 and 23, repeating measures 1, 2 and 3. No cadence is sounded, therefore, in measure 21 (= measure 1), and this causes the two-measure cadence-rhythm to falter, after measure 19. This accounts for the three-measure phrase of measures 20- 2, and also returns the two cadences on the mode-final to measures 22 and 23, one rising from the dominant to the final, and one reaching the final from the dominant through the mediant.

Such comments lead one to look more closely at beginnings and endings of the same two melodies. Is it too much to say that the comparative alignment of *Shinnō hajin-raku* and the Entering Broaching of *Ryō-ō* (Example 2) shows traceable connections between measures 1-2 of the former, and measures 1-4 of the latter? Not if note-patterns alone are recognized as materials of formulaic management capable of docile adaptations, apt for almost any set of contextual circumstances. Example 2, for instance, demonstrates that the first measure of the Entering Broaching finds only three notes of mutual contact in sequence with nine notes of the first measure of the tune above it; but those three notes are the thread of tonal movement in the first measures of each tune.

In measure 1 *Shinnō hajin-raku* follows a central line of notes: *d - c - b - a - g - e*, while in the same measure of the Entering Broaching it is only concerned with part of that sequence: *c♯ - b - a*. In measure 2, the common thread is more evident, rising from dominant to final. Put more simply, it can be seen that the *Ryō-ō* movement shapes its first four measures from the same basic material as the first two measures of *Shinnō hajin-raku*, the latter spending twice the amount of time to express itself, as does the former to do so more economically. *Shinnō hajin-raku* spends fourteen beats on the concave curve: *d - c - b - a - b - c - d*, whereas the Entering Broaching takes almost twice the time over the same curve by following it twice: *c♯ - b - a - b - c♯ - d*, repeating in slightly different form. This view is supportable, since the musical imagination is capable of unlimited transformations of note patterns, over and above the rudimentary level of the basic, tonal formula: the modal scale. Such patterns are not themes, motifs or melodies. They are small shapes of tonal substance that, subject to transient internal relations, hold together at moments of usefulness, and by frequency of appearance establish their existence as passing functional details.

Having observed the craft of the opening measures of these two melodies, it will be interesting to look at their closing measures. *Shinnō hajin-raku* ends with the same three measures with which it began – a feature that disappears in subsequent, consecutive repeats when a full performance is given. The Entering Broaching is not crafted in this way; it upholds its independent status by not returning to the formulae from which it set out. It does, however, refer back for its end, but not as far back as the beginning. The Entering Broaching is another example of many in this repertory, where the second quarter of a sixteen-measure tune (measures 5-8) is heard again as the last quarter (measures 13-16). This ABCB organization is very common; and the second B section refers back to the first B section.

A question now arises: if, perhaps, these melodies are variants of each other; or if conscious, or unconscious, connections – through musical or extra-musical circumstances – impinge on their composition, would not such connections be recognizable as distinctive features of the tunes? Unable to answer the rhetorical question, one shelters behind a defensive 'not necessarily'. Although the closing phrase of the Entering Broaching fails to return to its opening phrase, or a variant of it, it was shown (Example 2) that measures 1-4 of this movement are related to measures 1-2, and thereby to measures 1-3, and consequently to measures 21-3, of *Shinnō hajin-raku*.

It will now be shown (Example 3) that measures 14-16 of the Entering Broaching also resemble the initial and terminal measures of *Shinnō hajin-raku*, albeit in a relationship that pertains to a pair of compositions, regardless of which of them may have been first in the field. Similarities between the first and last sections of each movement add weight to the possibility – and it need not be pressed further – that the formation and consolidation of either tune may have influenced creation of the other. A technical relationship between them is established, while the intrinsic musicality of each conceals the craft that supports it.

Example 3. Three final measures of *Shinnō hajin-raku*, and of *Ryō-ō*, Entering Broaching, compared

In Example 3 the numbers of notes in sequence, common to the respective measures 21 and 14, and 22 and 15, of the two movements, are four and five notes respectively; and the cadence-formulae in measures 23 and 16 both rise from the dominant to the final. There are other connections between the last three measures of the melodies; but examples of detached pairs of common notes in similar order are themselves not necessarily enough to assume conscious connections between extended melodies of whole pieces.

Nevertheless, with Examples 2 and 3 before us, it is clear that the melodic lines of both tunes cover similar ground for similar purposes; and it can now be claimed that the first three, and the last three, measures of the Entering Broaching of *Ryō-ō* are shadowed (or echoed) in the first three, and final three, measures of *Shinnō hajin-raku*.

A difference to be noted – and it will not have been missed – is: that in *Shinnō hajin-raku* the return to the beginning is literal and palpable, whereas in the Entering Broaching it is concealed, not aurally recognizable, because orders of note-contacts in the final measures of the tunes are different from those encountered the first time. In the first measure of both tunes (Example 2), pitch-contacts occur on the notes *c* /*c♯*, *b* and *a*, while in their antepenultimate measures, 21 and 14 (Example 3), contacts are made on *f♯*, *a*, *g*/*g♯* and *e*. The second measures of both tunes meet on *a*, *b*, *c*/*c♯* and *d*, while in the penultimate measures, 22 and 15, contacts are made on *a*, *b*, *d*, *f♯* and *a*. In measure 3 there are no contacts: the melodies operate in opposing tetrachords; but in the ultimate measures of both tunes (23 and 16), cadence formulae are common patterns from *a* to *d*. Pursuit of possible interconnections, and interdependences, of these movements can be revealing and rewarding.

Shin Raryō-ō/Xin Luoling wang, 'A New "Prince of Luoling/Lanling" '

The first sentence of the historical and critical introduction to *Shin Raryō-ō* in this Volume (p.1) closes with the statement that 'the title is that of a later version of "The Prince of Lanling" ', that is, of the original 'Prince of the Grave-mound', the *Ryō-ō* of this Appendix, who was the same person as the original Prince of Lanling. L.E.R.P. points out that this military hero, Changgong (more aptly described as 'Prince' than King) was head of government of a regional territory under the Qi emperor (Fascicle 5, p.2). It is also pointed out in the presentation of *Shin Raryō-ō* in this Volume (p.1) that no similar Chinese title, with the lexigraph *Xin* as first character, occurs in Chinese records. Japanese sources, however, indicate that the piece was known in Japan by the early-ninth century, and that: 'it was evidently felt to be a military piece' since it was conferred on the Imperial Household Troops (this Volume, p.4). This part of the enquiry into compositions of royal tribute accepts *Ryō-ō* as 'The Prince of Lanling', that historically preceded 'A New "Prince of Lanling" '. Although no extant scores of *Ryō-ō* in tablature earlier than *c.*1171 (*SGYR*) survive, Chinese records of an item of related title date from the seventh century (*Beishi*).

  Shin Raryō-ō is a middle-sized composition in two movements, Broaching and Quick, each of sixteen drumbeats or measures (conflations: this Volume, pp.126,128); there is no Prelude. The movements exist in secondary, shorter versions – shorter in being part only of the primary version in the case of the Broaching, or shorter by ignoring a repeated phrase in the primary version of the Quick. Variant versions begin with the *Kandō*, as though taking up the melody for a second or later time in sequence, then to continue from measure 3. Another secondary version of the Quick, in six measures only, is mentioned in *SGYR* but lacks any tablature; it may have been the twelve-measure variant (in duple time) reduced to six drumbeat measures in quadruple time. An enquiry into pieces with titular reference to supreme rulers, as to whether such pieces inherit and share common materials, calls for comparison of movements of *Shin Raryō-ō* with each other, and with *Shinnō hajin-raku* and the Entering Broaching of *Ryō-ō*.

Example 4. Entering Broaching of *Ryō-ō* and the Broaching of *Shin Raryō-ō* compared

Placing the Broaching of *Shin Raryō-ō* beneath the Entering Broaching of *Ryō-ō*
brings out a number of similarities of form and structure. Both movements are of
equal length, dividing into equal parts of four, two-measure phrases. In both
tunes, phrases 7 and 8 repeat phrases 3 and 4; and cadences in measures 2, 4, 8,
10, 12 and 16, fall on the same notes in both tunes. Cadences of phrases 3 and 7
in measures 6 and 14 differ in each melody, and these differences are preserved
in both halves of the tunes; in phrases 3 and 7 of the Entering Broaching,
cadences fall on *f♯*, three notes above the final, while the same numbered phrases
of the Broaching cadence on *b*, three notes below the final. Otherwise there is
much in common. On comparison further evidence brings them still closer.
Weighted-scale data, drawn from the Entering Broaching of *Ryō-ō* and the
Broaching of *Shin Raryō-ō* (this Volume, pp.114,127) show the relative
importance of individual notes to each other in the determination of melodic
profiles.

Table 2. Weighted-Scales of Ryō-ō, *Entering Broaching, and* Shin Raryō-ō,
Broaching

	d	*e*	*f♯*	*g♯*	*a*	*b*	*c♯*	
Ryō-ō, Entering Broaching	58	28	32.5	25.5	81	62.5	31.5	= 319
Shin Raryō-ō, Broaching	48	9.5	36.5	12	66	82	25	= 279

Conversion of these figures to percentages of the total numerical data for each
movement establishes the relative tonal priorities of individual notes of the
modal scale in each entire melody.

Table 3. Conversion of weighted-scale ratings to percentages of the whole

	d	*e*	*f♯*	*g♯*	*a*	*b*	*c♯*	
Ryō-ō, Entering Broaching: percentages	18	9	10	8	25	20	10	= 100
Shin Raryō-ō, Broaching: percentages	17	3	13	4	24	30	9	= 100

253

The hierarchical orders of notes of the scales of both movements show that the tonal structures are similar.

Table 4. Notes in Order of Tonal Importance

Ryō-ō, Entering Broaching,
order of proportional weight   *a*, *b*, *d*, *f♯*, *c♯*, *e*, *g♯*

Shin Raryō-ō, Broaching,
order of proportional weight *b*, *a*, *d*, *f♯*, *c♯*, *g♯*, *e*

The structural and tonal resemblance of the Entering Broaching of *Ryō-ō* to the Broaching of *Shin Raryō-ō* is thus demonstrated. Evidence confirms that these movements, relics of an oral tradition, are related; but one has always to be mindful that what is written on paper is not the perceptible music but symbols of the music, be they notes, tablatures, numerals or other hieroglyphs that represent sounds to be sung, plucked, blown or struck.

When symbols are activated in sound, and submitted to prescriptions of time and rhythm, perception of the music becomes real, and musicality may be appreciated. For this reason it can be said for the moment, that there is technical evidence to prove affinity between these movements of differing titles; but what if the question is asked: 'Do they sound similar? Do they sound as if out of the same mould?' Answers are likely to differ according to individual, subjective responses. Experience, imagination and taste are called on to assess qualities of musicality; and it is a mature decision to delineate, in pure musical terms within a broad range of variation, what is like from what is unlike. For our purpose, the tunes are identifiable as independent creations; yet at the same time they are recognizable as related – as out of the same stock.

The same does not hold true of the Broaching of *Shin Raryō-ō*, 'A New "Prince of Lanling" ', and of *Shinnō hajin-raku*, 'The Prince of Qin Destroys the Formations'. These two compositions present opposing frames of reference. The search for evidence of modal practices and formulae shared in close and variant forms, has not, in the case of *this* pair, uncovered sufficient evidence to warrant further consideration at this time. Their contrary forms, lengths, subdivisions and cadence notes ensure individualities and profiles without common or related ancestries. In due course, however, comparison of *Shinnō hajin-raku* and the Quick of *Shin Raryō-ō* will prove more rewarding; but first the Broaching and Quick of *Shin Raryō-ō* must be examined.

Example 5. Broaching and Quick of *Shin Raryō-ō* compared

Measured against the Broaching of the same suite, sequences of notes of the Quick – the shorter movement – fall into place under notes of the longer tune, as they progress towards familiar cadence forms in measures 7-8, 9-10 and 15-16. Not all cadences are familiar, however. Two particularly distinctive phrases of the Quick (wrapped round the dominant and its *bian* – measures 5-6, repeated in measures 13-14) are not found in the Broaching; neither is the concise initial phrase of the Quick (measures 1-2), the amplitude of which announces promptly

255

that the melody rests in the *Gong*-mode scale. Nevertheless, there is much in common. The two movements share the same numbers of eight phrases in sixteen measures; the second, third and fourth phrases of each movement repeat in the sixth, seventh and eighth phrases, and the movements exhibit the same half-way divisions, albeit not identified as *hanjō* in the Quick. Of the eight cadences in each melody, the final and its dominant occur five times in the Broaching, and six in the Quick, with diversions being made to the sixth of the scale in the former, and to the fourth in the latter (measures 6 and 14).

Such unexpected gestures as those in the third and seventh phrases of the Quick (measures 5-6 and 13-14), are quite exotic. Identical penultimate phrases of both halves of the Quick, they nevertheless choose to cadence on the central *bian*-note of the scale, *g♯*, far removed from immediate proximity to the mode-final, in fact removed from it to the furthest tonal point, midway in pitch between the final and its octave. Distance from the mode-final in these phrases is contrary to its position in the first phrase, where the ambitus, *c♯ - g♯ - d*, draws attention to the *bian*-note, which looks back to the sub-final, and leads directly forward to the final. The presence of the fourth of the *Gong* scale is conspicuous in *Sada-chō* items in this Fascicle, but such prominence is rare in melodies in *Ichikotsu-chō* from Moronaga's great collections.

Both movements of *Shin Raryō-ō* consist of sixteen measures in binary form; an important difference between them is the presence of measures of eight beats in the Broaching, and of four beats in the Quick. The Quick is therefore half the length of the Broaching, and in consequence its phrases are brief and direct. Each phrase moves regularly through six quarter-note beats, and then pauses for two beats on all cadence notes. The Broaching exhibits three distinctive phrases that shape the progress of an organized and balanced composition: measures 1-2, 7-8 and 9-10. These are structurally the first, fourth and fifth phrases, to which all other phrases relate. (See aligned analysis of the Broaching, Example 4, p.130.)

The Quick is organized and balanced in simpler manner. Its distinctive phrases include the section of measures 5-8 that returns in measures 13-16. Repetitions of the same numbered phrases also occur in the Broaching; but in the Quick, cadence notes of the first, third, sixth and seventh phrases differ from those in the Broaching – the third and seventh phrases (the same in each half of the composition) noticeably so. In isolation this phrase sounds as a generally acceptable formula; but, in the present context, the three large melodic leaps in the mouth-organ versions (retained in the conflation) emphasize the cadence on the fourth of the mode-key, in between cadences on the dominant and final, in measures 4 and 8, and between mode-final cadences in measures 12 and 16. These leaps do not occur in the string versions of wider tonal range.

Positioning of this kind highlights the tonal and structural importance imposed on a comparatively non-essential, auxiliary *bian*-note, when thrown into

256

prominence beside its dominant and mode-final. Measures 5-6 and 13-14 have little in common with the Broaching. Of the nine appearances of *g♯* throughout the Quick (including duplicated phrases in Example 5), comparison of Broaching and Quick shows only two places where the Broaching matches the same note. As a whole, the Quick is the less close contender for a relationship with the Broaching; but there is sufficient evidence of affinity. It is difficult to assess physical likenesses between two pieces of 128 and 64 beats, cast in the same form, when a judgement of musical quality – a less tangible, but equally important element – bears on the final decision.

It is timely to be reminded here that the Prelude of *Ōdai hajin-raku* exhibits four rather striking cadences on *g*, one of which is the final cadence note of drum-beat period 25, while the other three are intermediate cadences in periods 19, 23 and 28 (conflation: Fascicle 2, p.77). The four cadences are approached through the same formula: *b - a - f♯ - a - g*, the formula almost identical with the third and seventh phrases of the Quick, where the pattern assumes increased prominence by repetition in a small composition.

Example 6. Comparison of two versions of an important melodic formula from two unrelated items

It is always of interest to discover exceptions to common practices and formalistic clichés. Cadences on the dominant are so frequent in items in this mode-key as to be expected, and accepted, in the normal course of events. Since dominant-cadences are next in importance to those on the mode-final, they are most likely to occur at definitive modal points: near the beginning, in the middle and near the end. Cadences on the fourth of the scale are unusual. They surprise the ear, not solely by their presence, but also by the approach through a formula that often predicts a dominant-cadence. Expectancy is aroused, but arrested, when the melody halts on the very beat where, in time and rhythm, the ear has learned to expect a dominant-cadence, anticipation having been alerted by formulae that habitually prepare for such a cadence. In the same Prelude, numerous cadences on the dominant are reached through patterns such as this: *f♯ - a - b - a - a* (drumbeat periods 2, 5, 9, etc.); or a variant thereof: *b - a - f♯ - a - a* (period 12).

In the light of this comparison of the two movements of *Shin Raryō-ō*, it would be hasty (at this stage) to claim a common origin. Technical differences, viewed objectively on paper, are heard more subjectively. It is the sum of the differences in their own contexts that makes the melodies what they are; and it is whole melodies that are perceived and assessed by the musical intelligence.

Identities of small note patterns are concealed beneath a limitless range of guises that musically inventive minds conjure up intuitively, when making music in accustomed styles. Within a traditional style, there is a comparatively free range of notes, time-values, rhythms, octave-placements, repetitions of notes, patterns and phrases, and additionally, there is freedom to add and subtract notes, embellishments and glosses.

All of these impulses of creativity are present (to greater or lesser degrees) in *Tōgaku* melodies, which are inevitably, and finally, appreciated subjectively. The music before us could not exist in its established styles without conscious, and unconscious, systematic manipulation of note patterns available in a fixed, seven-note scale. Of examples ready to hand, comparison of measures 7-8 of the Broaching, and of the Quick of *Shin Raryō-ō*, is a fair illustration (Example 5, p.255). The Broaching requires eighteen beats (counting the cadence note of measure 6 from which the phrase sets out) to make one, two-measure phrase move from *b* (of the previous cadence) through *f♯* to *d*, while the Quick fulfils the same task, on its own terms, with eight notes over eight beats. In short, although one observes interconnections of note patterns, the profiles and musicality of each tune are very different, though functionally they serve the same purpose.

Example 5 points up note-contacts between tunes but in itself does not necessarily prove them to be versions of each other, nor whether they are equally musical. It does, however, support the possibility that they are separate versions of a long-lost related tune. From this Example, no particular phrase of one tune could appropriately replace the equivalent phrase of the other; yet both are technically and musically satisfactory in their own contexts.

Following comparison of the movements of *Shin Raryō-ō*, it can be shown that the Quick also has structural and formulaic connections with the Entering Broaching of *Ryō-ō* (Example 7, p.259). The Quick and the Entering Broaching contain the same number of measures and phrases, but in 2/2 the Quick has just half the physical length of the Entering Broaching in 4/2 – the same relationship as was recognized between the Quick and Broaching in *Shin Raryō-ō*. The Quick and the Entering Broaching of *Ryō-ō* have the same ABCB form and binary divisions; and the melodic lines are seldom out of touch, although divergence occurs in measures 11-12. Five of the eight cadences of each piece fall on the same notes in variant forms of basic cadence formulae; but in measures 11 and 12, phrases do not align, each goes its own way, to come together again before the end of measure 12 of the Entering Broaching. Once more the third and seventh phrases, measures 5-6 and 13-14, exhibit the abnormal formations of the Quick; but in this instance the Entering Broaching agrees more closely (than does the Broaching of *Shin Raryō-ō*) with the melodic line backing these measures, and it includes the provocative *g♯*, cadence note of measures 6 and 14 in the Quick, nonetheless transferring its own cadence to *f♯*, one beat further on.

Example 7. Entering Broaching of *Ryō-ō* superimposed on the Quick of
Shin Raryō-ō

Shinnō hajin-raku and *Shin Raryō-ō*, Quick

The Quick of *Shin Raryō-ō* is remarkably versatile in that it has survived in its own right as the second part of a two-movement suite; it exhibits a discernible relationship with its Broaching (Example 5, p.255), and a more substantial one with the Entering Broaching of *Ryō-ō* (Example 7, p.259). The Quick also exhibits close affinity with *Shinnō hajin-raku*; Example 8 illustrates the two pieces in alignment. All the short, formulaic phrases of the Quick are shown in sequence beneath *Shinnō hajin-raku*, of necessity with gaps, since the tunes differ conspicuously in size. In addition, several phrases of the Quick offer alternative comparisons out of sequence.

Example 8. *Shinnō hajin-raku* and the Quick of *Shin Raryō-ō* compared

Example 9 offers a clear and more thorough breakdown, that shows how the sixteen measures of the Quick, detached from the full-length Example 8, can be located in continuity, in the first three measures of *Shinnō hajin-raku*. It is the nature of the language of this kind of traditional music that generates such extraordinary results as those here exposed by comparative analysis of the four selected compositions of this enquiry.

Example 9. The Quick of *Shin Raryō-ō*, accommodated in the first three measures of *Shinnō hajin-raku*

Similar creative impulses or influences are evident in the making of the two tunes; but there is nothing in particular to predicate: that each came from the same source, that each is a variant of the other, or that findings from a technical exposition of this kind presuppose rational or conscious composition. As melodies – individual melodies – they do not sound alike; and in various degrees they differ in style, length, form, structural organization and sequence of cadences. In support of this statement, Table 5 compares basic forms, internal organizations, and orders of cadence notes; numbers of measures and cadence notes are collated in horizontal lines. This is followed by the results of a weighted-scale procedure (Table 6), applied so as to obtain statistical information relating to the comparative importance of the various notes of the melodies, in their modal frameworks, and thereby to establish orders of priorities of notes, on the tonal surfaces of the two compositions.

Table 5. Shinnō hajin-raku (SŌHR:) *and* Shin Raryō-ō, *Quick* (SRRŌ);
lengths, sequences of cadence notes and phrase-structures, compared

Measures	1	2	3	4	5	6	7	8
SŌHR:		d	d ‖:		d		d	
SRRŌ, Quick	‖: d			a		g♯		d

Measures	9	10	11	12	13	14	15	16
SŌHR:	a		a		d		a	
SRRŌ, Quick		a			d	g♯		d ：‖

Measures	17	18	19	20	21	22	23	
SŌHR:	e		d			d	d	：‖

The impression here is of the apparent independence of two pieces of somewhat
similar titles, from the same repertory and in the same mode-key, although the
smaller composition could be said to be hidden in the first three measures of the
larger one (Example 9). In Table 6 the weighted-scale procedure brings relevant
detail to the surface, and thus clarifies tonal strengths of individual notes,
according to their functional behaviour in the melodies.

Table 6. Weighted-scales of Shinnō hajin-raku *and the* Quick *of* Shin Raryō-ō

	d	e	f♯	g♯	a	b	c♯	
SŌHR:	91	58	45	51	76	51.5	55.5	= 428
SRRŌ, Quick	35	11.5	22.5	17	34.5	25.5	11	= 157

The data here represent sum-totals of three prime factors of modal compositions,
as described in this Volume (pp.207-10). By converting figures for *Shinnō hajin-
raku* into percentages of the entire melody, the relative importance of various
notes to the whole is disclosed. The combined weight of dominant and final, 39
percent, and of *e, f♯, b*, 36 percent, confirms their importance; but what is high is
the combined weight of the *bian*-notes, 25 percent. The pentatonic scale,
therefore, provides just 75 percent (= 39 + 36) of the whole.

Conversions of figures from the Quick show rather different relationships.
Dominant and mode-final contribute 44 percent, while *bian*-notes, despite the
prominence of the *g♯*-cadences, account for 18 percent. The Five Notes therefore
provide 82 percent of the whole.

In *Shinnō hajin-raku*, the third note of the pentatonic scale is the weakest; even when combined with the sixth, the two notes are less important (23 percent) than the *bian*-notes, $g\sharp$ and $c\sharp$, with their combined weight of 25 percent, one quarter of the total operation of the scale of the entire tune. The *bian*-notes are well beyond the auxiliary status to which modal theory traditionally confines them. The Quick also inclines to abnormalities, partly consequent on the comparatively high exposure given to the fourth of the scale; as data indicate, $g\sharp$ earns one half the figure of the final, while in perspective it ranks only fifth in the hierarchy of notes in the tonal fabric of the movement. In the Quick, percentage-figures cover a wider range of variation. The final and dominant are pillars of the modal strength, each at 22 percent of total weight; but of the pentatonic scale, the super-final is the weakest element, registering only 7 percent. *Bian*-notes of the Quick together amount to 18 percent. In consequence the five-note *Gong* structure of the Quick is collectively stronger at 82 percent than that of *Shinnō hajin-raku*, in spite of the low rating of the super-final.

In Review: Observations on Pairings of the Various Compositions

Shinnō hajin-raku, *'The Prince of Qin Destroys the Formations'*
The two versions of this title from *GGKF* and *SGYR*, in *Taishiki-chō* (the Mixo-Lydian mode-key on *E*) are certainly versions of one item. That from *SGYR* is of the same standard, technically and stylistically, as are the thirty-one *Tōgaku* compositions in the mode-key on *D* from the same source (Fascicles 1-5). Measured throughout in well-defined phrases, there can be no doubt about the validity of the different tablatures, nor their transcriptions into Western notation. After reconciliation of the two versions (Example 1, p.242) with those of *KF/HSF/RK* and *SSSTF*, a conflated version of *Shinnō hajin-raku* was established for further reference; for this study, it is arranged in the heptatonic mouth-organ scale (except for writing *c'''* one octave lower) in the mode-key on *D*, for comparison with other movements in the same key. Being a one-movement item, and the only *Hajin-raku/Pozhen-yue* piece in this present investigation, it has been the focus of reference to which all other pieces under discussion have been referred; they too have been compared among themselves.

Shinnō hajin-raku and *Ryō-ō*, Entering Broaching

The two movements differ significantly in length, form and structure (Example 2, p.246). In its present condition the Entering Broaching is compact in form, clear in structure and thereby in phrasing, and its tonal scheme is well organized, in regular two-measure phrases that cadence on *d*, *a*, *f♯* and *d* in the first half, and on *a*, *a*, *f♯* and *d* in the second. *Shinnō hajin-raku*, operating on a different and less usual time-scale from other items, is not as compact nor as clear, and it displays an introductory three measures, made up from a two-measure phrase and a one-measure phrase; these three measures also serve as coda. Thus a long central span of seventeen measures forms the body of the work. In the conflation, physical details of the middle section are absorbed in a continuous line, mostly of quarter-note beats, measured off regularly according to Moronaga's *hyaku* markings. The questioning ear is uncertain how the seventeen measures adapt to the binary system that governs the music of this entire repertory, nor is it certain what the rationale of phrasing is, that orders so long a stretch of melody.

When measure 21 is reached, measure 1 is immediately recalled as first of the three introductory measures from the start of the movement, and the same three measures return as coda. Nevertheless, over the major part of the comparative alignment (Example 2), there are many places where note patterns and formulaic groups meet, with contacts continuing as far as measure 16 in the larger piece, and measure 14 in the shorter.

The absence of connections with measures 17-21 is due to the disparate lengths of the two movements. When the melodies come together again, in measures 22 and 23, eighteen of the twenty-three measures of *Shinnō hajin-raku* are by then known to be related to the sixteen measures of the Entering Broaching. 78 percent of *Shinnō hajin-raku* has connections with the *Ryō-ō* movement. Clearly there is some musical connection between the two items; equally clearly, however, the connection is more tenuous than that between several other pairs of melodies previously examined.

Ryō-ō, Entering Broaching; and *Shin Raryō-ō*, Broaching

These movements are of the same form: sixteen measures of binary structure, with measures 4-8 repeating as measures 12-16, and with identical cadence notes in measures 2, 4 and 8, and in measures 10, 12 and 16 (Example 4, p.252). Repetition to this extent leads to the same phrasing in both melodies. Eight phrases of the two Broachings divide the movements into equal parts, with like structural patterns in two-measure phrases. In the Entering Broaching, the structural organization of phrases of the two halves is: A, A', B, C, and D, A', B, C; and in the Broaching, the equivalent structural organization is A, A', A, B, and C, A', A, B. Cadence notes follow in similar sequences in the Entering Broaching: on *b*, *a*, *f♯*, *d* and on *a*, *a*, *f♯*, *d*; and in the Broaching: on *b*, *a*, *b*, *d* and on *a*, *a*, *b*, *d*. No two tunes could be stronger in tonality, or more predictable in modal practices. Comparison of conflations of the Entering Broaching of *Ryō-ō* with the Broaching of *Shin Raryō-ō* asserts the close affinity between the two pieces, an affinity due to technical features described, and to palpable sharing of formulae in undisguised variant forms.

Measures 1-4 of the two tunes sound convincingly alike, the Broaching disclosing slight variations of patterns present in the same-numbered measures of

265

the Entering Broaching, where formulae appear abruptly as if in a mode-key on *a*. Tonality is not clarified, indeed, until the fourth phrase (measures 7-8) halfway through the movements. Formulaic material, a determinant in both melodies, delays modal definition until the *hanjō*. The Entering Broaching is dominant-oriented through measures 1-4, and mode-final oriented through measures 5-8 – a balance of dominant-final tensions. The Broaching retains dominant-focus longer, through measures 1-6; and both movements leave the preparation and delivery of the first, mode-final cadence, until as late as measures 7-8.

The difference between them is one of degree. Intrusion of tonal implications into modal conventions is due to the nature of the particular formulae engaged and manipulated in the manner described. The same kind of manipulation continues through the second parts of the melodies. The working material of both movements is a small assortment of formulae, which brings the pieces close to being variations of each other, and thus to stemming from like impulses and musical memories. It may be thought that there is one formula – measure 5 of the Entering Broaching – exposed and not shared; but a variant form of it is present in the Broaching, not in the vicinity of measure 5, but in the notes *d - f♯ - a - g♯ - b - a* of measure 12, the complement (in the second half) to measures 4 and 5 (in the first). In measure 5 of the Entering Broaching, the formula does not cadence, but moves on to cadence on *f♯* in the next measure; in measure 12 of the Broaching, however, it is the end of a phrase and cadences forthwith.

Over all, the two melodies are corresponding expressions of a cognate creative experience. The titles are significantly apt so far as these movements are concerned: 'The Prince of Lanling' and 'A New "Prince of Lanling" '. Can there be doubt that the Entering Broaching of 'The Prince of Lanling' is the composition to which 'A New "Prince of Lanling" ' refers? The next step is to summarize the Quick of *Shin Raryō-ō* against the Broaching of the same suite, to see whether the Quick, before referring it back to the Entering Broaching, carries the hallmarks of the design and material of the Broaching.

Shin Raryō-ō, Broaching and Quick

It has been shown that the Broaching and Quick of this suite are alike in structure (Example 5, p.255). The total number of measures in each is the same, with the second, third and fourth phrases of the first half of each tune repeating in their second halves, even though the phrases are not matched between one movement and the other. One striking difference between the tunes is that the third and seventh phrases of the Quick highlight, and cadence on, the fourth of the scale, *g♯*, which does not occur in any other of the melodies under discussion. Apart from this, notes of the Quick retain their linear order in the Broaching – of necessity allowing for gaps, since the the number of beats in the Quick is half that in the Broaching – and the cadences (of the first, second and fourth phrases, and of the fifth, and final phrases) rest on the same notes in both pieces.

It was said earlier that there is sufficient evidence here to establish a perceptible affinity between the movements, not as close a relationship, say, as that between the Entering Broaching of *Ryō-ō* and the Broaching of *Shin Raryō-ō*, but enough to suppose (in the absence of written documentation) that the Quick of *Shin Raryō-ō* influenced composition of the Broaching of the same suite; and that the rugged nature of the Quick was subjected to a degree of 'refinement' in the making of the Broaching.

Ryō-ō, Entering Broaching and *Shin Raryō-ō*, Quick

In all regards these movements are a pair: they have the same number of measures, and phrases of equal length; the same ABCB form; and comparative alignment (Example 7, p.259) shows the two melodies to be compatible through much of their durations, although one is twice the length of the other in number of beats. The two exotic phrases of the Quick (measures 5-6 and 13-14), unmatched in other comparative pairs of melodies, accord in this pair; and it is feasible that the Quick of *Shin Raryō-ō* is an actual reduction of the Entering Broaching of *Ryō-ō*. If such feasibility be postulated, it would establish a strong and intimate relationship between three movements out of our selected four: the Entering Broaching of *Ryō-ō*, and the Broaching and Quick of *Shin Raryō-ō*.

Shinnō hajin-raku and the Quick of *Shin Raryō-ō*

Earlier comparison of these two movements established that they have enough in common (Example 8, p.260) to substantiate the view that one of the pair may have come into being under influence of the other. Yet it was said above that '...there is nothing to predicate: that each came from the same source, that each is a variant of another, or that findings from a technical exposition of this kind presuppose rational or conscious composition.' Indeed, there is nothing in Chinese and Japanese historical writings of the first millennium, or since, to suggest that people were at any time aware of the nature and degree of commonality between the movements; or that possible connections between the circumstances of creation of the compositions, singly or collectively, were known or suspected.

What evidence is assembled here, surrounding Example 8, is musicological, analytical and technical, and may have been applicable to the movements in earlier forms; but these particular versions survive in Japanese sources alone, dating from about seven centuries after consolidation of the dynastic house of Tang by the middle of the seventh century.

The two pieces are similar in some respects; but what they have in common is primarily established by choice of tone-material, and by organization and manipulation of similar formulae over disparate stretches of musical time: *Shinnō hajin-raku* has nearly three times the number of beats as does the Quick of *Shin Raryō-ō*. Nevertheless, within the formal dimensions adopted, the physical structures differ, and this causes hesitation before making direct statements about musical relationships. When attempting to clarify relatedness, or degrees of similarity between musical compositions, one is bound to exercise caution when visual appearance is a principal arbiter. The visual image is not the same as, nor (finally) as important as the aural experience. The latter is more immediate, direct and subjective.

When more of the Tang repertory has been examined and transcribed, items in other modal groups, with titles of similar relevance to those investigated here, may be found. Two such are mentioned now, in the hope that further research may increase interest in, and knowledge and understanding of, music and musicians of the Tang court, and the musicianship of those who made and played it.

One such, with imperial connotation, is *Ōdai santai / Huangdi santai* (皇 帝 三 臺), 'The Emperor's "Three Terraces"', a single movement in sixteen drumbeats or measures, in the *Ōshiki*-mode. It is included in the Japanese manuscript *Hakuga fue-fu* (Fascicle 1, p.9), completed in 966, and transcribed from flute-tablature by Marett (1977, p.39).

Another item is *Ōjō / Huang zhang* (皇 獐), 'The Imperial Roebuck', of which two movements survive in the *Hyō*-mode. Three ten-measure Sections make what is left of a Broaching; and there is a Quick of twenty measures, transcribed from *SGYR* and other sources by Wolpert (1981, pp.78-80). The Quick of *Ōjō* includes the striking figure (measures 6-7, 16-17) present in the Quick of *Shin Raryō-ō*, at the same pitch, but in the Dorian-type scale on *E* instead of the Lydian-type scale on *D*.

These pieces may not yet attract concentrated enquiry; but it would be hasty to dismiss the possibility that other items may emerge that could be embraced within a larger critical study.

By reputation and design, and by technical organization, the most important composition of the first mode-key group *Ōdai hajin-raku/Huangdi pozhen-yue* has yet to be fully examined, relative to compositions that acknowledge qualities of emperors and other ruling leaders. 'The Emperor Destroys the Formations' has not yet yielded all its secrets, although much of its history, circumstances and attributes has been discovered and clarified since the first transcriptions were published in Fascicle 1 (1981). In view of its popularity and regard in Tang China, and the admiration and esteem it subsequently enjoyed in Japan, it is difficult at this juncture to accept that this Large Suite has not influenced, nor been influenced by, other music of royal distinction and association, in China and Japan.

From time to time, comparative aligned examples from various items, including 'The Emperor Destroys the Formations', have drawn attention to similar phrases and formulaic sequences in a variety of pieces (Nickson, 1988; and see Fascicle 5, pp.60-2, p.92 and p.105), albeit some of which are short extracts not necessarily implying indebtedness of one whole piece to another.

Where movements have been aligned to show conscious (or unconscious) acknowledgement of each other they have usually been movements within a multi-movement title; and there are splendid examples of these in analyses of *Toraden /Tuanluanxuan,* 'The Whirl-Around' and *Shunnō-den / Chunying-zhuan,* 'The Singing of Spring Warblers' in Fascicle 3 (pp.77-90) and of *Koinju / Hu yin jiu,* 'Sogdians Drinking Wine' in Fascicle 5 (pp.57-61).

To identify the whole, or a major part, of a single or multi-movement title, as being related to another title, is what this experimental enquiry set out to do; but whereas progress has been made in this direction, it has not as yet brought one of the most prestigious items of the entire repertory, *Ōdai hajin-raku,* into that extended family of Tang compositions acclaiming the honour and glory of celebrated imperial and military leaders. An extension of this preliminary exploration remains an exercise for the future.

Because of its extraordinary length and complexity, 'The Emperor Destroys the Formations' excluded itself from the present selection of items appropriate to the topic. In its place, focus has centred upon 'The Prince of Qin Destroys the Formations', a similarly named, single item of unusual form, made available here in transposition ahead of publication in its customary mode-key classification. In the course of inquiry, 'The Prince of Qin Destroys the Formations' has been important, not alone due to latent analogies with other items, but rather, paradoxically, to the nature and validity of patent disparities that justified its integrity within the group, despite its technical independence.

The three other movements are of similar length and form; but even so, none of the comparative pairs of aligned, sixteen-measure tunes could be sustained without intermittent lapses of continuity. Variation between kindred pieces can be presumed – one might say it is inevitable – given the unpredictable and hazardous processes confronting survival of intangible cultural treasures from the first millenium such as: unconnected, unilateral, oral transmissions; the extent of geographical terrain traversed over time from early Tang to late Heian; and the high risks of infiltration by extrinsic, cultural elements over the long voyage through time and space.

Summary Observations

Of the four movements of the sample group, *Shinnō hajin-raku* manifests a close correlation with the Entering Broaching of *Ryō-ō* (Example 2, pp.246,247), and with the Quick of *Shin Raryō-ō* (Example 8, p.260). Formulaic material of the

Quick is adaptable and accommodating; its phrases are short and concise to the point that patterns themselves form regular phrasing, in fundamentally the same rhythm. The brevity of the Quick – its length is only 35 percent of that of *Shinnō hajin-raku* – lends itself to comparisons, in which its short phrases have more time and space to stretch out within the longer tune; indeed, some phrases connect at random more than once. In addition, there is that astonishing illustration, where the entire Quick can be accounted for within the first three measures of *Shinnō hajin-raku* (Example 9, p.262) – including the phrases that cadence on the fourth note of the scale.

Beside *Shinnō hajin-raku*, the Entering Broaching of *Ryō-ō* offers a more varied comparison, though its sixteen, eight-beat measures give it twice the length of the Quick. Aligned with *Shinnō hajin-raku*, the first four measures of the Entering Broaching reflect its first three measures, and then continue through measures 5-14, following a line similar to measures 4-16 of *Shinnō hajin-raku* – such is the peculiar form of the latter. Materially and technically, the two pieces trace similar but individual profiles, in which the structural organization of the Entering Broaching proceeds in regular phrases, with four measures of the first half repeating in the second half, although this particular attribute is not clear in *Shinnō hajin-raku*. Nevertheless, the two melodic lines are maintained, fairly coherently, from measures 4 and 5 to measures 14 and 16, respectively.

Comparison of *Shinnō hajin-raku* with the Entering Broaching and the Quick confirms the malleability of the Tang musical language, adding further proof of the ingenuity of musical intelligence of these people, and of their capability of producing compositions of diversity and distinction from what was, theoretically, a strictly limited modal system. The various comparisons included in the essay support this statement and its implications (Example 7, p.260). The Entering Broaching shares formulae of both *Shin Raryō-ō* movements in undisguised forms, in continuity and in length. The two related movements of the suite are corresponding instances of creative energy and the re-creative process; their affinity is apparent, in so far as they are associated in a relationship, not as close as that of the Entering Broaching, but close enough to suggest that the Quick may be the older of the two, and consequently could have had bearing on the formation of the Broaching. [The sharply defined form of the Quick, and its bold foreign style, resemble the same features of several other short, popular pieces of the repertory, for instance: *Shukoshi*, 'The Wine Puppet' and *Butokuraku*, 'Martial Virtue' (conflations: Fascicle 5, p.90 and p.100).]

Comparative analysis (of the kind demonstrated) has been *enlightening* and *rewarding*; but the selection of movements for comparison arose from *titles* of compositions that praise the qualities of high-born, military leaders, renowned in life and legend for outstanding bravery, heroism and personal prestige. The items were therefore selected on non-musical grounds. Results of the study are *enlightening* because it brought together melodies not previously known to have musical affinity, and proved them to share a common musicality, evident both in material and manner of treatment.

Limited information about the origins and reputations of these items is recorded in Chinese historical sources, but nothing of their qualities, and little of their fates. They were evidently an esteemed part of the Court Entertainment Music from the sixth century onwards, and lapsed into oblivion during the decline of Tang. By then they had become well established and admired in Japan where, after something like twelve centuries, two of the four selected movements, though now changed beyond recognition, are still performed by the court musicians.

Over many hundreds of years, written history has no hint of connections between repertory compositions, other than similar circumstances of functional purpose. The present study has been *rewarding* in that it has led to confirmation: of the resilience of the raw material of the Tang musical language; of the extent of its compliancy, subject to a creative process; and of the ability of Tang musicians to create compositions from familiar, diatonic elements – compositions of which the outstanding properties are a natural musicality and tunefulness, a balanced structure and phrasing, and a variety of style and disposition.

Can it now be said that the four selected movements are of the same stock? Their various distinctions – forms, structures, outward appearances, physical contours and individualities – add contrasts within their identities, and their identities are inseparable from their integrities. On the surface, the four pieces fall within a frame of titular and musical reference; beneath the surface there is evidence of a complementary, less precise, frame of reference, one of familial group relationship. The movements are mutually agreeable, collectively compatible and physically comparable, while at the same time each stands on its own merits, self-contained and self-evident.

It will have been noticed that the most distinctive incipit of the group is the first phrase of the Quick of *Shin Raryō-ō*. From the first note through to the first cadence – seven notes only – the ear recognizes the heptatonic *Gong*-mode, its scale and the positions of the auxiliary notes; these perceptions are formed from aural perception of the two semitone-steps, and the placing of the cadence note. The opening statement is factual, precise and dogmatic. From the *bian*-notes and the cadence note, the scale and mode-final are established immediately in the ear. The style of utterance is economical and concise; from the outset it intimates that the piece is likely to be short – many short phrases in the rhythm of the first phrase would quickly tire if extended at great length.

Another interesting first phrase from one of the four selected pieces (but of interest for different reasons) is that of *Shinnō hajin-raku* (Example 1, in the original mode-key on *E*, and transposed in part in Example 2, in the mode-key on *D*). Though not compressed like the first phrase of the Quick, *Shinnō hajin-raku* announces its mode and key at the outset: scale, mode-final and dominant, ostensibly with forthright clarity. Yet, because of the contour and ambitus of the notes of the first measure (Example 2), *d - c - f♯ - g - cb - a - g - e*, and the nature of the four-note formula, *d - c - f♯ - g*, the initial impression is that of the *Gong*-mode on *c*, which is temporarily misleading. As explained earlier, the scale here is the *Shang* octave-series, with the first cadence in measure 2 sounding on *d*, and with *d* confirmed as mode-final in measure 3. (It will be remembered that the original classification of *Shinnō hajin-raku* was in the *Taishiki*-mode on *E*, a *Shang*-mode octave-series. In transposition, for whatever purpose, the *Shang* octave-series, a Mixo-Lydian-type scale, remains intact.) In passing, it will be noted that the recurrence of measure 1 in measure 21 rests in the broader context, logically and without doubt, in the mode-scale on *d*.

Those who have followed our Tang research through the years will need no reminding of the adaptability and versatility of the modal system as practised in the repertory of this tradition. One of the fascinating discoveries rising from this investigation has been the ingenuity of the musical mind breaking through the old, received modal system. There is an inventive energy in some of these movements, generated, albeit unwittingly, from two authentic pentatonic structures present in the *Gong*-mode scale, and from the increasingly free participation of auxiliary (*bian*) notes of modal scales in the burgeoning melodic style.

Discussion of the two incipits of *Shinnō hajin-raku* and the Quick of *Shin Raryō-ō* invites a look back to Example 8 (p.260), where the movements are aligned in the mode-key on *D*. The openings of each are cogent in their different styles. Alignment of initial phrases in this Example does not necessarily prove a close musical relationship, although notes of the shorter tune are all located in sequence in the longer one. What is important is that the "feel" of each is so different; they do not mean the same to the musical intelligence, nor does familiarity bring them closer together in musical terms. Each incipit fulfils its obligations and purpose in its own context; but this very aptness does not preclude the same or other patterns from appearing in numberless compositions, given manipulation and variability. The innate compliancy of this kind of simple, musical material has always provided scope for creative expression in many a folk and traditional culture throughout history.

Comment on the physical and tonal plasticity of melodic formulae is supported by detaching from the two versions of *Shinnō hajin-raku* (Example 1, p.242) the distinctive note pattern that forms the first phrase of the Quick of *Shin Raryō-ō*. As pointed out, relevant facts about the Quick are delivered in the smooth and concise opening which, in addition to offering essential information at the start of the movement, arrests attention by its brevity. Not everywhere will replicas and variants of this pattern have the same qualities of importance and self-containment as demonstrated in the Quick. As a formulaic pattern it is part of the vocabulary of the musical language that furnishes the modal context in which it functions, and that affords freedom to adapt its physical form to demands of the moment.

This is not the place to examine fully the theory and practice of note-patterns in traditional musical languages, nor to attempt anything so precise as definitions of note patterns in general, except in so far as analysis and appreciation of formulaic practices are relevant to music from the Tang court. It would be difficult to say categorically from *Tōgaku* experience, just what a note-pattern is in this repertory. Equally difficult is it to decide degrees of variation to which note patterns may be subjected, before losing their identities and becoming other patterns. The practice of making music from tiny note patterns is extremely free in intuitive composition in familiar styles; this very freedom confers the viability of formulaic structures in this form of traditional music.

An illustration will make the point. As already stated, the first two measures of the Quick of *Shin Raryō-ō* form an orderly tonal structure; they also form a phrase that comprises seven notes through eight beats. Meeting this phrase in isolation, it might be described in various ways, for example, as consisting of two groups of four and three notes respectively, and there would be nothing to contradict this or any other similar description; but to a musician it means little. In context, however, the opening of the Quick can be seen in terms of the entire composition – its form, structure, texture and style – and may then be described as a melodic unit, or as a compound pattern of tiny note-sets making one phrase. Might it not be fairly and acceptably described as several things at the one time? Much has been said in this enquiry of the idiosyncrasy of this opening phrase.

In pursuit of the formula in the musical language of Tang, the two oldest surviving forms of one of the selected compositions of undoubted Tang origin: *Shinnō hajin-raku*, have been searched for the presence of the initial phrase of *Shin Raryō-ō*, in some recognizable form.

The following instances of occurrences of the phrase, and its variants, are taken from the transcribed versions of *Shinnō hajin-raku* in *GGKF* and *SGYR* (Example 1, p.242). For comparison with the Quick, excerpts from both versions of *Shinnō hajin-raku* are presented (Example 10), slightly reduced, and transposed into the mode-key on *D*.

Example 10. Measures 1-2 of the Quick of *Shin Raryō-ō*, seen as a melodic formula in two versions of *Shinnō hajin-raku, GGKF* and *SGYR*

Example 10 is of special interest at this stage, when attention can be given briefly to characteristics of note patterns, their variant forms, and the ease with which they meet every kind of textural requirement. The two versions of *Shinnō hajin-raku* furnish eleven forms of the first phrase of the Quick, at various pitch levels. If we accept these patterns (for the purpose of clarifying the issue in hand), they illustrate a number of useful points.

Notes in the chosen excerpts identifying with the incipit-pattern are marked (+); other notes, unmarked, are supplementary to the pattern, without being essential to it.

The patterns are recognizable visually; but aurally, and in context, their presence is usually unobtrusive. Literal repetition of variant forms of prosaic patterns occurs, and may be noticed; but unitary prominence is not to be expected in the formulaic, centonate style. Tonal tesserae are not themes or motifs, but naïve building materials, capable of limitless flexibility in their capacity to fit anywhere into any modal texture. The skeletal form of the first phrase of the Quick is this: four conjunct notes in descent, a small upward leap in the opposite direction, followed by three conjunct notes in ascent. Neither group of notes needs to be repeated exactly. There are examples of the pattern at pitch levels other than that of the Quick; but the *Shang* scale can only produce the distinctive tritone when the pattern commences on *f♯* – which does not occur in either

274

source. If, however, the excerpts are read in the *Gong*-mode (Lydian-type) scale of *Shin Raryō-ō* – that is, with the mode-key signature of three sharps – some of the sample passages resemble the opening measures of the Quick quite strongly.

Of value at the centre of the exercise are several pairs of variants taken from the same contextual places in both primary versions of *Shinnō hajin-raku*, and they are unaffected by the independent styles and lengths of the transcribed sources. Excerpts B and J, and C and K, illustrate the point, and their differences are not incompatible. All excerpts in Example 10, however, are integral parts of the language of the repertory; and all retain their own jot of individuality and importance in the total structure.

Samples E and K may have similar practical value in that E commences the repeat that leads back to the sign at beat 16 (in the *GGKF* version), while K, in measure 20 (of the *SGYR* version) is followed by measures 21-3, the same as measures 1-3, and *then* (after measure 23) repeats from measure 4. Thus measures 21-3 fulfil the functions of coda and *kandō* at the same time; and the composition settles down, in all its repetitions, to a regular form of twenty measures.

When planning exploration of musical relationships of a chosen set of items, the aim was to determine whether pieces with related titles 'are composed from similar musical materials, or perhaps owe their origins to one piece, of which others are descendants or kindred versions.' The study was intended to penetrate more deeply than previously into the nature of the musical language of the Tang, as evidenced in items from the Tang repertory, to see whether like titles imply like music, whether such items are musically related, or share a common parentage. Pursuit of answers to these questions has involved comparative investigation, with the aim of extracting visual and statistical evidence from the earliest extant versions, in the hope that the melodies themselves might yield answers relevant to their identities.

Starting from written historical references, the enquiry advanced by collecting and comparing data acquired from the items in their earliest known forms, and by assembling them in numerical Tables and staff notations. This led to comparison of all the melodies in paired alignments. The procedure afforded a firm basis of statistical and physical information, from which a search for possible correlations between hitherto disparate compositions could be made.

It is concluded that the four movements are composed of similar materials. That they all derive from a prototype is probable in the case of the three movements of sixteen measures duration (Examples 4, 5 and 7). In comparative analyses, all four compositions have yielded recognizable evidence of melodic materials shared along similar lines of continuity, but showing that similarity is disguised by elements of style, and by degrees of variation applied (or acquired) in the course of time and transmission. The three movements in sixteen measures belong to compositions in the name of the Prince of Lanling/*Lingwang/Ryō-ō*; and it is probable, therefore, that the Entering Broaching of this title is the prototype of the movements, Broaching and Quick, of the medium-sized suite, 'A New "Prince of Lanling" '/*Shin Raryō-ō*.

This conclusion adds weight to the Entering Broaching being indeed a Tang composition, this one movement of *its* suite being categorically of Tang or pre-Tang origin, and certainly of Tang origin so far as the Japanese were concerned.

Returning to *Shinnō hajin-raku*, it must be asked whether the comparative and paired analyses (Examples 2, 8 and 9) support the inclusion of *this* item in the set of like compositions, named after military and imperial leaders honoured in their day, or posthumously. The analyses insist that its inclusion cannot be rejected outright although, because of the piece's unusual form, it cannot be accepted forthwith without reserve. In Example 2, the Entering Broaching of *Ryō-ō* is unable to furnish material matching measures 17-21 of *Shinnō hajin-raku*; furthermore, the gap would not be effectively reduced, even when the final measures of *Shinnō hajin-raku* and the Entering Broaching are realigned, as in Example 3, where measures 14-16 underlie measures 21-3. If measure 14 of the Entering Broaching (Example 2) were removed to the realigned position of Example 3, measures 15-20 (inclusive) of *Shinnō hajin-raku* would not match the Entering Broaching for as many as six measures, whereas the gap (in Example 2) is five measures.

Example 2 nevertheless makes an interesting comparison, in that ten measures of the Entering Broaching (measures 5-14) are accommodated without difficulty in fourteen measures of *Shinnō hajin-raku* (measures 3-16); the first four measures of the shorter tune nestle in the first two measures of the longer one; and the last measures of each piece follow very similar lines. It would seem then, that at some stage *Shinnō hajin-raku* acquired additional material unrelated to the Entering Broaching; alternatively, that a one-time longer Entering Broaching lost measures, over the years, before becoming established in the form known in the context of *Ryō-ō*. If serious consideration is to be given to either hypothesis, the former appears more feasible: (1) the balance and wholeness of the Entering Broaching, in its present form, are historically practicable, strong and convincing; (2) its form and structure are very close to the movements of *Shin raryō-ō*, the melodic profile of which it complements.

Comparison of *Shinnō hajin-raku* with the Quick of *Shin Raryō-ō* (Example 8) reveals that the Quick has many connections with the larger tune. Not only do its phrases follow in sequence – admittedly with some quite long gaps between – but detached phrases of the Quick find other connections, at random, in various parts of *Shinnō hajin-raku*, even though the Quick is just one third (35 percent) of the length of that movement.

In addition to random placings of phrases of the Quick in Example 8, there are further instances (not shown here) where the Quick could match measures of *Shinnō hajin-raku*: measures 5-6 of the Quick with measures 1 and 21; measures 1-2 might lie across the bar-line that separates measures 19 and 20; and measures 7-8 might underlie measures 3 and 23. On the surface, tonal materials of both movements appear to be entirely different; but the Quick delivers itself precisely and to greater effect. The inherent differences lie in the time scales, and in the manner of self-presentation.

How then is the question to be answered, whether *Shinnō hajin-raku* should be admitted to the group of compositions in which titles, and the music itself, share common factors? It is the one tune of the four in a different style, a piece of greater length and somewhat discursive in delivery. Identifying each piece by a letter: let *Shinnō hajin-raku* be A; *Ryō-ō*, Entering Broaching, B; and the Broaching and Quick of *Shin Raryō-ō*, C and D, respectively. The question about relationships can now be restated. If B, C and D appear to be closely related, and A is related in a lesser degree to B and D, is A related to C?

When the various pairs of tunes were examined in turn, it was felt at first that *Shinnō hajin-raku* and the Broaching of *Shin Raryō-ō* did not warrant comparison, because of their palpable variance: in forms and structures; in individualities and profiles; and in technical matters concerning use of the musical language. In spite of such dissimilarities, it has now to be admitted in hindsight that, on the basis of shared formulaic elements of the musical language, this study has established that the four movements are related, some more closely than others. It may justifiably be claimed that B, C and D are near relatives; that (to a lesser degree) A is related to B and D; and that through its relationship to B and D, A's family connections with C can now be recognized.

From the outset, the items subjected to close examination posed important questions. These can now be answered in a few words. The four movements are composed of numerous, diverse, tonal elements, many of which are widely shared in one form or another in the Tang musical language. All these elements are concealed, absorbed in the idiosyncratic linear textures of the musical language. They are not perceived, and consequently they are not heard, as specifically intrinsic to the profiles and musical qualities of the compositions; undoubtedly, however, they are part of the physical fabric and structure of the music. In the case of the selected specimens, 'like titles' predict 'like music' – where 'like' applies primarily in the technical sense to the presence of a large number of like note patterns, of freely adaptable clichés, and of loosely constructed fragments. These have little to do *per se* with what the ear perceives, the imagination appreciates, or the mind understands, as compositions known by their given titles. The musical identities of the four pieces are therefore independent, and they have their own distinctive individualities. What inferences may be drawn, regarding musical likenesses of like-titled compositions, can go no further than the above reservations permit.

It may be claimed, however, that the Entering Broaching of *Ryō-ō* is the exemplar from which the movements of *Shin Raryō-ō* have come, which claim implies that the Entering Broaching of *Ryō-ō* (the single movement) antedates both movements of *Shin Raryō-ō*. Where *Shinnō hajin-raku* is to be placed is a question beyond further consideration at the present time. It seems certain, however, that the two *Shin Raryō-ō* movements are derived from the *Ryō-ō* Entering Broaching, as also (in all probability) is *Shinnō hajin-raku*.

This investigation has probed, more deeply than hitherto, into the musical language of the Tang. It was a musical medium of great flexibility and adaptability, capable of supporting well-organized, large- and small-scale compositions, attractive as music for their accessible tunefulness. The traditional modal system worked well in Tang times and was respected, if not always heeded. What maintained the viability of productive and reproductive processes over three centuries was the ingenuity of musicians in transcending its limitations. Tang music represents creative achievement equal to the requirements of cultivated and common tastes. At court and in the cities, musicians made music in their own ways, abundantly and on all occasions, and avidly gathered in music from tributary states and beyond. A large contemporary repertory was developed and sustained over centuries. Titles and compositions inform and reward musicians and historians alike. The people of Tang are long since gone; but a substantial part of their music and musical culture remains for those who care to read and listen.

Cumulative bibliography

Abraham, O. and Hornbostel, E.M. (1903-4) 'Phonographierte indische Melodien', *Sammelbände der Internationalen Musikgesellschaft* 5, pp.348-401, Leipzig

Arai, Hakuseki 新 井 白 石 (1964) *The Armour Book in Honchō-gunkikō* (本 朝 軍 記 考) translated by Y. Ōtsuka 大 塚 ed. H. Russell Robinson, Rutland (Vermont), Tokyo

Baqiong shi jinshi buzheng 八 瓊 室 金 石 補 正 (Lu Zengxiang 陸 增 祥, 1924); reprint 1967, Taipei

Bäumker, W. (1886) *Das katholische deutsche Kirchenlied in seinen Singweisen* (Freiburg i.B.), I, 252, 1, No.7; reference from Dr Rajeczky

Bei Qi shu 北 齊 書 (Li Baiyao 李 百 藥, 565-640), Zhonghua shuju 1974, Beijing

Beishi 北 史 (Li Tingshou 李 廷 壽, 7th century), Zhonghua shuju 1974, Beijing

Biji manzhi 碧 雞 漫 志 (Wang Shuo 王 火勺 1149) Zhongguo wenxue cankao ziliao xiao congshu, I, 6, 1957

Birrell, Anne (1982, 1986) *New Songs from a Jade Terrace*, London

Boltz, William G. (1993) *Shuo wen chieh tzu* 説 文 解 字 in Loewe, Michael (1993)

Bronson, B.H. (1959-72) *The Traditional Tunes of the Child Ballads*, Princeton, N.J.

(1980) 'Folk and popular balladry', *The New Grove Dictionary of Music and Musicians*, ed. Stanley Sadie, vol. 2, p.73b, London

Cefu yuangui 冊 府 元 龜 (between 998 and 1023; Wang Qinruo 王 欽 若 and others), Zhonghua shuju, 1960, Beijing

Chavannes, Edouard (1895, 1905) *Les Mémoires historiques de Se-Ma Ts'ien* 5, p.398, n.4, Paris

Chuci 楚 辭 (attributed in part to Qu Yuan 屈 原, 400 BC). Wang Yi 王 逸, first editor of the *Quci zhangzhu* 楚 辭 章 句, early second century AD. This is usually incorporated with the 'amplification' by Hong Xingzu 洪 興 租 (1090-1155) and other Song scholars, and may be found in both the *Sibu congkan* 四 部 叢 刊 and *Sibu beiyao* 四 部 備 要 series.

Chū Ōga ryūteki yōroku-fu 註 [注] 大 神 龍 笛 錄 譜, Tenri Library *MS*. See Marett, 1988.

Coedès, G. (1948) *Les Etats hindouisés d'Indochine et d'Indonésie*, Paris

Condit, Jonathan (1976) 'Differing transcriptions from the twelfth-century koto manuscript *Jinchi-yōroku*', *Ethnomusicology* 20 (1), pp.87-95, Ann Arbor, Michigan

Cooper, Arthur R.V. (1973, 1986) *Li Po and Tu Fu*, London
(1985) 'Exploring etymographic origins of Chinese characters', Paper for 'British Association for Chinese Studies Conference', Durham, 21 September

Couvreur, S., *S.J.* (1896, 1926) *Cheu King* Texte chinois avec une double traduction en français et en latin (Sien Hien imprimérie de la mission catholique); see pp.5, 6.

Cramp, Stanley (ed.) *Handbook of the Birds of Europe, the Middle East and North America: The Birds of the Western Palaearctic*, Volume 1 (1977), Ostrich to Ducks, Oxford. For sonograms from Sture Palmér and S. Wahlstrom, see p.395.

Crawcour, Sydney (1965) *An Introduction to Kambun*, Ann Arbor, Michigan

Dai jimmei jiten 大 人 名 辭 典 (1953) Heibonsha, Tokyo

Dainihonshi (*DNHS*) 大 日 本 史 Tokugawa Mitsukuni 德 川 光 國 and others (1810-51, 1928-9) 卷 之 三 百 四 十 七, 志 五, 禮 樂 十 四, 樂 曲 一, 左 部 樂 *Ichikotsu-chō* 壹 樂 調 二 十 五 曲, pp.215-21, *Sada-chō* 沙 陀 調, pp.221-4, Tokyo

[*Da*]*Tang Liu Dian* (*DTLD*) [大] 唐 六 典 completed in 738; compiled by Li Linfu 李 林 甫, Wenhai chuban she, Taipei; reprinted in 1962. See p.287. The text corrects a mis-writing of *zhen* 陣. For a further note on this work, and on Li Linfu, see P.A. Herbert: ' "A Hawk among Rabbits": an appraisal of the T'ang Chief Minister, Li Lin-fu' in 布 目 潮 渢 博 士 古 稀 記 念 論 集, 東 アシアわ 法 社 會 1990 年 5 月, 汲 古 書 院 刊.

Demiéville, P. (1925) 'La Musique Čame au Japon', *Etudes Asiatiques*, *Publications de l'Ecole française d'extrême-orient*, Nos. xix, xx, Paris, G. van Oest, t. 1, pp.199-226; for Minamoto no Jun/Shitagau see p.209, n.1.

Eckardt, Hans (1952) '*Ryō-ō*', *Sinologica*, III, 2, pp.110-28, Basel
(1956) *Das Kokonchomonshū* 古 今 著 聞 集 *des Tachibana Narisue* 橘 成 季 *als musikgeschichtliche Quelle*, Wiesbaden

Eide, Elling O. (1982) 'Li Po's riddle naming Cloud-ritual Hsü in relation to the Feng Sacrifice of 742 and the Great Heavenly Treasure scandal to which is appended a note on the Stamping Songs and a Sino-Turkish name for the Huns', *Tang Studies*, Number One, pp.8-20, Wisconsin

Fu, Yunzi 傅 芸 子 (1940) '*Wuyue Lanling wang kao*' 舞 樂 蘭 陵 王 考, *Tōhō-gakuhō* 東 方 學 報 10, pp.85-93, Kyoto

Fujiie Reinosuke 藤 家 禮 之 助 (1988) 日 中 交 流 二 千 年, Tōkai daigaku, Tokyo

Fukushima, Kazuo and Nelson, Steven G. (1983) *Descriptive Catalogue of the Eighth Exhibition* 'Musical Notations of Japan' Research Archives for Japanese Music, Ueno Gakuen College, Tokyo

Fushimi no Miya bon biwa-fu 伏 見 宮 本 琵 琶 譜, copy of an original manuscript completed in 920/1 by Prince Sadayasu (Fujiwara no Sadayasu 藤 原 貞 保 (新 王) (Facsimile published by Kunaichō Shoryōbu in 1962, Tokyo)

Gakkaroku (GKR) 樂 家 錄, Abe Suehisa 安 倍 季 尚 (1690); ed. Masamune Atsuo 正 傑 敦 太 and others (1935-6), 5 volumes (*Nihon Koten Zenshū* 日 本 古 典 全 集 edn), Tokyo

Gakukō mokuroku (GKMR) 樂 考 目 錄; see *Gakkaroku*, pp.964-94, 卷 之 三 十 二 , *Ichikotsu-chō* pp.967-72, *Sada-chō* pp.973-4

Gamō Mitsuko 蒲 生 美 津 子 (1986) 'A study of Ranjō (*Ranjō shōkō* 亂 聲 小 考)', *Shominzoku no oto* 諸 民 族 の 音 Collected memorial essays for Koizumi Fumio (小 泉 文 夫 先 生 追 悼 論 文 集, pp.237-56) (summary pp.818-9), Tokyo

Garfias, R. (1964) *Music of a Thousand Autumns*, Berkeley, Los Angeles, London

Genji monogatari no ongaku – see Yamada, Yoshio.

Gibbon, Edward (1776 vol.1; 1781 vols 2, 3; 1781 vol.4) *The Decline & Fall of the Roman Empire*, London

Gimm, Martin (1966) *Das* Yüeh-fu tsa-lu *des Tuan An-chieh*, Wiesbaden

Gulik, R.H. van (1940) *The Lore of the Chinese Lute*, Tokyo
(1961) *Sexual Life in Ancient China*, Leiden

Hanshu 漢 書 (begun in AD 54, completed in the second century) Zhonghua shuju, 1964

Harich-Schneider, Eta (1954) *A History of Japanese Music,* Oxford

Hawkes, David (1959) *The Songs of the South, an ancient Chinese anthology* (Oxford: Clarendon Press); Second revised edition: *The songs of the south: an anthology of ancient Chinese poems by Qu Yuan and other poets*, Harmondsworth: Penguin Books Limited. See *Ch'u tzu*, David Hawkes, in: Michael Loewe, *Early Chinese Texts*...(1993)

Hayashi, Kenzō 林 謙 三 (1969) *Gagaku – Kogaku-fu kaidoku, Tōyō ongaku sensho* 雅 樂 – 古 樂 譜 解 讀, 東 洋 音 樂 選 書; see *Biwa-fu shinkō* 琵 琶 譜 新 考 (pp.235-62: p.258), Tokyo
(1974) *Ongaku kongen shō* 音 樂 根 源 鈔, *Kogaku sho iju* 古 樂 書 遺 珠, *Zempon sōsho* 全 本 叢 書 16, pp.103, 119, 123, Tenri; see note (p.24) and in particular p.25.

He, Changlin 何 昌 林 (1985) '變 于 闐' – 於 邾 應 時 同 志 討 論, 1, pp.94-9 (p.96) Hua ishu chuban she, Beijing

Herbert, P. A.(1979) 'Japanese Embassies and Students in T'ang China', University of Western Australia, Centre for East Asian Studies, Occasional Papers no.4

Herzog, George (1928) 'The Yuman Musical Style', *Journal of American Folklore* 41, pp.183-231

Hirade, Hisao 平 出 久 雄 (1982), entry: *Gagaku*: 雅 樂, *Ongaku daijiten* 音 樂 大 字 典, 2, pp.527-35, Heibonsha 平 凡 社, Tokyo

Hirano, Kenji 平 野 健 次 (1977) 'The intake and transformation of Chinese music in Japan', *Proceedings of the Second Asian Pacific Music Conference*, Seoul, pp.26-9

Holzman, Donald (1957) *La Vie et la Pensée de Hi Kang*, Leiden

Honchō gunkikō 本 朝 軍 記 考 (c.1850), Osaka

Honpō gakusetsu (HPGS) 本 邦 樂 説; see *Gakkaroku* 卷 之 三 十 一, pp.918-63, *Ichikotsu-chō* pp.918-24, *Sada-chō* pp.924-8, (1936), Tokyo

Hornbostel, E.M. (l905-6) 'Die Probleme der vergleichenden Musikwissenschaft', *Zeitschrift der Internationalen Musikgesellschaft,* 7(3), pp.85-97, Leipzig

Hulsewe, A.F.P. (1993): see Loewe (1993), '*Han Shu* 漢 書', pp.129-36.

Hymns Ancient and Modern (1st edn 1861; 2nd edn ed. W.H. Monk; Standard edn = 2nd edn with two Supplements 1916, 1940). The tune *Ravenshaw* appears on p.258 as Hymn 243. The statement that it was abridged from a tune in the collection of M.Weisse appears in the *English Hymnal.*

Ishida, Mikinosuke 石 田 幹 之 助 (1948) *Tō-shi sōshō* 唐 史 叢 鈔, Tokyo

Ishihara, Akira and Levy, Howard S.(1969) *The Tao of Sex, an annotated translation of the twenty-eighth section of The Essence of Medical Prescription* (Ishimpō), Yokohama

Jiaofangji (JFJ) jianding 教 坊 記 箋 訂. The *Jiaofangji* was composed by Cui Lingqin 崔 令 欽 of the Tang dynasty. The *Jiaofang* itself was established in the *Kaiyuan* period (713-41) of the reign of the Xuanzong Emperor, commonly known as Minghuang. See Ren Bantang (1974).

Jiegulu (JGL) 羯 鼓 錄 (Nan Zhuo 南 卓 *fl.* 847), 中 國 文 學 參 考 瓷 料 小 叢 書, 的 一 輯, pp.1-16, Gudian wenxue chubanshe

Jinchi-yōroku (JCYR) 仁 智 要 錄, Manuscript copy (of 12th-century original) made in *Temmei* 天 明 元 年 (1781) (item 593 in the Catalogue of *Kunaichō Shoryōbu* 宮 內 廳 書 陵 部 (Library of the Imperial Palace, Tokyo), 音 樂, 雅 樂. For *Ichikotsu-chō* items **1 - 7** (our numbers) see 卷 第 四, 壹 越 調, 上; for the remaining items in this mode-key (**8 - 23**), and for all those in *Sada-chō* (**24 - 31**) see 卷 第 五, 壹 越 調 曲, 下, and 沙 陀 調.

Jinshi cuibian 金 石 萃 編 (Wang Chang 王 昶) (1805)

Jiu Tangshu (*JTS*) 舊 唐 書 (Liu Yun 劉 昫 and others, completed 945) Zhonghua shuju 1975, Beijing

Jones, Stephen (1990) 'A note on Xi'an Ancient Music and its *Yousheng*', *Music from the Tang Court* 5, pp.127-8

(1995) *Folk Music of China*: *Living Instrumental Traditions*, Oxford, Clarendon Press

Jones, Stephen and Picken, Laurence (1987) 'Tunes of T'ang date for the "Get treasure song" ?', *T'ang Studies*, *Number Five*, pp.33-44, Boulder CO

Joseph, H.K. (1976) 'The Chanda', *T'oung Pao*, 62, pp.167-98, Leiden

Kabu hinmoku 歌 舞 品 目 (1930, 1978) *Nihon koten zenshū* edn, Kyoto

Karlgren, B. (1931) 'The early history of the Chou Li and Tso Chuan texts', *The Museum of Far Eastern Antiquities*, *Bulletin* 3, pp.1- 59, Stockholm

(1957) *Grammata Serica Recensa*, *The Museum of Far Eastern Antiquities Bulletin* 29, Stockholm

Keizū sanyō 系 圖 纂 要 (1973) Heibonsha, Tokyo

Kikkawa, Eishi 吉 川 英 史 (1979) *Nihon ongaku no shikaku* 日 本 音 樂 の 思 格, Tokyo; see p.73.

(1984) *Vom Charakter der japanischen Musik*, Aus dem Japanischen übertragen von Petra Rudolph, Durch Quellenhinweise ergänzt, mit Anmerkungen versehen und redigiert unter Mitwirkung von Heinz-Dieter Reese von Robert Günther, Kassel; see p.64.

Kishibe, Shigeo 岸 邊 成 雄 (1966, 1981) The Traditional Music of Japan, Ongaku no tomo sha, Tokyo. See pp 51-3.

(1985) *Tempyō no hibiki* 天 平 の 響, Tokyo

Kofu Hōshō-fu ryokan/ritsukan 古 譜 鳳 笙 譜 呂 卷 律 卷, *MS* in the Collection of Ueno Gakuen University, Tokyo: 上 野 樂 園 日 本 音 樂 瓷 料 室, directed by Professor Fukushima Kazuo 福 島 和 太. The two sewn volumes are stamped: 日 本 音 樂 瓷 料 室 藏 書 No. 6009. For further details see our Fascicle 1 (1981), pp.33,34.

Kokonchomonshū (*KKCMJ*): see Tachibana Narisue and Eckardt, Hans.

Ko sō-fu 古 箏 譜 (10th Century?), *Kogakusho ishu* 古 樂 書 遺 珠 (Volume 16 of *Zenpon sōsho* 全 本 叢 書, Tokyo 1974, pp, 4-55, with commentary by Hayashi Kenzō 林 謙 三)

Kyōkunshō (*KKS*) 教 訓 抄, *Nihon shisō taikei* 日 本 思 想 大 系 23, 1984, pp.10-215, ed. Ueki Yukinori 植 木 行 宣, Tokyo

Lai, Chun-Yue (1979) '*Lao Liuban*', *Chinese Music* 2, pp.47-51, Woodbridge, Illinois

Lidai yudi yan'ge xian yaotu 歷 代 興 地 沿 革 險 要 圖 (1879), compiled by Yang Shoujing 楊 守 敬, 觀 海 堂

Li, Linfu 李 林 甫 and others (738) [*Da*] *Tang liu dian* [大] 唐 六 典, Wenhai chubanshe, Taipei, 1974

Li, Shigen 李 石 根 (1982) 西 安 古 樂 曲 集 *Xi'an guyue quji* Shaanxi sheng qunzhong yishuguan 陝 西 省 群 眾 藝 術 館; also n.1, p.127, Fascicle 5

Liu, Feng-Shüeh 劉 鳳 學 (1986) *A Documented Historical and Analytical Study of Chinese Ritual and Ceremonial Dance from the Second Millennium BC to the Thirteenth Century.* Ph.D. Dissertation, Laban Centre, University of London, Goldsmiths' College

Loewe, Michael, ed.(1993) *Early Chinese Texts* A Bibliographical Guide, The Society for the Study of Ancient China and The Institute of East Asian Studies, University of California, Berkeley

Lunyu 論 語 (*c.*465-50 BC) Guyi congshu 3, 1882

Marett, Allan J. (1976) 'Hakuga's flute-score: a tenth-century Japanese source of "Tang-Music" in tablature', Ph.D. Dissertation, University Library, Cambridge, No.9823

(1977) 'Tunes notated in flute-tablature from a Japanese source of the tenth century', *Musica Asiatica*, 1, pp.1-59, Oxford

(1979) '*Hakuga no fuefu no sho kifuhō ni tsuite* 博 雅 の 笛 譜 の 諸 記 譜 法 について', *Gagakkai* 雅 樂 會 54, pp.171-88, Tokyo

(1985) '*Tōgaku*: where have the Tang melodies gone, and where have the new melodies come from?', *Ethnomusicology* 29, pp.409-31

(1986) 'In search of the lost melodies of Tang China: an account of recent research and its implications for the history and analysis of *Tōgaku*', *Musicology Australia* vol. 9, pp.29-38, Canberra

(1988) 'An investigation of sources for *Chū Ōga ryūteki yōroku-fu*, a Japanese flute-score of the 14th-century', *Musica Asiatica*, 4, pp.210-67, Oxford

Markham, Elizabeth J. (1983) *Saibara – Japanese Court Songs of the Heian Period* (2 vols.), Cambridge

Markham, E.J., Picken, L.E.R., Wolpert, R.F. (1987) 'Pieces for *biwa* in calendrically correct tunings from a manuscript in the Heian Museum, Kyoto', *Musica Asiatica* 5, pp.191-209, Cambridge

Mathews, R.H.(1931, 1943) *A Chinese-English Dictionary* compiled for the China Inland Mission, Shanghai, China Inland Mission and Presbyterian Mission Press, 1931; photolithographed by the Murray Printing Company Cambridge, Mass.

Matsushima Yorimasa 松 島 順 正 (1952,1953) *Shōsō-in ko retsu meimon shūsei* 正 倉 院 古 裂 銘 文 集 成, *Shoryōbu kiyō* 書 陵 部 記 要, Archives and Mausoleum Division, Imperial Household Agency: No.2, March 1952, No.3, March 1953

(1978) *Shōsō-in hōmotsu meimon shūsei* 正 倉 院 寶 物 銘 文 集 成, Tokyo

Mengqi bitan 夢 溪 筆 談 (Shen Gua 沈 括 1086-93) Congshu jicheng 1937

Mommsen, Theodor (1854-6; 1976) *Römische Geschichte*, Leipzig; Munich

Morris, Ivan (Ira) (1964) *The World of the Shining Prince*, London

Moule, A.C. (1909) 'On the musical and other sound-producing instruments of the Chinese', *Journal of the North-China Branch of the Royal Asiatic Society*, London, etc.

Moule, A. C. and Yetts, W. Percival (1957) *The Rulers of China* 221 BC - AD 1949, London

Murasaki Shikibu 紫 式 部 (10th century) *Genji monogatari* 源 氏 物 語 1, *Nihon koten bungaku taikei* 日 本 古 典 文 學 大 系 (1958) 14, Iwanami shoten kankō 岩 波 書 店 刊 行, Tokyo. For the Flower Banquet (*Hana no en* 花 の 宴), see p.304, column 12.

Nanchikufu 南 竹 譜 = *Nangūfu* 南 宮 譜 = the lost score of Prince Sadayasu 貞 保 親 王 (921), perhaps incorporated in that of Minamoto no Hiromasa (Hakuga).

Needham, Joseph (1971) in collaboration with Wang Ling and Lu Gwei-Djen, *Science and Civilisation in China*, volume 4, Physics and Physical Technology, Part III: Civil Engineering and Nautics; pp.306ff.

Nettl, Bruno (1964) *Theory and Method of Ethnomusicology*, London

Nickson, Noël (1988) 'Structural design of "Chinese" melodies known in Japan before 841', *Conspectus Carminis* – Essays for David Galliver, *Miscellanea Musicologica, Adelaide Studies in Musicology*, volume 15, pp.58-73 Adelaide

Nihon Gagakkai Kaihō 日 本 雅 樂 會 會 報, 第 9 回 *Nara Gagaku Kenkyūgai* 奈 良 雅 樂 研 究 會, Heisei 4 (1992) '蘭 陵 王 の 墓 前 て 舞 う p.3, Tokyo

Nihon-koku genzaisho mokuroku 日 本 國 現 在 書 目 錄. See the edn of Yashima Kurosuke 矢 島 玄 亮 (1984), subtitled *Shūshō to kenkyū* 集 証 と 研 究, Kyūko shoin 汲 古 書 院. The book-list is believed to date from 891.

Nihon Ongaku Daijiten 日 本 音 樂 大 字 典 (1989) eds Hirano Kenji 平 野 健 次, Kamisango Sukeyasu 上 參 鄉 祐 康, Gamō Satoaki 蒲 生 鄉 昭, Heibonsha, Tokyo

Ongaku daijiten 音 樂 大 辭 典, vol.2, Heibonsha, Tokyo, 1982

Parry, C. H. Hubert 'CODA' in *Grove's Dictionary of Music and Musicians* (1879), London; 1, p.376

Picken, L.E.R. (1954) 'Instrumental polyphonic folk music in Asia Minor', *Proceedings of the Royal Musical Association*, 80th Session, London (1955) 'The Origin of the Short Lute', *The Galpin Society Journal* 8, pp.32-42, London
(1956, 1957, i) 'Twelve Ritual melodies of the T'ang dynasty', *Studia Memoriae Belae Bartók Sacra*, pp.147-73, Budapest

(1957, ii) 'Chiang K'uei's "Nine Songs for Yüeh" ', *The Musical Quarterly* 63, pp.201-18

(1965) 'Early Chinese Friction-Chordophones', *The Galpin Society Journal* 18, pp.84-9

(1966) 'Secular Chinese songs of the twelfth century', *Studia Musicologica Academiae Scientiarum Hungaricae*, vol.8, pp.125-72, Budapest

(1969, i) 'T'ang music and musical instruments', *T'oung Pao* 55, pp.74-122, Leiden

(1969, ii) 'Music and musical sources of the Song dynasty', *Journal of the American Oriental Society*, 89, pp.600-21, NewYork

(1969, iii) 'The musical implications of line-sharing in the *Book of Songs* (*Shih Ching*)', *Journal of the American Oriental Society* 89, pp.408-10, New York

(1969, iv) 'Tunes apt for T'ang lyrics from the *shō* part-books of *Tōgaku*', *Essays in Ethnomusicology – a birthday-offering for Lee Hye-ku*, Seoul

(1971, i) 'Some Chinese terms for musical repeats, sections, and forms, common to T'ang, Yüan, and *Tōgaku* 唐 樂 scores', *Bulletin of the School of Oriental and African Studies, University of London*, 34/1, pp.113-18, London

(1971, ii) 'A twelfth-century secular Chinese song in zither-tablature', *Asia Major* 16, pp.102-20, London

(1974) '*Tenri toshokan shozō no jūyōna Tōgaku-fu ni kansuru oboegaki*' 天 理 讀 書 館 所 藏 の 重 要 な 唐 樂 譜 に 關 す る 覺 書, *Biblia* 57, pp.2-12, Tenri

(1975) *Folk Musical Instruments of Turkey*, Oxford

(1977) 'The shapes of the *Shi Jing* song-texts and their musical implications', *Musica Asiatica* 1, pp.85-109, Oxford

Picken, L.E.R. and Mitani, Yōko (1979) 'Finger-techniques for the zithers *sō-no-koto* and *kin* in Heian times', *Musica Asiatica* 2, pp.89-114, Oxford

Picken, L.E.R. and Wolpert, R.F. (1981) 'Mouth-organ and lute parts of *Tōgaku* and their interrelationship', *Musica Asiatica* 3, pp.79-95, Oxford

Pulleyblank, E.G. (1949-50) 'The *Tzyjyh tong jiann kaoyih* and the sources for the history of the period 730-63', *Bulletin of the School of Oriental and African Studies, University of London*, vol. 13, pp.448-73, London

(1960) 'Neo-Confucianism and Neo-Legalism in T'ang intellectual life, 755-805' in *The Confucian Persuasion*, ed. A.F. Wright, Stanford, California

Qian Lezhi 錢 樂 之 (Astronomer Royal of the (Liu) Song (劉) 宋 dynasty, *ca* 435).

Qinding da Qing huidian (1818) 欽 定 大 清 會 典

Quan Tangshi 全 唐 詩 (1986, 1990) 上 海 古 籍 出 版 社 Shanghai guji chubanshe (2 volumes)

[*Quxian*] *shenqi mipu* (1425) [膠 仙] 神 奇 秘 譜 (Facsimile printing, with introduction by Zha Fushi 查 皀 西) Yinyue chuban she, 3 volumes, 1956

Reese, Heinz-Dieter (1986) 'Picken, Lawrence [*sic*] (ed.) *Music from the Tang Court*. Fascicle 2. Cambridge London New York: Cambridge University Press, 1985. 108pp. music, charts, illustrations.' *The World of Music*, 28, 2, pp.80-2, Florian Noetzel Verlag, Wilhelmshaven

Reid, James Lany (1946) *The Komagaku Repertory of Japanese Gagaku (Court Music)*: a study of contemporary performance practice, U.C.L.A., Ph.D. Music

Ren Bantang 任 半 塘 (1972) *Jiaofangji jianding* 教 訪 記 箋 訂, Taipei, Hongye shuju; an edition of the Tang *Jiaofangji* (Cui Lingqin 崔 令 欽 758) with commentary

(1984) *Tang xinong* 唐 戲 弄, Shanghai guji chubanshe, Shanghai

Rikkokushi 六 國 史, 9, *Nihon rekishi sōsho* 日 本 歷 史 總 書 7, ed. Sakamoto Tarō 土反 本 太 郎 (1970), Tokyo

Ruijū sō-fu 類 聚 箏 譜 *Classified Zither-Scores* (Editorship attributed uncertainly to Fujiwara no Tadazane 藤 原 忠 實 (1078-1162) (see *Nihon Ongaku Daijiten* 日 本 音 樂 大 事 典，平 凡 社，1989; p.734b). However, as stated in Fascicle 1, p.36, upper marginal glosses in both *JCYR* and *SGYR* affirm that *Ruijū sō-fu* was 'edited by Nochi no Ujidono', and this is the usual name of Fujiwara no Morozane 藤 原 師 實 (1042-1101). As such this zither-collectaneum has disappeared, but it is believed that much of its contents survive in the next.

Ruisō-chiyō 類 箏 治 要 *Essential Information for the Zither-Kind*. The University Library, Cambridge has a microfiche of a copy in the library of *Tōkyō Geijutsu Daigaku* あ152.

Ryūmeishō 龍 鳴 抄: Ōga no Motomasa 大 家 惟 政 (1133) *Gunsho Ruijū* 群 書 類 從 19, *Kangenbu* 管 絃 部, Tokyo

Sandai jitsuroku 三 代 實 錄, 卷 14, p.357 (see *Rikkokushi*)

Sango-yōroku 三 五 要 錄 (Fujiwara no Moronaga compiler) Lute (*biwa*) manuscript of *Karyaku* 嘉 曆 3 (1328) in *Kunaichō Shoryōbu* 宮 內 廳 書 陵 部, Library of the Imperial Palace, Tokyo. For *Ichikotsu-chō* items **1 - 7** (our numbers) see 卷 第 五，壹 越 調 曲，上; for the remaining items in this mode-key (**8 - 23**), and for all those in *Sada-chō* (**24 - 31**) see 卷 第 六，壹 越 調 曲，下 and 沙 陀 調 曲.

Schafer, E.H. (1963) *The Golden Peaches of Samarkand*, Berkeley and Los Angeles

(1967) *The Vermilion Bird*, Berkeley and Los Angeles

Seidensticker, E.G. (1976) *The Tale of Genji*, London

Shiba, Sukehiro 芝 祐 泰 (1955) 'The Tones of Ancient Oriental Music and those of Western Music', *KBS Bulletin* (*Kokusai Bunka Shinkokai* 國 祭 文 化 新 古 會) No. 13, July 25, pp.6-8, Tokyo
(1972) *Gosen-fu ni yoru Gagaku-sōfu* 五 線 譜 に よ る 雅 樂 總 譜 (4 vols), Tokyo

Shiji 史 記 (Sima Qian 司 馬 遷, 145 – *ca* 86 BC) Zhonghua shuju 1964, Shanghai

Shilin guangji 事 林 廣 記 (1100-1250, a popular encyclopaedia, first printed in 1325), compiled by Chen Yuanjing 陳 元 靚

Shinsen shōtekifu 新 選 笙 笛 譜 *MS. Yōmei Bunko* 陽 明 文 庫 Library: item 94487, Kyoto; see Fascicle 1, p.30.

Shōchū-yōroku-hikyoku 掌 中 要 錄 秘 曲 (1263) *Zoku gunsho ruijū* 530, pp.420-36, Tokyo

Shoku Nihongi 續 日 本 紀, *Shin Nihon koten bungaku taikei*, 1-3, 1989, 1990, 1992, Tokyo

Shominzoku no oto 諸 民 族 の 音 (1986), Memorial Volume for Professor Koizumi Fumio 小 泉 文 夫 先 生 追 擇 文 集, ed. 柴 田 南 雄, Tokyo

Shujing 書 經 (c.450-221 BC) *Shinshaku kambun taikei* 25, 26; ed. Katō Jōken (1983) Tokyo

Shuowen jiezi 説 文 解 子 (AD 121), compiled by Xu Shen 許 慎. For editions, etc., see Boltz, 1993.

Sipos, Janos (1994) *Török Népzene* I., MTA Zenetudományi Intézet, Budapest

Soothill, W.E. and Hodous, L. (1937) *A Dictionary of Chinese Buddhist Terms*, London

Suishu 隋 書, Wei Zheng 魏 徵 and others, 14, pp.345-6, Beijing, Zhonghua shuju, 1973

Sui Tang jia hua 隋 唐 嘉 話 (Liu Su 劉 餗, *c.*750) *Zhongguo wenxue cankao ziliao xiao congshu* 中 國 文 學 參 考 資 料 小 叢 書 (1958) I, 2, Shanghai (1986) Hangzhou Zhejiang Guji 杭 州 折 江 古 籍

Tachibana no Narisue 橘 成 季 (1254) *Kokonchomonshū* 古 今 著 文 集; some read:*Kokonchomonjū*. See Eckardt, Hans.

Takakusu Junjirō (1929) 'Le Voyage de Kanshin en Orient (742-54), par Aomi-no Mabito Genkai (779)', Bulletin de l'Ecole française d'extrême orient, vol. 28, 1928, pp.1-41
ibid., vol. 29, 1929, pp.47-62

Tanabe, Hisao 田 邊 尚 雄 (1926) *Nihon ongaku kōwa* 日 本 音 樂 講 話, Tokyo
(1930) *Nihon ongaku shi* 日 本 音 樂 史, Tokyo

Tangdai wudao 唐 代 舞 蹈 (1980), Ouyang Yuqian 歐 陽 予 倩 ed. Shanghai wenyi chuban she, Shanghai. See pp.122-4.

Tang huiyao (THY) 唐 會 要 (As *Huiyao* presented to the Throne in the recension of Su Mian 蘇 冕 in 801; today, known only in the recension of Wang Pu 王 溥, presented to the Throne in 961) (1955) *Guoxue jiben congshu*, 國 學 集 本 叢 書, Zhonghua shuju, Beijing

Tang Li Shou *mu fa jue tong bao* 唐 李 壽 墓 發 掘 簡 報 (陝 西 省 博 物 館, 文 管 會) *Wenwu* 文 物 1974, 9, pp.71-88. For plates see pp.84-6. See also: 壁 畫 試 探, pp.89-94.

The Music of Japan (1962) Record 2, *Gagaku*, Bärenreiter Musicaphon

Thrasher, Alan R. (1985) 'The melodic structure of *Jiangnan sizhu*', *Ethnomusicology* 29, pp.237-63, Bloomington, Illinois
(1988) 'Hakka-Chaozhou instrumental repertoire: an analytic perspective on traditional creativity', *Asian Music, New York*, 19-2, pp.1-30

Tōdaiji yōroku 東 大 寺 要 錄 (Heian to Kamakura) ed.Tsutsui Eishun 筒 井 英 俊 (1971), Kyoto

Tongdian (TD) 通 典 (Du You 杜 佑 – 801 or 803), Siku shanben congshu shibu 1965, Taipei

Twichett, Denis Crispin and Anthony Christie (1959) 'A medieval Burmese orchestra' in *Asia Major*, 7, pp.176-95, London

Twitchett, Denis Crispin (1992) *The Writing of Official History under the T'ang* 劍 橋 中 華 文 史 叢 刊, Cambridge. For *The Monograph on Music*, 音 樂 志, see pp.212-19.

Vaurie, Charles (1959, 1965) *The Birds of the Palaearctic Fauna* (1) Order Passeriformes, (2) Non-Passeriformes, London; *Anser fabalis serrirostris*: see (2) pp.98-101.

Waley, Arthur (1928,1945, 1949) *The Analects of Confucius*, London
(1935) *The Tale of Genji*, London (first one-volume edn)
(1937) *The Book of Songs*, London
(1949)*The Life and Times of Po Chü-i,* London

Wamyō ruijū shō (WMRJS) 倭 名 類 聚 鈔 (10th Century, by order Minamoto no Jun/Shitagau 源 順 between 923 and 930.) Facsimile of printing of 1617, published by 風 間 書 房 刊, Tokyo,1954. For *Tōgaku* repertory see Chapter 4. This chapter is much later than the tenth century, as pointed out by Demiéville (1925). See Fascicle 3, p.31, and reference p.98.

Wechsler, Howard J. (1979) 'The founding of the T'ang dynasty: Kao-tsu (reign 618-26)', *The Cambridge History of China* eds Denis Twitchett and John K. Fairbank, Chapter 3, Volume 3: Sui and T'ang China, 589-906, Part 1, Cambridge
(1979) 'T'ai-tsung (reign 626-49) the consolidator', Chapter 4, Volume 3

Weisse, M. (Michael) (1531) ed. *Ein neu Gesengbuchlen*, Zum jungen Buntzel (Facsimile, Hrsg. von K. Ameln. Kassel, 1937)

Wenwu 文 物 1974, pp.71-94. See *Tang* Li Shou.

Wenxian tongkao (*WXTK*) 文 獻 通 考 by 馬 端 臨 Ma Duanlin (late 13th
century or *ca* 1308) ed. Wang Yunwu 王 雲 五 (1936), Shanghai

Wilhelm, Helmut and Knechtges, David R. (1987) 'T'ang T'ai-tsung's Poetry',
T'ang Studies 5, 1-23, Boulder CO

Wolpert, R.F. (1975) *Lute Music and Tablatures of the Tang Period*, Ph.D.
Dissertation, University Library, Cambridge, No. 9447

(1977) 'A ninth-century lute-tutor', *Musica Asiatica* 1, pp.111-65, Oxford

(1979) 'The evolution of notated ornamentation in Tōgaku manuscripts for
lute', *Sino-Mongolica, Festschrift für Herbert Franke, Münchener
Ostasiatische Studien* 25, ed. W.Bauer, Wiesbaden

(1981) 'A ninth-century score for five-stringed lute', *Musica Asiatica* 3,
pp.107-35, Oxford

(1985) 'Colour and the notation of rhythmic variation and modal rhythm in
12th- to 14th-century sources for the *Tōgaku* 唐 樂 "Tang Music" repertory
of Japanese Court Music', *Zinbun* 人 文, *Memoirs of the Research Institute
for Humanistic Studies*, 20, pp.51-80, Kyoto

(1988) 'Frogs more frogs', 24 *Deutscher Orientalistentag: Ausgewählte
Vorträge* (Stuttgart, 1990)

Wolpert, Rembrandt; Marett, Allan; Condit, Jonathan; Picken, Laurence (1973)
' "The Waves of Kokonor": a dance-tune of the T'ang dynasty', *Asian
Music, New York*, 1973, pp.3-9

Wright, Arthur F. (1960) *The Confucian Persuasion*, Stanford, Cal.

(1978) *The Sui Dynasty*, New York

Xin Tangshu 新 唐 書 (Song 宋: Ouyang Xiu 歐 陽 修 and Song Qi 宋 祁)
Zhonghua shuju 1975, Beijing

Yamada, Yoshio 山 田 孝 雄 (1934, 1969) *Genjimonogatari no Ongaku* 源 氏
物 語 の 音 樂, Hōbungan zōban shuppan, Tokyo

Yang, Hong 楊 泓 (1980) *Zhongguo gu bingqi luncong* 中 國 古 兵 器 論 叢,
Wenwu chuban she, Beijing

Yang, Yinliu (1980) *Zhongguo gudai yinyue shigao* 中 國 古 代 音 樂 史 稿
(A draft history of ancient Chinese music), Renmin yinyue chuban she,
Beijing

Yili jingzhuan tongjie 儀 禮 經 傳 通 節 (Zhu Xi 朱 熹 *c.*1220) Lü shi
Baogaotang edn, *c.*1700 (A unique copy in the Rylands Library,
Manchester.)

The work was first published posthumously during the Southern Song (南
宋) between 1217 and 1232 (Jiading 10 to Shaoding 4) (嘉 定 丁 丑 (十
年) 至 紹 定 辛 卯 (四 年).

A copy of this first printing exists in the Taipei Municipal Library. Even this
copy, however, is incomplete and lacks the fifteenth *juan* of the entire work.
A printed note in the original text asserts this. Following the heading for the

15th *juan* is the statement: 'This one Section is wanting.' (此 一 篇 闕);
presumably it was never available to the printer.

The music for the 12 *Shijing* songs occurs in the fourteenth chapter
(*juan*) of the entire work. This is entitled 'Song Music' and numbered 24th
(詩 樂 第 二 十 四), it is also the seventh part of 'Ritual Studies' (學 禮).
The original page numbers for the *Xiao Ya* items (小 雅) run from 1 to 6;
those of the *Zhou Nan Guo Feng* (周 南 國 風) from 7 to 11.

Yokoyama Shigeru 横 山 重(1964, 1967, 1968) *Sekkyō shōhon shū* 説 經 正 本 集, Tokyo

Yuefu shiji (*YFSJ*) 樂 府 詩 集 (Guo Maoqian 郭 茂 倩, *ca* 1150-1200)
Zhonghua shuju 1979, Beijing

Yuefu zalu (*YFZL*) 樂 府 雜 錄 (*c*.890, Duan Anjie 段 安 節), in 中 國 古 典 戲 曲 論 著 集 成, Beijing 1959, volume 1, pp.31-89

Yueji 樂 記 (a component of the *Liji* 禮 記) The *Liji* itself, and in its entirety, cannot be earlier than about AD 100. Parts of the *Yueji* may once have belonged to the *Xunzi* 荀 子 (see Riegel, 1993). Xunzi himself may have died in 238 BC; but there are considerable doubts as to the authenticity of the text as a whole, as it now exists, in 32 *pian* 篇.

Zdeněk, Nejedlý (1955): *Dějiny husitského zpěvu* III (Prague, 1955: pp.222-3)

Zhongguo minge 中 國 民 歌 (1959) *Zhongguo yinyue yanjiu bian* 中 國 音 樂 研 究 遍, Yinyue chuban she, Beijing

Zhonghua dazidian 中 華 大 字 典, p.80, Zhonghua shuju yinhang Shanghai (1952)

Zhongwen ciyuan 中 文 辭 源 (1980): ed. Ding Daichen 丁 戴 臣, Taipei, Taizhong

Zhu Xie 朱 契 ('Xie' requires determinative 人) (1962) 中 區 運 河 史 料 選 輯. See pp.16,20.

Zizhi tongjian (*ZZTJ*) 資 治 通 鑑 (1067-84) ed.1956, Beijing

Zoku Kyōkunshō (*ZKKS*) 續 教 訓 抄 (13th century), Tokyo

12032208R00171

Printed in Great Britain
by Amazon.co.uk, Ltd.,
Marston Gate.